American Public Opinion, Advocacy, and Policy in Congress

What the Public Wants and What It Gets

Between one election and the next, members of Congress introduce thousands of bills. What determines which become law? Is
it the public? Do we have government "of the people, by the
people, for the people"? Or is it those who have the resources to
organize and pressure government who get what they want? In
the first study ever of a random sample of policy proposals, Paul
Burstein finds that the public can get what it wants – but mainly
on the few issues that attract its attention. Does this mean
organized interests get what they want? Not necessarily – on
most issues there is so little political activity that it hardly
matters. Politics may be less of a battle between the public and
organized interests than a struggle for attention. American
society is so much more complex than it was when the
Constitution was written that we may need to reconsider
what it means, in fact, to be a democracy.

Paul Burstein is Professor of Sociology, Adjunct Professor of
Political Science, and Samuel and Althea Stroum Chair in
Jewish Studies at the University of Washington, Seattle. He is
the author of *Discrimination, Jobs, and Politics: The Struggle
for Equal Employment Opportunity in the United States
since the New Deal* and has published on topics including
policy change; public opinion; social movements; interest
organizations; congressional action on work, family, and
gender; and the mobilization of law. His articles have appeared
in the *American Sociological Review, American Journal of
Sociology, Social Forces, American Political Science Review,
Political Research Quarterly, Sociological Forum, Law and
Society Review*, and other journals. He has been elected to the
Council and the Publications Committee of the American
Sociological Association and to the position of Chair of the
ASA's Political Sociology section. He has also served on the
editorial boards of twelve journals in sociology, political science,
and other fields.

American Public Opinion, Advocacy, and Policy in Congress

What the Public Wants and What It Gets

PAUL BURSTEIN

University of Washington

CAMBRIDGE
UNIVERSITY PRESS

CAMBRIDGE
UNIVERSITY PRESS

32 Avenue of the Americas, New York, NY 10013-2473, USA

Cambridge University Press is part of the University of Cambridge.

It furthers the University's mission by disseminating knowledge in the pursuit of education, learning, and research at the highest international levels of excellence.

www.cambridge.org
Information on this title: www.cambridge.org/9781107684256

© Paul Burstein 2014

First published 2014

Printed in the United States of America

A catalog record for this publication is available from the British Library.

Library of Congress Cataloging in Publication Data
Burstein, Paul.
American public opinion, advocacy, and policy in Congress : what the public wants and what it gets / Paul Burstein, University of Washington.
  pages cm
ISBN 978-1-107-04020-5 (hardback)
1. Political participation – United States.   2. Public opinion – United
States.   3. Lobbying – United States.   4. Pressure groups – United
States.   I. Title.
JK1764.B88   2013
320.60973–dc23   2013021177

ISBN 978-1-107-04020-5 Hardback
ISBN 978-1-107-68425-6 Paperback

For Florence, my life's love

Contents

List of Tables

Acknowledgments

This book owes the most to two people who probably weren't even aware of how much influence they had on me. First, Bill Gamson, whose work has always been an inspiration to me, for his creativity, willingness to take intellectual risks, and commitment to social justice. I got an idea that proved crucial to the development of the book and my conclusions – the idea of studying a random sample of policies – from his path-breaking study of a sample of challenging groups in *The Strategy of Social Protest* (1975). True, it was 25 years after publication that the idea really hit me, but the slow pace was my fault, not his. Second, Claude Fischer, who not only read and commented on an entire earlier draft of the book, but whose support and advice have been important to me since we met our first year in graduate school.

I also owe a great deal to three graduate students who started off as research assistants and became co-authors – Shawn Bauldry, Paul Froese, and Elizabeth Hirsh – whose work is reflected most significantly in Chapters 2 and 6. Evan Jewett was the graduate research assistant who helped make the impossible (or at least the unprecedented) possible; his work on the ideas and data collection that are central to Chapters 4 and 5, and his dedication to the project well beyond what I could have reasonably asked, played a critical role in the book.

There are many others to thank as well. Some provided feed-
back on earlier versions of the work, others technical advice, still
others support and inspiration at important moments. I hadn't
realized how long the list would be: Frank Baumgartner, John
C. Berg, Clem Brooks, Allan Cigler, Bill Domhoff, George Farkas,
Patty Glynn, Lowell Hargens, Michael Hechter, Alex Hicks, Kim
Quaile Hill, Robert Max Jackson, Lawrence Jacobs, Craig
Jenkins, Bryan D. Jones, David Knoke, Liz Lammert, John
D. McCarthy, Debra Minkoff, Alan Monroe, Steve Pfaff, Sarah
Sausner, Wendy Schiller, Mark A. Smith, Kate Stovel, Ann
Swidler, Stewart Tolnay, John Wilkerson, and Christopher
Wlezien. I also benefited from feedback during presentations at
the University of California, Irvine; the University of Washington;
Indiana University; and the University of Uppsala. A grant from
the National Science Foundation, SES-0001509, made the work
possible, and for that I'm greatly appreciative. And I want to
thank Lew Bateman, my editor at Cambridge University Press,
for his open-mindedness and support.

Three chapters in the book appeared previously in other forms.
Thanks go to my co-authors for granting permission to include the
articles we published, and to the following:

Sage Publications, for permission to include parts of "Bill
   Sponsorship and Congressional Support for Policy Proposals,
   from Introduction to Enactment or Disappearance," by Paul
   Burstein, Shawn Bauldry, and Paul Froese, published in
   Political Research Quarterly 58 (2005): 295–302, in
   Chapter 2.
Oxford University Press, for permission to include much of "Why
   Estimates of the Impact of Public Opinion on Public Policy Are
   Too High: Empirical and Theoretical Implications," by Paul
   Burstein, published in *Social Forces* 84 (2006): 2273–90, in
   Chapter 3.
John Wiley and Sons, for permission to include much of
   "Interest Organizations, Information, and Policy Innovation
   in the U.S. Congress," by Paul Burstein and C. Elizabeth
   Hirsch, *Sociological Forum* 22 (2007): 174–99, in Chapter 6.

Finally, I want most to thank my family, though I feel as though I hardly know how. Nathan, Anna, and Deborah grew up hearing more about policy change than they wanted to; they made me keep my priorities straight, even if they may not have realized it at the time. Florence read and edited, listened and supported, loved and was loved; her worth is indeed far above rubies.

1

Introduction

The first day of the 101st Congress, January 3, 1989, was a busy one, as the first day of a new congress always is. Four hundred and thirty-three bills were introduced in the House of Representatives. Some were potentially important to everyone in the United States (such as H.R. 16, "to provide a program of national health insurance"), some to a smaller but nevertheless substantial number of people (H.R. 1, "to establish a National Housing Trust to assist first-time home buyers), some to only a few (H.R. 27, "to direct the Secretary of the Interior to acquire certain real property adjacent to the Andrew Johnson National Historic Site in Greeneville, Tennessee, for inclusion within the national cemetery located in that site").

By the time the 101st Congress adjourned on October 27, 1990, 5,977 public bills had been introduced in the House and 3,271 in the Senate. Some of these were taken seriously enough to be the subject of committee hearings; some of these were debated in the House or Senate; and some of those debated were enacted into law. But the winnowing process was intense. Of the 433 bills introduced on the first day, only eleven became law. Of the thousands introduced during the entire congress (some of which were duplicates), 650 became law – a small fraction of the total.

What happened to the bills that failed to win enactment in the 101st Congress? Their sponsors could have tried again and reintroduced the bills in the next congress. Many did not; their proposals for policy change disappeared from the congressional agenda. Some persevered; sponsors of H.R. 181, calling for changes in benefits for some beneficiaries of Social Security, had been introducing the same bill in each congress since 1985 and would continue to do so through 1999 before giving up; sponsors of H.R. 2273, prohibiting discrimination against individuals with disabilities, had been trying to win enactment since the 92nd Congress (1971–72) before their efforts were rewarded with passage in 1990 of the Americans with Disabilities Act. Some specific proposals were abandoned, while the general issue remained on the congressional agenda, sometimes, as in the case of national health insurance, well into the 21st century.

What happened during the 101st Congress happens during every congress and raises the same questions. Why do so many bills vanish immediately after being referred to committees, never to win serious congressional attention? Why do some win serious attention but fail to gather the support needed to become law? What influences Congress as it decides which policy proposals to reject and which to enact into law?

Two answers to these questions are most often proposed. The first is that our democratic institutions really work – that we actually have, as Lincoln hoped, "government of the people, by the people, for the people." In contemporary terms, that would mean that Congress is affected most strongly by public opinion – members of Congress nearly always want to win reelection and believe that winning depends on doing what their constituents want. As Stimson, MacKuen, and Erikson (1995:543, 560) write, "Constitutional mechanisms harness politicians' strategies to the public's demands. . . . This is dynamic representation, a simple idea and an old one. Public sentiment shifts. Political actors sense the shift. And then they alter their policy behavior at the margin."

The second proposed answer is that Congress is affected most strongly, not by public opinion, but rather by organizations and individuals with the resources to get what they want by putting pressure on elected officials. They provide the campaign contributions, labor, expertise, and other resources likely to help members of Congress win reelection; then they lobby members of Congress, telling them what they want, and very often getting it. Social scientists often describe those pressuring Congress as organized interests (Leech 2010; Lowery, Gray, and Baumgartner 2010). In the eyes of journalists and the public, they are "special interests."[1] Congress, responding to the wishes of the wealthy and powerful, adopts policies that enrich elites at the expense of everyone else. "For those committed to core principles of democratic governance," Hacker and Pierson (2005:49) write, "the picture that emerges is unsettling.... It is now possible for policy makers to venture far from the average voter on important matters."

There are strong arguments in favor of both these answers, but also strong arguments against them. The most obvious argument against each answer is the argument for the other. If Congress must be attuned to public opinion, it cannot be swayed by other forces. When Erikson, Wright, and McIver (1993:80) find that the relationship between public opinion and policy in American states is "awesome," they go on to say that its impact "leaves little variance to be accounted for by other variables ... state opinion is virtually the *only* cause of the net ideological tendency of policy in the state" (p. 81, emphasis in original). The finding of Stimson et al. (1995:557) that "there exists about a one-to-one translation of preferences into policy" carries the same implication.

Conversely, organized interests have a great many advantages over the general public when trying to influence policy; they have ready access to information and resources useful to elected officials, are able to continually monitor what elected officials do to help or hurt them, and can easily communicate with supporters and urge them to vote for or against incumbents (Clemens 1997; Granados and Knoke 2005; Lohmann 1998, 2003). More power for organized interests almost necessarily means less power for the general public. Public opinion and the activities of those especially

---

[1] On the power of organized interests, see, for example, Hacker and Pierson 2005; Jacobs and Page 2005; Winters and Page 2009; Lopipero, Apollonio, and Bero 2007–8; for reviews, see Lowery and Gray 2004; Leech 2010.

concerned about particular policies may be seen as arrayed against each other in battle, with each struggle over policy having winners and losers.

This book contributes to the debate between these competing views by analyzing the impact of public opinion, organized interests, and other forces on some policy proposals considered during the 101st Congress; for proposals that had been introduced in earlier congresses, or would be introduced again later, the book traces their entire history, from first introduction until they were either enacted into law or they disappeared from the congressional agenda. My hope is that learning about those proposals will increase our understanding of the democratic political process more generally.

But the book goes beyond addressing the debate between those who believe public opinion matters most, and those who believe power belongs to organized interests. It proposes a third alternative – that on many issues there may be little struggle, and the victory of one side may not mean the defeat of the other.

Normally we say that if Congress responds strongly to public opinion, the democratic political process is working well; if Congress does not respond to public opinion, it must be responding to organized interests instead, and the democratic political process is working badly. But the public cares very little about most of the hundreds of issues on the congressional agenda at any particular time. On issues people care little about, they have no reason to acquire much information or to think about the issues very much. They may have no opinion on such issues at all. If public opinion does not exist, Congress cannot very well respond to it. Yet that does not imply that the democratic political process is working badly.

What about the power of organized interests? It seems obvious that people will try to affect policy on issues that matter most to them. They can engage in a wide variety of activities supporting or opposing policy change – activities collectively described here as "advocacy." They can create political action committees to raise money for candidates; stage rallies, write letters, and collect signatures on petitions to let members of Congress know they care;

and lobby members of Congress to provide information about how best to satisfy their wishes. Yet there are reasons to think they will seldom do so. They aren't likely to create organizations because of the collective action problem. As Olson (1971) explained, organizations attempting to affect policy seek a collective good that will benefit every member. Because everyone will benefit, whether or not they have done anything to win the collective good, it is rational for everyone to let others do the necessary work. The result will be little or no collective action. The same argument holds for individuals: why try to influence policy when letting others do the work will produce the same benefit? And if little effort is made to influence Congress, such efforts cannot very well have much impact.

Thus, there are very good arguments that public opinion will be the prime determinant of policy change, and that it won't; that organized interests will be the prime determinant of policy change, and that they won't; and that on many issues there may be neither public opinion nor advocacy – perhaps that's why most bills go nowhere.

There have been thousands of studies of how public policy is affected by public opinion and advocacy. What do they tell us?

PUBLIC OPINION

To say that views about the impact of public opinion on policy vary widely would be an understatement. On one side are those who find the impact of public opinion so strong that nothing else can matter – as Stimson et al. (1995:557) conclude, "there exists about a one-to-one translation of preferences into policy" in American national policymaking; Erikson et al. (1993:80) reach the same conclusion for policymaking at the state level. On the other side are the many political sociologists who consider the idea that public opinion influences policy so absurd that they refuse to consider it in their own research and simply dismiss other views (see the review by Manza and Brooks 2012).

Few researchers would go as far as Stimson et al. (1995) and Erikson et al. (1993), but, on balance, there is great support for the view that public opinion consistently influences policy, sometimes very strongly, not only in the United States, but in other countries as well, over time and on a wide range of issues. Soroka and Wlezien (2010:182) conclude their book on the relationship between public opinion and government spending in major policy domains in the United States, the United Kingdom, and Canada by writing that "Democracy works . . . the people ultimately decide" what policy will be, especially on issues the public cares about. Brooks and Manza (2007) reach similar conclusions, finding public opinion having a powerful influence on social welfare spending in 15 economically advanced countries. Even in the Russian Federation – a country not thought of as especially democratic – the strength of the relationship between opinion and policy proves to be "surprisingly high" (Horne 2012:215). In a massive review of work on public opinion and policy in the United States, Shapiro (2011:999) concludes that although there are aspects of the relationship still subject to debate, "the overall evidence – qualifications, contingencies, and all – provides a sanguine picture of democracy at work." According to Manza and Brooks (2012:106), there is so much evidence that opinion matters that no one studying the determinants of policy can afford to ignore it.

ADVOCACY

Public opinion is a huge field of study. There is a massive amount of research being pursued, and a great deal of theoretical work as well. Though there is wide consensus about public opinion affecting public policy, there are many disagreements about how this occurs, how strong the impact is under varying circumstances, how often and how extensively opinion is manipulated by elites, and which research methods, both conventional and innovative, are most likely to advance our understanding (Shapiro 2011). But the field may be described as relatively coherent and well organized; with the exception of the political sociologists who refuse to consider public opinion, those who study it are for the most part in agreement, are aware of each other's work, and take each other seriously.

That is not true for the study of advocacy – indeed, there is no such thing as the study of advocacy as such (Harris and Gillion 2010). There are many studies of the impact of particular types of activities on policy, including lobbying, campaign contributions, protest demonstrations, media coverage, and letter writing. But no one has conceptualized the entire range of such activities – indeed, there has been no term used to describe all the activities people engage in as they try to influence policy. "Political participation" is often defined as including only the sorts of political activity traditionally seen as conventional – voting, lobbying, letter writing, and the like, but not protests or actions involving violence (Verba, Nie, and Kim 1978: 1). "Collective action" includes protests but excludes the actions of individuals (Earl, Soule, and McCarthy 2003:587; Opp 2009:47–48). "Claim-making" is intended by some authors to be more inclusive than collective action, but still excludes some types of activity and, more importantly, is defined simply as a list of types of activities – "the purposive and public articulation of political demands, calls to action, proposals, criticisms or physical attacks" (Koopmans et al. 2005:254) rather than analytically. Major works on lobbying (e.g., Baumgartner et al. 2009) will claim to be concerned about the determinants of policy but ignore social movements. Works on social movements may decry how narrow the field has become (McAdam and Boudet 2012:ch. 1) and argue that ignoring other forces may lead to an exaggerated sense of movements' importance (p. 24) but cite almost no works on lobbying or interest groups. Researchers may have data on 68 kinds of political activity engaged in by Americans during the second half of the 20th century, including press conferences, speeches, and lawsuits as well as demonstrations, yet lump them altogether under the rubric of "protest" (Walker, Martin, and McCarthy 2008:35) and pay almost no attention to work on any other kind of political activity.

To encompass all of these activities, I will use the term "policy advocacy" (or just "advocacy"). "Advocacy" is a term often used in studies of policy change (e.g., Baumgartner et al. 2009:6–8; Jenkins, Leicht, and Wendt 2006); it is rarely formally defined but generally refers to any kind of activity aimed at achieving some policy goal. Sometimes it is defined more narrowly, limited to the presentation of arguments in support of a policy proposal (Smith 1984:45) or to "systematic efforts" as opposed to "sporadic outbursts" (Prakash and Gugerty 2010:1). Sometimes the definition is complex. The sociologists Andrews and Edwards (2004:481) define advocacy organizations as making "public interest claims either promoting or resisting social change that, if implemented, would conflict with the social, cultural, political, or economic interests or values of other constituencies or groups." This definition goes beyond the political and requires making judgments about the consequences of an activity before deciding if it is advocacy. Here policy advocacy will be defined simply as all kinds of publicly reported activity supporting or opposing specific policies.

Just because there is no unified study of advocacy, that doesn't mean that study of various types of advocacy doesn't contribute to our understanding of policy change. In fact, it does. But there is much less agreement about the impact of advocacy than there is about the impact of public opinion.

McCammon (2012:11) begins her study of the movement for the inclusion of women in juries by writing that "Social movements are one of the primary agents of social change in modern society.... In fact, a sizable body of scholarly study provides evidence of the far-reaching effects of collective action" (see also Snow, Soule, and Kriesi 2004 for a similar view). In a recent review on "The Political Consequences of Social Movements," Amenta and his co-authors (2010) are quite a bit more cautious: "Determining whether a movement has had any consequences and, if so, which ones, is not an easy task" (p. 300). They conclude, a bit vaguely, that "The biggest and best-studied movements have been shown to be politically influential in various ways, and movement protest is especially influential in helping to set policy agendas," while noting how little we know about the less-studied – that is, the vast majority – of movements. McAdam and Boudet (2012:24) warn that "we should be wary of the affirming evidence" about movement impact because so many studies leave out other forces, part of whose impact may be incorrectly attributed to movements (see also Amenta and Caren 2004:476).

The study of interest groups is a bit different only in that the contrast between expectations and findings is so stark. Leech (2010:534) notes that "politicians, the public, and most other political scientists all are convinced that interest groups are so powerful," yet the actual influence is amazingly difficult to "pin down" in their research. Review articles find that sometimes interest groups influence policy and sometimes they don't, leaving conclusions about impact at best "inconclusive" (Baumgartner and Leech 1998:187: Smith 1995:123; also see Francia 2010). Ansolabehere, de Figueiredo, and Snyder (2003:117) confront a similar paradox in their analysis of campaign contributions – although everyone is sure that contributions affect how legislators vote, contributions in fact "have no detectable effects on the behavior of legislators" once legislator ideology is taken into account. In my own review with April Linton of many articles in major journals (Burstein and Linton 2002), we found social movement organizations (SMOs) and interest groups together (collectively called "interest organizations") affected policy less than half the time. Confronting all the negative findings in light of their own theoretical arguments, Baumgartner et al. (2009:22) begin with an expectation that must be viewed as counterintuitive – that "the relation between control over material resources and gaining the policy goals that one wants in Washington is likely to be close to zero."

Thus, oversimplifying only a little, we may say that there is considerable evidence for the view that policy is clearly affected by public opinion and that the evidence about the influence of advocacy is mixed. As to the possibility that often neither public opinion nor advocacy will affect policy because neither exists for many issues, there seems to have been no research, and so we can't reach any conclusions at all.

These conclusions may seem unlikely to some and inadequate to others (certainly the total absence of conclusions about the latter possibilities is inadequate). No one would agree more than many of the researchers who have done the studies and written the reviews; they often highlight major problems in their own work and that of their colleagues. Here I will summarize some of their major concerns, and add some of my own, in order to point the way to improving our research. The book will then try to address the concerns with new approaches to research that will advance our understanding of the policy process.

CONCERNS ABOUT THE STUDY OF POLICY CHANGE

Sampling

Although it is widely believed that public opinion strongly affects policy, Page (2002) disagrees – he believes that the actual impact is much weaker than we think. We overestimate the impact of opinion on policy, he argues, partly because we mostly study issues on which the impact is especially likely to be strong – issues especially important to the public. It is on those issues that legislators are most likely to do what the public wants – the legislators know that the public is paying attention to what they do, and feel they have little choice other than doing what the public wants, because they want to be reelected (Page 2002; Shapiro 2011:986, 991). Our estimates of the impact of opinion are too high, in other words, because of sampling bias; if we studied a random sample of issues, we would get a more accurate – and lower – estimate of the impact of opinion on policy.

Leech (2010:540) contends that those studying organized interests make the same mistake. Political scientists trying to gauge the impact of organized interests on policy tend to analyze issues that are especially prominent and provoke a lot of interest group activity. "All these factors," she writes, "increase the interest group's chance of success." McAdam and Boudet (2012:181) state that past work has "dramatically exaggerated the frequency and causal significance of true social movements." Why? In large part because the movements studied most often are "wildly nonrepresentative" of all such movements. Other scholars also express concern about how our conclusions about policy change may be undermined by our studying a biased sample of issues (e.g., Baumgartner et al. 2009; Gamson 1990; Jacobs and Tope 2007:1486–87; Jones and Jenkins-Smith 2009:54; Krehbiel 1995:921; Schroedel 1986; Wittman 1995).

There have been two major attempts in the study of policy change to overcome sampling bias: Gamson (1990) analyzed a random sample of SMOs, and Baumgartner et al. (2009) a random sample of issues on which there had been lobbying in Washington, D.C. So why not study a random sample of policies? Because, writes Nicholson-Crotty (2009:196), "gathering a random sample of policies is effectively impossible because of the difficulty of identifying the universe of observations." We have no comprehensive list of policies from which to select a sample. The reason, I claim, is that we have no good definition of "policy" that could provide the basis for such a list.

Defining "Policy"

Gamson's analysis of a random sample of SMOs (which he called "challenging groups") was highly praised – "among the most significant early works in the emerging field of social movement studies," according to McAdam and Boudet (2012:30) – but never emulated. The reason? It would be too much work, or, as McAdam and Boudet (ibid.) put it, "it is hard to empirically command as many as fifty-three cases." Both Gamson (1990) and Baumgartner et al. (2009:ch. 1 and methodological appendix) show that it was indeed very hard work to create lists of SMOs and issues, respectively, but they managed to do so. Why should proceeding in a similar way with regard to policies be "effectively impossible"?

Implausible as it may seem, a key issue is definitional. Baumgartner and Leech (1998:38) wrote that despite the vast amount of attention devoted to the study of issues, there was no good "single definition" of an issue, and because there was no definition, "there can be no universe of issues from which to sample." Within a few years, though, they developed an operational definition of "issue," created a universe from which to sample – issues mentioned in nearly twenty thousand reports on lobbying filed under the terms of the 1995 Lobbying Disclosure Act – and based their research on the sample (Baumgartner and Leech 2001; Baumgartner et al. 2009). Perhaps not everyone would agree with their definition and procedure, but what they did had the tremendous advantages of enabling research on a sample to proceed, and making generalization possible.

"Policy" is like "issue" – there is no single definition of the term, and therefore no universe of policies from which to sample. Social scientists study an extremely diverse set of things under the heading of "policy," including the sum of government actions on many important laws seen as liberal or conservative (Erikson, MacKuen, and Stimson 2002), expenditures by government agencies or on large sets of policies (Meyer and Minkoff 2004; Brooks and Manza 2007; Soroka and Wlezien 2010), numbers of laws enacted in a policy domain (Olzak and Soule 2009), number of congressional votes (McAdam and Su 2002), specific legal provisions in laws enacted (Lax and Phillips 2009), and many others. In contrast to Gamson and to Baumgartner and Leech, those who study policy have not felt the need to develop an operational definition of policy and a list of policies from which to sample. There has thus been no way to overcome sampling bias in the study of policy, and no way to overcome uncertainty about the credibility of our conclusions about the determinants of policy change.

Chapter 2 proposes a definition of policy – the "policy proposal," meaning the content of a bill (or set of identical bills) introduced into Congress – identifies a universe of observations – all the non-appropriations public bills introduced – from which to sample, and selects for analysis a stratified random sample of 60 policy proposals. The general approach is similar to that of Baumgartner et al. (2009) but differs in significant ways. It may be possible to think of the two approaches as complementary attempts to improve our ability to generalize about the process of policy change.

Causality

It seems obvious that when assessing the impact of public opinion on policy, the measure of public opinion should match the measure of policy. If members of Congress are voting on a bill proposing a particular policy, we need to see what public opinion is on *that particular bill*, and not on something else, to gauge meaningfully the impact of opinion on policy.

Yet that is not how research on public opinion and policy proceeds. According to Jessee (2009:63), until his own research was conducted in 2005 and 2006, "there ha[d] not been *any* large-scale data sets capable of measuring citizen views on the same scale as the votes of legislators or the positions taken by the president" (emphasis added). The reason is essentially practical – survey organizations seldom ask the public's opinions about specific policy proposals, so we lack the public opinion data on such proposals necessary to reach meaningful conclusions.

This means that, for example, research on congressional voting to end American involvement in the Vietnam War does not have data on whether the public thought the United States should get out of Vietnam; instead, the research relies mainly on a question about whether American entry into the war had been a mistake (Burstein and Freudenburg 1978; McAdam and Su 2002). Research on congressional action on civil rights uses data not on the public's views of civil rights bills being considered, but rather on views about integration and race relations (see the extensive discussion in Burstein 1998b:ch. 3).

The consequence of proceeding this way should be apparent; as Jones (2011:767) writes, "any resulting estimate of congruence between the two [opinion and policy] will be inaccurate" – probably lower than it would be if the public opinion questions were closely matched to the policy being considered.

The same may be said of advocacy. The biggest and most widely used American set of data on advocacy activities (described in Walker et al. 2008) provides detailed information about such activities in major policy domains, including the environment, civil rights, women's rights, peace, social policy, and education. The data are widely used in studies of federal policy to estimate the impact of advocacy on policy (e.g., Johnson, Agnone, and McCarthy 2010; McAdam and Su 2002; Olzak and Soule 2009). But the data do not gauge advocacy on any particular policy. The studies include measures of congressional action and measures of advocacy, but not measures of advocacy directed at particular congressional actions. The consequence of this must be the same as with public opinion – the estimates of impact must be inaccurate, probably lower than they would be if the advocacy were matched to the policies being considered.[2]

Chapters 3–5 consider the problems involved in trying to gauge the impact of opinion and advocacy on policy, when conventional measures of opinion and advocacy are not closely matched to policy and therefore cannot be said to be intended to cause policy change.

Ignorance

Most people know little or nothing or about most policies – and can't be expected to. Sometimes major pieces of legislation very important to the public are so complex that it almost impossible to understand them in detail. The "Patient Protection and Affordable Care Act" (often called "Obamacare"), Public Law 111–148, is 906 pages long (http://www.gpo.gov/fdsys/pkg/PLAW-111publ148/pdf/PLAW-111publ148.pdf). The public consistently favored major provisions of the law but was much more divided about the law as a whole, a result attributed by some to its complexity and the capacity of elites to confuse people about it (Jacobs and Mettler 2011:919; Kaplan 2012).

More generally, the public has neither the time, the interest, nor the ability needed to understand most policies being considered by

---

[2] The largest data sets about advocacy in Europe suffer from the same problem, but European social scientists focus on describing the development and nature of advocacy, and less than the Americans on trying to gauge the impact of advocacy on policy; see Koopmans and Statham 1999, 2010; Koopmans et al. 2005.

Congress, and this is inevitable – people devote themselves to things that are far more urgent or interesting to them on a day-to-day basis than policy, such as earning a living, dealing with family, and, if possible, having a good time (Converse 1964; Althaus 2003; Luskin and Bullock 2011).

When the level of public ignorance was discovered by polling organizations and social scientists in the 1940s and 1950s, it appeared to represent a serious challenge to the concept of representative government. How can the government be said to respond to the public if the public has no opinion on most issues? And how can the public be said to control the government if it doesn't know or care what the government is doing on most policies?

There have been at least two major ways to address these concerns while trying to hold onto the belief that "democracy works" (Soroka and Wlezien 2010:182; see also Shapiro 2011:999). The first has been to argue that although individuals may be ignorant, the public as a whole may be seen as rational (Page and Shapiro 1992). Collectively, public opinion responds to events in ways that seem sensible; changes in the overall distribution of preferences are the product mostly of changes of mind by citizens who are relatively knowledgeable about politics, while the errors of the ignorant more or less cancel out (Stimson 2004 also discusses this possibility). There is some debate about whether this view is plausible – Stimson (2004) prefers to use the term "orderly" rather than "rational," while Ellis and Stimson (2012:192) argue that measures of ideology are "fraught with substantial systematic misrepresentation" – but it still wins considerable support (Ansolabehere, Rodden, and Snyder 2008).

Second, many social scientists who study opinion and policy go to where the public is. That is, they focus on policy questions the public is able to respond to – not questions about specific policies, but rather about the direction in which they'd like to see public policy move, in a general way, in broad policy domains. Very often the focus is on whether the public wants government expenditures increased, decreased, or kept the same in domains such as education, defense, health, or social welfare (Erikson et al. 2002: ch. 6; Soroka and Wlezien 2010; Stimson 1999). This approach has proven extremely fruitful, as researchers have been able to show that public policy responds strongly to such measures of opinion, and, even more significantly, public opinion then responds to what the government does, creating the meaningful mutual responsiveness – in what Soroka and Wlezien (2010) call their "thermostatic model" – that is the basis for their conclusion that democracy works.

Soroka and Wlezien's (2010) conclusions are very powerful, but what about specific policies? As important as it is to discover that in broad policy domains, the government and the public respond to each other, their picture is incomplete – they can't say whether the government responds to the public on specific policies, or vice versa. Their argument is, essentially, that it makes no sense to study issues about which the public is ignorant, writing that "expecting representative democracy to represent preferences that do not exist, in domains about which people do not care, is unreasonable" (p. 182).

It may very well be unreasonable to expect representative democracy to respond to opinions that do not exist, but it seems very reasonable to ask what the implications are for our understanding of democracy. If the government is not responding to the public on most issues, because the public has no opinions, to whom is it responding? If it is responding to the needs of particular powerful organizations and individuals, doesn't that matter? And how are we to understand the democratic political process if we ignore those issues? Chapter 3 addresses these questions, not to question others' conclusions, but rather to complement what they say in order to provide a more complete picture of the democratic political process.

Advocacy

As noted above, though the number of studies considering the impact of public opinion on public policy is vast, there are no comparable studies considering the impact of advocacy as such. Instead, scholars focus on particular types of advocacy – protest, lobbying, etc. – and on advocacy by particular types of organizations – SMOs and interest groups.

During the last few years, there has been something of a revolt against the narrowness of conventional approaches, with both American and European scholars saying that those concerned about political mobilization and policy should broaden the range of the activities and organizations they study (Koopmans and Statham 1999; McAdam and Boudet 2012). This view has been implemented most comprehensively by the European scholars who argue that it is essential to take into account all "political claims" (their term; Koopmans et al. 2005:254), "regardless of the form in which they are made (statement, violence, repression, decision, demonstration, court ruling, and so on) and regardless of the nature of the actor (governments, social movements, NGOs, individuals, anonymous actors, and so on)" (see also Koopmans and Statham 1999; Koopmans and Statham 2010b).

It is difficult to disagree with the logic of their argument, though the practical difficulties of following through on their research agenda are tremendous – there is a reason why most researchers stick to more limited sets of activities and actors. Indeed, the researchers calling for a broader approach generally limit themselves to activities reported in newspapers, paying little attention (at least for now) to the insider activities reported in official records and elsewhere (for example, lobbying of the sort analyzed by Baumgartner et al. 2009). And the task of collecting data on what I call advocacy seems so immense that those who do so seldom try to gauge the impact of such advocacy on policy – they stick more to the study of mobilization itself.

Chapters 4 and 5 try to address many of the concerns discussed above – sampling, causality, the desirability of analyzing all types of advocacy – by examining publicly reported advocacy directed specifically at the 60 policy proposals, collecting data not from just one or a handful of newspapers per country (as is the case for the large American and European data sets), but rather from a major electronic database, finding data on advocacy in a total of 116 newspapers and periodicals. On the one hand, narrowing the focus to advocacy on specific policy proposals may limit the amount of advocacy discovered; on the other hand, searching so widely should make it possible to discover more than others do.

I also ask what it is that matters most about advocacy. Researchers often make broad arguments about why the kinds of advocacy they study should affect policy, but often the arguments are rather vague and the predictions are along the lines of: the more advocacy, of whatever type, the more impact the advocates will have on policy. I am more specific, drawing on the arguments of others to suggest that what matters especially greatly to legislators is information[3] – about the importance of policies, the efficacy of proposed solutions, and the potential impact of their stances on their reelection chances – meaning that advocacy is especially likely to be effective when it provides information to legislators that they find useful. Chapters 4–6 consider the impact of information on members of Congress, particularly Chapter 6, which focuses on information provided at a venue designed to enhance the flow of information, namely, committee hearings.

How much impact can we expect advocacy to have on policy? The arguments presented so far lead in two opposing directions. By focusing on advocacy directed at particular policies, rather than, as is more customary, advocacy simply expressed in broad policy domains, I should find advocacy having a stronger impact than others have. Here potential cause – advocacy aimed at specific policies – is more tightly linked to potential effect – impact on Congress – than in most previous work. However, the theoretical arguments made by Olson (1971) and others suggest that I will find very little advocacy directed at most proposals – perhaps too little to have much impact. In that case, I should find advocacy having less impact than others have.

PLAN OF THE BOOK

In line with the logic of this chapter thus far, Chapter 2 will focus on the very desirable (Gamson 1990; Baumgartner et al. 2009) but allegedly "effectively impossible" (Nicholson-Crotty 2009:196)

---

[3] For example, Arnold 1990:38; Baumgartner et al. 2009:54–57; Hansen 1991:12; Kingdon 1995:210; Krehbiel 1991:20, 62; Leyden 1995; Smith 1995:98, 101.

task of developing an operational definition of policy, specifying a population of policies, drawing a stratified random sample of 60 such policies, and showing both that the procedure is feasible and that it immediately leads to findings that enhance our understanding of the congressional policy process.

Chapter 3 examines the impact of public opinion on policy and, in contrast to most past work, considers what we find when we take into account the public's lack of knowledge about most policies and assesses the implications of the findings for our thinking about the struggle between public opinion and advocacy for influence over policy.

Chapters 4 and 5 move on to the study of advocacy. Chapter 4 describes how much publicly reported advocacy there is directed at the 60 policy proposals, who advocates, and what they do. Chapter 5 considers the impact of publicly reported advocacy on congressional action.

Chapter 6 moves farther into the policy process, analyzing testimony at congressional hearings on the 27 policy proposals for which hearings were held, considering the testimony of almost a thousand witnesses, with a special focus on the information they provide to members of Congress and the impact of such information on congressional action.

Chapter 7 concludes the book, assessing its implications for our understanding of democratic politics and making suggestions for future work.

2

Policy Change

It seems obvious that if we want to understand policy change, we should agree on what we mean by "policy." That shouldn't be a problem. Policy has long been studied by political scientists, sociologists, economists, historians, lawyers, scholars in other fields, and journalists. We could use their definition.

Unfortunately, they don't have an agreed-upon definition precise enough to be useful. "Policy" is formally defined at the beginning of many textbooks, but researchers rarely pay attention to such definitions. Instead, they treat their subject as both broad and intuitively obvious – it has to do with things the government, or some part of a government, does, might do, or might decline to do, or the views of particular people as to what the government should do. In the final chapter of *The Oxford Handbook of Public Policy* (Moran, Rein, and Goodin 2008), Klein and Marmor (2008:892) call public policy a "chameleon concept" and write that they "define public policy quite simply. It is what governments do and neglect to do. It is about politics, resolving (or at least attenuating) conflicts about resources, rights, and morals." While this type of definition is very common, as a guide to research it's not very useful – it is too broad and too vague to be of much value.[1]

---

[1] As noted in Chapter 1, Baumgartner and Leech (1998:38) make much the same point about another concept central to the study of politics – "issue."

As a practical matter, policy is defined operationally – it's whatever people study when they say they're studying policy. Under that rubric, researchers study a vast array of different things, conceptualized and measured in a great many ways. Policies have regularly been defined and measured in terms of:

- Specific, narrowly drawn laws or policy proposals, such as the Lee amendment to the Social Security Act Amendments of 1939 (Amenta, Caren, and Olasky 2005), state ratifications of the ultimately unratified Equal Rights Amendment (Soule and Olzak 2004), and state laws allowing women to serve on juries (McCammon et al. 2007; McCammon 2012);

- Large numbers of laws on many issues, summarized in numerical indexes, including the liberalism of major laws enacted by Congress during the second half of the 20th century (Erikson, MacKuen, and Stimson 2002), the overall liberalism of a variety of state laws (Erikson, Wright, and McIver 1993; Gray et al. 2004; Monogan, Gray, and Lowery 2009); and the stance of all U.S. statutes enacted between 1789 and 1968 on capitalism, internal sovereignty, redistribution, and other dimensions (Ginsberg 1976);

- Expenditures, including spending on U.S. civil rights policy (Meyer and Minkoff 2004), social welfare and foreign aid cross-nationally (Brooks and Manza 2007; Therien and Noel 2000), welfare, health, education, the environment, and urban areas in the United States (Wlezien 2004); and health, welfare, crime, education, and other policy domains in the United States, the United Kingdom, and Canada (Soroka and Wlezien 2010);

- What laws say about particular topics, such as same-sex sexual relations (Frank and McEneaney 1999), hate crimes (Grattet, Jenness, and Curry 1998), sex (Frank, Camp, and Boutcher 2010), smoking (Shipan and Volden 2006); childhood (Boli-Bennett and Meyer 1978), and wages and working hours legislation (Steinberg 1982);

– Policy preferences of elected officials and other elites, as expressed in roll call votes on the Vietnam War (McAdam and Su 2002) and surveys concerning foreign policy (Jacobs and Page 2005).

Some researchers justify what they do in great detail and try to show why their measures are particularly good (e.g., Erikson et al. 2002; Brooks and Manza 2007:ch. 3; Grattet et al. 1998:291–93). Many are much more casual, doing little more than stating that it is convenient to define and measure policy a particular way. Yet social scientists very seldom take differences among the measures into account when trying to generalize about policy change. They infrequently suggest in literature reviews that the results of some studies should be discounted because their measures of policy were of poor quality. They do not propose that a study analyzing 10 policies, or policies in 10 countries, should be weighted more heavily than a study analyzing one policy, or policies in only one country. They rarely consider whether conclusions about the determinants of policy change are affected by how policy is measured – for example, whether public opinion affects policies measured in terms of expenditures the same way it affects policies measured in terms of how liberal they are. They fail to ascertain whether statistical results might be affected by the quality of measurement – whether, for example, a finding that protest has no effect on a policy means that protest really has no impact, or only that policy was measured so poorly that the impact could not be detected.

In sum, though individual researchers may thoughtfully and carefully develop measures for their own purposes, they don't see themselves as contributing to the study of policy measurement more broadly conceived. There are experts on the measurement of public opinion, lobbying, protest demonstrations, and other forms of advocacy (see, e.g., Schuman and Presser 1996; Tilly 2008; Baumgartner and Leech 1998; Earl et al. 2004), but no experts on the measurement of policy as such. It is hard to believe that the neglect of measurement hasn't impeded our advance in understanding policy change.

This chapter tries to advance our thinking about the conceptualization and measurement of policy. It argues that good measures of policy should meet at least three criteria. First, the measures should be objective. This would seem to go without saying, but some researchers use subjective measures – in some instances, because the development of objective measures is so challenging.

Second, measures of policy should be politically meaningful to the public, at least in studies of the impact of advocacy. If we want to understand how people influence policy, we must think in terms of policies people would *want* to influence and *might be able* to influence. We can easily imagine people wanting to influence specific policies being considered by a legislature. It is more difficult to imagine people caring about or wanting to influence levels of legislative activity – how many laws are passed on some issue or how often members of Congress vote, for example – yet there are studies that measure policy in terms of such activity (e.g., Johnson, Agnone, and McCarthy 2010; McAdam and Su 2002). People might want to influence government spending on social welfare, but standard measures of social welfare are often the sum of expenditures on many different policies adopted one at a time over long periods of time (e.g., Brooks and Manza 2007; Soroka and Wlezien 2010); trying to study advocacy on all the relevant policies over a long period would be incredibly difficult. Indeed, researchers who study aggregated measures of spending seldom include measures of advocacy among the likely determinants of policy change and never try to assess the impact of advocacy on all the relevant laws separately.

Third, measures of policy should, if possible, provide a basis for generalization. If we want to generalize about policy change, it is very important we be able to identify a population of policies and sample from it. Gamson (1990) has shown the utility of this way of thinking with regard to SMOs and Baumgartner et al. (2009) with regard to issues on which there has been lobbying. It is time to build on their work with regard to policies.

This chapter contends that a particular measure, the "policy proposal" (based on congressional bills), can serve especially well as the basis for work on policy change, describes a stratified random sample of policy proposals addressed by the U.S. Congress, and considers how long policy proposals stay on the congressional agenda and what this suggests about the policy process. Subsequent chapters try to explain what happens to the policy proposals – why some never get beyond being introduced into Congress, while others proceed well into the legislative process and some are ultimately enacted into law.

CONCEPTUALIZING POLICY

Measuring Policy Objectively

It may seem obvious that measures of policy should be objective, but in fact much research measures policy subjectively. Subjective definitions take two forms. The first is when policies are put into very broad categories, such as environmental policy, tax policy, or defense policy. Because the terms are commonsensical, it seems clear in a general way what is being referred to; but close analysis will often show room for disagreement. For example, are expenditures on highways part of defense policy? Many people would say no, but the law creating the interstate highway system in the United States was called the "National Interstate and Defense Highways Act of 1956" – Congress was willing to support the system only if it was portrayed as contributing significantly to national defense. What about advanced placement courses in high schools? Created under the auspices of the National Defense Education Act. Federal policy on tobacco? Sometimes part of agricultural policy, sometimes health policy (Baumgartner and Jones 1993:114–17, 209–10). When different researchers discuss broad topics like environmental policy, it may appear that they are discussing the same thing, but there may be substantial differences among them (Agnone 2007:1598).

Policies are also defined subjectively when thoughtful, careful researchers bump up against current limits in our concepts and methods. Baumgartner and Leech (1998:38) describe how seriously our understanding of the policy process was impeded by the lack of an objective definition of "issue" – a term very much like policy – and yet, in their recent work (with others) on lobbying (Baumgartner et al. 2009:3), they let issues be defined subjectively by the lobbyists they're studying. Similarly, in their effort to gauge the impact of public opinion on policy, Erikson et al. (2002) meticulously try to create an objective measure of public opinion, but, as careful as they are, their state-of-the-art measure of policy is based in significant ways on subjective decisions about the relative importance of different laws, whether laws were of national or local concern, and whether they moved in a liberal or conservative direction. "Obviously, our judgment is subjective," they write (p. 330), and, in a statement suggesting the difficulties they faced, go on to say that "Readers who disagree with our measure may find reason to invent their own." Objectivity is a critical goal, but sometimes so difficult to attain that researchers decide to proceed with less-than-ideal measures. This is quite understandable, but objectivity should remain the goal (as it is for Erikson et al.).

Politically Meaningful Measures of Policy

If we want to gauge the impact of public opinion and advocacy on policy, policy should be measured in a way that makes sense politically – it must be possible to imagine the public having opinions about it, advocates expressing their views on it, and Congress acting on it.

Many measures of policy lack these qualities. Some studies claim to measure policy, but actually measure legislative activity – for example, the number of laws enacted in a particular policy domain, or the number of times Congress votes on an issue (e.g., Agnone 2007; McAdam and Su 2002; Olzak and Soule 2009). But citizens, advocates, and legislators rarely care about how many laws are enacted or how many times Congress votes; they care about particular laws that say particular things. It matters whether Congress votes on a bill, but not how often.

Other studies use measures of policy that are substantive but cannot be voted on. These are generally measures that are the product of much legislative activity, often taking place over a

substantial period of time. For example, measures of welfare state
effort and similar concepts (spending on a range of social welfare
programs relative to gross national or domestic product) essentially summarize the impact of many laws, enacted and amended
over many years, on expenditures for particular purposes (Brooks
and Manza 2006; Hicks and Misra 1993; Huber and Stephens
2000; Pampel and Williamson 1988; Wilensky 2002:ch. 5); measures of state policy liberalism sum up the general direction of
policy in U.S. states across a number of policy domains (Erikson
et al. 1993; Gray et al. 2004); measures of federal policy liberalism
sum up congressional action on many laws over the course of
several decades; and other indexes also aggregate legislative
action on many programs, sometimes dozens (Jenkins, Leicht,
and Wendt 2006).

Such aggregate measures are often useful descriptions of exist-
ing policies, but they're not politically meaningful during the
policy process for the public, advocates, or policymakers.
Legislators don't vote on welfare state effort, state policy liberalism, or state economic development policy; they vote on specific
bills. And policy advocates don't generally try to influence broad
composite measures of policy. Though advocates express general
policy preferences – more spending on welfare, more spending on
defense – most of their efforts will be devoted to affecting legislative action on particular bills. Study of the correlates of broad
measures of policy can teach us a lot about the general circumstances associated with variations in policy – for example, public
opinion, economic development, union membership – but not
about the policy process – not about how the public's preferences
on particular policies, or advocacy efforts directed at those policies, influence legislative action on those policies.

Generalizing about Policy Change

There are thousands of studies of policy change in democratic
countries. But can we generalize about the causes of policy
change? No. Our studies focus very disproportionately on some
policy domains while paying little attention to others, and within

those domains they focus on policies seen as especially important and neglect the rest (Burstein 1998c). We study, that is, a very biased sample of policies, meaning that attempts to generalize from our sample to the policy process in general are likely to be wrong. In fact, we already know some generalizations are wrong – public opinion is often said to strongly influence policy, for example, yet we know this is much more likely for policies highly salient to the public than for the vast majority of policies the public cares less about (Page 2002). How much impact does public opinion or any other likely cause of policy change have across the entire range of policies on the political agenda? Books and articles often conclude with confident-sounding generalizations, but because our studies focus on atypical issues, the confidence is unwarranted.

What to do seems obvious: define a population of policies, draw a random sample, analyze the determinants of the sample of policies, and generalize. Yet this has never been done, for at least two reasons.[2]

First, even though most social scientists understand sampling and its importance for generalization, many don't see its relevance to their own fields. On subjects where sampling is not the conventional approach to research, its utility may simply not occur to researchers; sometimes it is not taken seriously, or even rejected on principle. As Becker (1998:84) has written, social scientists often "concentrat[e] their efforts in any particular field of study on a few cases considered to be archetypal, apparently in the belief that if you can explain those, all the other cases will automatically fall into line." "Generalizations meant to describe all the organizations of a society," he continues (p. 94), "have rested on the study of a nonrandomly selected few, with the result that sociology suffered from a huge sampling bias." In the study of politics, researchers have been pointing out since the 1970s how sampling bias in the analysis of both organizations and issues may lead to inaccurate conclusions (e.g., Baumgartner et al. 2009; Burstein, Bauldry, and Froese 2005; Gamson 1990; Krehbiel 1995:921;

---

[2] Baumgartner et al. (2009) come closest, but their definition of issues is subjective.

Page 2002; Schroedel 1986; Wittman 1995), but their arguments have had almost no impact on the study of policy change.

Second, those who see the value in defining a population of policies and then sampling shortly find themselves confronting a very significant barrier to progress: without an objective, politically meaningful definition of policy, there is no way to define a population of policies from which to sample. Yet Nicholson-Crotty (2009:196) writes that "gathering a random sample of policies ... is effectively impossible because of the difficulty of identifying the universe of observations."[3] The rest of this chapter is devoted to showing that while the task may be difficult, it is not impossible.

DEFINING POLICY – THE "POLICY PROPOSAL"

What does Congress address that might be thought of as a policy, can be described objectively, is politically meaningful, and belongs to a readily identifiable population? One plausible answer would be what Kingdon (1995:150) calls a policy proposal – a particular proposed solution to a policy problem, one out of possibly many alternatives that might be considered by a legislature (Kingdon uses the terms "proposal," "solution," and "alternative" interchangeably). Intuitively, it is easy to imagine tracing the rise and fall of support for a particular proposed solution to a policy problem.

But what does this mean operationally? How are we to identify a particular proposal and distinguish it from others? How might we define a proposal in a way consistent with conventional, informal discussions of policy, yet formal and precise enough to be used in research? There are no good, widely accepted answers to these questions.

One possibility is to define a policy proposal as a bill. Kingdon (1995:150–51) does this at one point, writing with regard to

---

[3] He does not attribute the impossibility specifically to definitional problems, but it would be difficult to describe more forcefully the importance of sampling policies and the difficulty of doing so.

airline deregulation that "Senators Howard Cannon and Edward Kennedy had agreed on a proposal, and the administration simply adopted that bill wholesale." Kingdon provides this as an example, not a formal definition, but there is a lot to be said from a social-scientific perspective for focusing on bills: bills are distinct, readily identified entities; they are at the heart of the legislative process; and it is easy to see a bill as a particular proposed solution to a public problem.

Such a definition seems too narrow, though, because it doesn't conform to how we normally discuss politics. Those who write about politics often assess support for what they probably think of as policy proposals, stating, for example, that congressional support for repeal of the estate tax increased over the course of a few years, or that support for a balanced budget amendment to the Constitution increased a few years ago but then declined. Such descriptions seem to convey important information, but they are not descriptions of support for single bills. Multiple identical bills are often introduced in each two-year congress, and they all die at the end of the congress – if a proposal has not been enacted, supporters must reintroduce it as a new bill after the next congress convenes.

It would be more reasonable to think of a policy proposal as a particular alternative, potentially manifested in any number of identical (or at least highly similar) bills. All such bills, introduced in a single congress, or in different congresses, could be seen as manifesting the same policy proposal. Analyzing policy change would mean analyzing congressional action on the proposal, not on any single bill.

Unfortunately, such a definition seems problematic in its own way. How similar must bills be to be viewed as manifestations of the same policy proposal? When bills are identical, this is no problem – same content, same proposal. And when they are very different, it is no problem either – different content, different proposal.

But what about intermediate cases in which bills are similar but not identical? On one side would be bills that address the same problem and share some elements, but express different, possibly even competing, approaches. This is what observers often mean when they say that there are "three patients' rights bills" or "two welfare reform bills" on the agenda. It would not make sense to think of these as representing the same policy proposal. On the other side would be bills that differ only slightly. Arguably, such bills should be treated as manifestations of the same proposal. The problem, then, would be to decide where the dividing line should be, between bills so similar they may be treated as identical, and those not similar enough.

If the number of alternatives proposed on an issue is small, and it is easy to distinguish among them, then each could readily be treated as a different proposal, and support for each described in a meaningful way. If, in contrast, the number is large and it is difficult to distinguish among them, it would not make sense to think of congressional support for a clearly delineated policy proposal; describing congressional action would be far more difficult.[4]

What is a reasonable expectation – that proposals on an issue during a particular period will be few in number and readily distinguishable, or many that blend into each other? If there were strong reasons to expect many proposals, not distinctly different, it might make no sense to proceed. There are some reasons to expect this to be the case. Policymaking might often proceed through a winnowing process, starting with many proposals and gradually eliminating most of them, or through an elaboration process, starting with a few and developing more as policy ideas are refined (Burstein and Bricher 1997; Burstein, Bricher, and Einwohner 1995; Polsby 1984).

Yet there are also reasons to expect proposals to be few: legislators may lack the resources to develop many proposals, and the need to develop and maintain coalitions may lead legislators to stick to a proposal they've won agreement on

---

[4] I am not considering here amendments to bills being debated on the floor; my focus is on the earlier part of the policy process, when proposals are first conceptualized and introduced.

(Baumgartner and Jones 1993; Burstein 1998b; Kingdon 1995; Schneider and Ingram 1988). And there may be no point disagreeing about details before a proposal is further along in the policy process and has a reasonable chance of being enacted.

There has been very little research on similarities and differences among congressional bills on the same subject, but it is consistent with the "few proposals" view: on antidiscrimination bills, at least, Congress considers very few policy proposals at any given time – very often, just one (Burstein 1998b, 2002). More generally, debates within policy domains typically focus on a very small number of alternatives (Boli-Bennett and Meyer 1978; Burstein et al. 1995; Burstein and Bricher 1997; Gamson and Modigliani 1987, 1989). Thus, I thought it worthwhile to see if policy could be defined in terms of policy proposals. And if it were practical to study policy proposals, I wanted to be able to analyze the forces affecting what happened to them – what happened historically, as some proposals were ignored and others moved through the policy process, from introduction to committee hearings and then, potentially, floor debate, passage by one or both houses of Congress, and enactment.

To determine whether studying policy proposals was feasible, I first had to define a population and then develop a sampling procedure. I began with the 5,977 public bills introduced into the 101st Congress, 1989–90 (U.S. Library of Congress 1998: table 6-1) – a congress relatively recent when the research was started, but sufficiently far in the past to make it possible to track each proposal forward through time and find out what eventually happened to it – was it enacted or did it disappear from the congressional agenda?

I wanted to focus on bills explicitly proposing new policies, so I excluded appropriations bills. I then selected a stratified random sample of bills introduced in the House of Representatives: 50 chosen at random, and then, to ensure the inclusion of some bills that had proceeded well into the legislative process, 10 more randomly chosen from among bills that had been reported out of committee. A sample of 60 may not seem large, but tracing their history was an unprecedented and, as it turned out, extremely labor-intensive task.[5] I had to go back historically far enough to be sure I had found the very first introduction of the proposal, and far enough into the future to be sure I found what ultimately happened to the proposal (including the possibility of its being reintroduced after a hiatus). The sample is large enough to show the utility of trying to generalize about policy change and contrasts strongly with most studies of policy change, which consider one issue, or at most a handful, with no thought about generalizability.[6]

Summaries of the 60 bills were found in the *Thomas* database of the U.S. Library of Congress (2001). To determine whether the bills could be seen as manifestations of a policy proposal – of a particular set of elements, duplicated (or nearly duplicated) in a set of identical (or nearly identical) bills – the following procedure was devised: "Bill tracking reports" were found in the *Lexis-Nexis Congressional Universe* (2001), and the Congressional Research Service index terms at the end of each report were used as key words to search for bills in the *Thomas* database. (The CRS index terms were more useful than those in the *Thomas* database, but the latter had more information on the bills themselves.) Where it seemed appropriate, variations in key words and in their order were used as well – for example, "handicapped" as well as "disabled" with regard to the Americans with Disabilities Act. If the original bill was an omnibus bill, subdivided into parts called "titles," each addressing a different subject, the first substantive title was selected and treated as a bill.

---

[5] Studies of policy often consider relatively small numbers of cases in statistical analyses – fewer than 35 in parts of Soroka and Wlezien's (2010:92) analysis and 45 in Brooks and Manza (2007:137); Gamson's (1990) sample was 53, while Baumgartner et al.'s (2009) was a somewhat larger 98.

[6] Bernhagen and Trani (2012) discuss what they call policy proposals in the British context, but their definition refers to statements by members of government showing intent to change policy, as reported in the press – meaning that it is the press that defines the population. Their concerns about advocacy in the policy process overlap with mine and that of Baumgartner et al. (2009), however, and their article very usefully attempts both to extend a similar approach to the British case and demonstrate the challenges involved in trying to do so.

The next step was to find all bills with identical or virtually identical summaries in the 101st Congress – both House and Senate – and previous and subsequent congresses. The search went back in time until the first such bill was found, and forward in time until the policy proposal was either enacted or disappeared from the congressional agenda (see Figure 2.1; no proposals remain on the agenda).

Bills with virtually identical summaries were treated as identical bills, and sets of such bills were all treated as manifestations of the same policy proposal. It is these bills that make up the data set. The 60 proposals proved to have been manifested in 417 bills over a 28-year period.[7]

Here is an example of the process. One of the bills initially selected was H.R. 5598, the "Patent Competitiveness and Technological Innovation Act of 1990." This was an omnibus bill, so Title I was treated as a bill. The summary of this bill, in *Thomas*, was

Title I: Patents in Space – Patents in Space Act – Amends Federal patent law to provide that any invention made, used, or sold in outer space on a space object or component under the jurisdiction or control of the United States shall be considered made, used, or sold within the United States unless: (1) it has been specifically identified and otherwise provided for in an international agreement which the United States has signed; or (2) it is carried on the registry of a foreign state in accordance with the Convention on Registration of Objects Launched into Outer Space. Declares that any invention carried on such registry shall be considered made, used, or sold within the United States if it has been specifically so agreed in an international agreement between the United States and the state of registry.

A search for bills in the 101st Congress under "patents" produced 48 bills; "space policy" produced 38, some duplicating those related to patents. Three of the summaries were identical to that of H.R. 5598: H.R. 352, 2946, and S. 459 (enacted as Public Law

---

[7] In the future it might make sense to sample policy proposals rather than bills, but when this research began, it was not even known if the "policy proposal" would be a practical unit of analysis. Nor was there any way to group all the bills introduced into Congress into policy proposals.

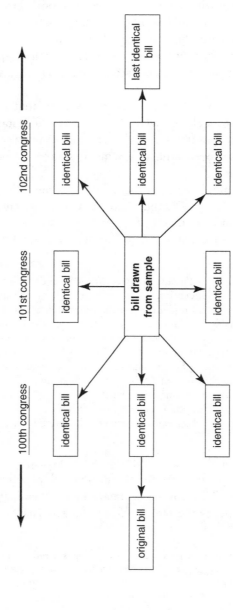

FIGURE 2.1. Schematic Representation of the Content and History of a Policy Proposal

101–580), while the summary of Title III of H.R. 5145, which I will give shortly, was seen as sufficiently similar for it to be treated as the same policy proposal. By way of comparison, H.R. 5145 says that it relates to inventions made in outer space "on a vehicle or payload" instead of H.R. 5598's "space object or component" and that it applies "except for a vehicle or payload (1) under an international agreement" instead of H.R. 5598's "unless: (1) it has been specifically identified and otherwise provided for in an international agreement":

> Title III: Intellectual Property Disposition – Amends Federal law relating to patents to require that any invention made, used, or sold in outer space on a vehicle or payload under U.S. jurisdiction or control be considered to be made, used, or sold in the United States for purposes of the title of the U.S. Code relating to patents, except for a vehicle or payload: (1) under an international agreement; or (2) carried on the registry of a foreign state in accordance with the Convention on Registration of Objects Launched into Outer Space. Requires that a commercial provider making an invention under contract with the Government have the same rights as would a small business firm under specified provisions of Federal patent law.

Other bills found in the search were very different; bills with the keyword "patents" dealt with transgenic farm animals (H.R. 1556), patent infringement by state governments (H.R. 3886), and renewable energy sources (S. 488), among other topics, while those found under "space policy" dealt with weapons in space (e.g., H.R. 966), the export of satellites (H.R. 2624), space transportation (H.R. 2674), and other topics unrelated to patents. There were no bills on patents in space that took another approach to the issue. Other keywords (e.g., "inventions") led only to bills that had already been found.

Identical searches conducted in earlier congresses found relevant bills in the 99th and 100th congresses, but none earlier. Because S. 459 was enacted into law, there was no need to search subsequent congresses, but such searches were conducted for every bill not enacted during the 101st.

It is indeed useful to think of legislative activity in terms of policy proposals. Sets of nearly identical summaries were not difficult to identify, or to distinguish from other summaries.

Rarely were summaries in the gray area between extremely similar and clearly different. When they were, the entire bills were read and compared; a few times, interpretations of the bills in the *Congressional Quarterly Almanac,* academic journals, and the *New York Times* were read to decide if the bills could be considered manifestations of the same policy proposal. The additional information always made it clear whether they were.

THE POLICY PROCESS

The most important finding – the one that underlies all the others – is that the policy proposal is a useful, practical way to describe policy for purposes of research.

Its basic building block is a bill – a unit of analysis that can be identified and described objectively. Within a congress, the population of bills is easily identified and sampled, opening up the possibility of generalizing from a sample to the entire set of bills Congress considers, across the entire range of subjects Congress addresses.

But the bill itself is not a good unit of analysis because bills die at the end of every congress. Members of Congress may persistently fight for the enactment of a particular policy over a period of years, but in each congress the policy will be expressed in a different bill. To study the ebb and flow of support for particular policies over time, it is necessary to find bills with identical (or virtually identical) content, think of the shared content as manifesting a *policy proposal*, and trace what happens to policy proposals from the time they are introduced until they are either enacted into law or disappear from the congressional agenda.

Within particular congresses, multiple members of Congress will introduce identical bills. When the desire to trace proposed policy changes over multiple congresses forces a shift from particular bills to policy proposals, it becomes clear that the same thing should be done within congresses – the focus shifts from particular bills to particular content. Thus, within as well as across congresses, bills with the same content should be seen as manifestations of the same policy proposal. As a unit of analysis, the policy proposal is politically meaningful, in that it is policy proposals – bills with particular content – toward which members of Congress orient their activities, trying to win or block passage when the policy proposals become relevant to them in the course of the policy process. And because policy proposals are based on random (or stratified random) samples, they can be used as the basis for generalizations.

But policy proposals would be very difficult to study if members of Congress regularly introduced bills that shared goals but varied in content – significantly enough to be distinguishable but similar enough to seem equivalent. It turns out – and this could definitely not be taken for granted – that members of Congress regularly introduce bills summarized in virtually identical ways, both within congresses and over time, and rarely propose alternative ways of expressing the same policy ideas. The legislative process in this sample does not involve winnowing down from many proposals to few or elaborating a single proposal into many. Instead, it is consistent with the "few proposals" view derived from the modest amount of roughly comparable research already available. Thus, the very process of trying to determine whether the policy proposal is a useful unit of analysis leads to findings about how new policy ideas are introduced and processed. Thinking of congressional action in terms of policy proposals rather than bills leads to new insights about the policy process, even before gauging the impact of public opinion and advocacy.

What the Policy Proposals Address

The 60 bills varied widely by subject and potential impact, not surprising in a stratified random sample. Among the bills of great importance were those enacted as the Americans with Disabilities Act (S. 933) and the Financial Institutions Reform, Recovery, and Enforcement Act (popularly known as the "savings and loan bailout," H.R. 1278). Arguably less important were the bills enacted as the Student Right-to-Know and Campus Security Act (H.R. 1454) and the Amtrak Reauthorization and Improvement Act (H.R. 2364). Of likely importance to relatively few people

were bills dealing with tanker traffic in Puget Sound (H.R. 2423)
and pecan, mushroom, and lime promotion and research programs (H.R. 3664). Other bills addressed foster care (H.R. 178),
taxes on capital gains (H.R. 499), the admission of refugees on an
emergency basis (H.R. 1605), the disposal of solid waste (H.R.
3264), and the boundaries of Rocky Mountain National Park
(H.R. 1606). A complete list is in Appendix Table 1.

Bills versus Policy Proposals

How is our sense of the policy process affected by focusing on
policy proposals rather than bills? For one thing, policy proposals
could have considerably more support than any single bill. For
another, the history of a policy proposal could be very different
from the history of a single bill. A particular bill might never even
win consideration by a committee, but an identical bill, manifesting the same policy proposal, might be enacted.

The 60 policy proposals were manifested in a total of 417 bills.
Seventeen were manifested by only one bill, and another 13 by
two; but 13 were manifested by 10 or more, and one by 76. The
average was seven and the median between two and three.

Conventionally, support for bills is gauged by how many votes
they get in roll call votes. But the vast majority of bills are never
voted on. How can we measure how much support they have?

There have been two approaches to measuring congressional
support for policy proposals early in the policy process. Both
conclude that sponsorship is a plausible measure of support.

The first approach is based on commonsense notions of what it
means to say that congressional support for repeal of the estate tax
is rising, or that support for a balanced budget amendment rose
and then fell. For many historians, political scientists, and journalists, sponsorship is a good measure of such support (see the review
in Burstein 1998b:ch. 2).

A second approach is that of political scientists arguing on
more theoretical grounds that sponsorship (including cosponsorship) may indicate support for policy change. As part of the public
record, sponsorship may be like roll call voting, signifying support

for particular policies (Krehbiel 1995:906, 910; Schickler, Pearson, and Feinstein 2010; Talbert and Potoski 2002); it may be used by legislators to win constituents' support or by their challengers to arouse opposition (Schiller 1995:189); and it may be used by some legislators to signal others about commitment to a bill.[8]

Though both approaches point toward using sponsorship as a measure of support, neither provides a satisfactory way to do so. The first gauges changes in support over time, but does not carefully define what is being supported, typically focusing on a vaguely defined set of bills that vary among themselves in ways not described. The second approach is clear about what is being supported – nearly always, single bills – but because bills die at the end of each congress, it cannot describe changes in support over time (see, e.g., Browne and Ringquist 1985; Campbell 1982; Kessler and Krehbiel 1996; Krehbiel 1995; Regens 1989; Wilson and Young 1997). Schickler et al. (2010) provide the rare example of tracing sponsorship over time, but they do so for a broad policy area – civil rights – including bills on many specific topics, and therefore they don't track support for any particular policy proposal.

Here it is possible to gauge support for policy proposals by combining the strengths of both approaches, gauging support for sets of highly similar bills for as long as any are on the congressional agenda. Doing so shows that support as gauged by sponsorship of single bills underestimates support of policy proposals and provides additional information about the policy process.

Focusing first on the 101st Congress, the 60 original bills had a total of 1,190 sponsors, the 60 policy proposals (manifested in 417 bills), 2,643. If the entire history of the policy proposals, from initial introduction to enactment or disappearance, is considered,

---

[8] Talbert and Potoski 2002; Wawro 2000:30–32; Wilson and Young 1997:28. Although it is sometimes important to distinguish between sponsorship and cosponsorship, often both together are seen as measures of support (Wawro 2000:ch. 2). Here "sponsor" includes both.

the disparity is even greater – the 60 policy proposals had 7,090 sponsors during the entire time they were on the agenda.[9]

Cumulative support for policy proposals is much greater than support for individual bills not only at introduction but at ultimate outcome as well. During the 101st Congress itself, 10 of the original 60 bills were enacted, but 15 of the policy proposals. Five more were enacted later, for a total of 20, twice the number of the original bills. An analysis of congressional action on particular bills would underestimate by half the likelihood of the policies they represent becoming law (cf. Wawro 2000:31–32).

The Pace of the Policy Process

A view of the policy process popular among political scientists suggests that policy change comes about through the conjunction of long- and short-term processes. Developing a proposal and winning attention to it often take a long time, as proponents refine the proposal and try to soften up the system, pushing for consideration in many ways and in many forums (Kingdon 1995:210, 226).

For proposals in the system, though, ultimate success or failure may be determined very quickly. Often, according to Kingdon, enactment depends upon the opening, typically for a short time, of a "policy window," a conjunction of circumstances that moves some proposals onto the decision agenda, to be either enacted or decisively rejected (Kingdon 1995:174–75). If ingredients necessary for policy change are present – a well-articulated definition of a public problem, a proposed solution, mobilized interest groups, engaged political entrepreneurs – then rapid, dramatic change will occur; if key ingredients are missing, the opportunity will be lost.

Some aspects of this scenario have been examined in detail (Baumgartner and Jones 1993), but not what happens to specific

---

[9] Within a congress, sponsors of a policy proposal are counted only once. Over time, though, sponsors are counted separately for each congress in which they sponsor a particular proposal; because it requires action to reintroduce a proposal at the start of every congress, "reintroductions" convey useful information about support.

policy proposals. Are many proposals actually on the agenda for a long time, as sponsors introduce and reintroduce bills, try to build support, and wait for a policy window to open? Or might proposals first be introduced when a window appears about to open, only to be withdrawn shortly if they fail to pass, as members of Congress conclude that the window never really opened, or opened and closed too quickly? Ideas for policy change may have been developed in other venues and promoted over a long period of time, but the focus here is on Congress, after a policy idea has been turned into a bill.

It turns out that Congress tends to act on proposals quickly or not at all. Proposals were on the agenda for an average of 2.6 congresses; only 22 percent were considered for four or more. Half the proposals enacted were enacted in the congress in which they were first introduced, and four in each of the next two – 18 of 20 within three congresses. Proposals that fail are on the agenda longer than those that succeed – 2.8 congresses versus 2.2 – but the difference does not seem large and is not statistically significant.

Seldom do members of Congress try patiently to build support for a policy proposal while waiting for a policy window that will make enactment possible. Rather, they act more as if they believe the possible opening of a policy window provides an opportunity for quick enactment of a new proposal. If they prove wrong, they usually abandon their effort, acting as if one try, or maybe two or three, suffices to show that further effort would be pointless.

This is not to say that *issues* are on the agenda for only a short time, only particular ways of addressing them. Those who fail to win support for a policy proposal may abandon it, but maintain their general goal; they may try to reframe the issue and win support for a new proposal very different from the old (Baumgartner and Jones 1993, especially ch. 10). But the logic of the preceding argument suggests that when they do so, they are likely to proceed as they do when conflict focuses on a single proposal, introducing only one or two alternative proposals rather than trying many alternatives and hoping that one will succeed (for an example of how this worked with regard to policies pertaining to work, family, and gender, see Burstein et al. 1995).

This finding may seem implausible to some readers, who may recall policy proposals on the agenda for a long time. Indeed, the sole previous analysis of a policy proposal (Burstein 1998b) found some sponsors persisting for 30 years before winning most of what they wanted. It is here that the importance of random sampling becomes apparent. I analyzed an equal employment opportunity proposal, part of an extraordinarily long and intense struggle for civil rights – the sort of struggle likely to stay in the minds of those who lived through it and mislead them about how long most proposals are on the agenda.

CONCLUSIONS

This chapter began by highlighting three problems in the study of policy change: first, there is no good, widely applied definition of policy; second, studies of policy change focus on a small, biased sample of policies and cannot be the basis for generalization; and third, there seem to be no measures of policy that are simultaneously objective, politically meaningful, and able to serve as the basis for generalization.

This chapter has proposed such a measure: the policy proposal. I am not claiming that it is the one best measure of policy or that it is necessarily suitable for all types of analyses of policy change. But it does have a number of advantages. It is objective; bills are easily identified, and identical (or virtually identical) bills may be found using conventional modes of searching (indeed, technological advances since this research was carried out are likely to make searching for identical bills significantly easier). It is politically meaningful: policy proposals are stated in the very words that members of Congress themselves find meaningful, and the proposals are the focus of activities by both members of Congress and those trying to influence them. And it can provide the basis for generalization: the population of bills can be straightforwardly defined and sampled.

The attempt to operationalize the concept of policy proposal leads to several new insights into congressional activity, showing both the feasibility of studying policy proposals and some benefits of doing so, even before beginning to analyze the impact of public opinion and advocacy on policy change. First and foremost, it is possible to operationalize the concept. Members of Congress *could* introduce a variety of bills on the same topic, with generally similar goals but so many variations in approach that no particular bill could be identified as especially important. But that is not what happens. Members of Congress introduce a single policy proposal, often manifested in multiple bills, and stick with it until it is either enacted or disappears from the legislative agenda. They neither winnow many proposals down to a few nor elaborate on an initial proposal and produce many variations. Thus, the investigation into whether policy proposals exist in a way useful for research discovers both something significant about how Congress operates, and a useful way to define and measure policy.

Second, the analysis of policy proposals produces a different view of congressional support for policy change than a focus on single bills would. If sponsorship is viewed as a reasonable measure of support for bills that have been introduced but not acted upon, it turns out that support for the 60 policy proposals is more than six times greater than support for the original 60 bills on which the policy proposals were based. And twice as many policy proposals were enacted as original bills.

Third, the analysis of policy proposals shows something important about the pace of congressional action that could not be discovered if only single bills were being analyzed. Congress tends to act quickly on proposals or not at all. Very seldom do supporters of a policy proposal begin with little support and work gradually, congress after congress, to win adherents and then, after patient, long-term coalition building, succeed in getting their proposal enacted. For the most part, supporters may try to win support for two or three congresses, sometimes four; if they don't succeed, they give up, and the policy proposal disappears from the legislative agenda.

The attempt here to provide a basis for generalizing about policy change may be viewed as a very modest step. I propose a way to generalize about policies, but analyze only one legislature –

the U.S. Congress – in one country at a particular time. But I hope that subsequent research using this approach will show that the approach can be utilized to study state legislatures as well as Congress over longer periods of time, and, with suitable adaptations, to analyze the legislative process in other democracies as well.

At this point, the analysis turns from the policy proposals themselves to the environment in which they are introduced, fairly often debated, and sometimes enacted. How is congressional action on policy proposals affected by public opinion?

3

Public Opinion

Debates about the impact of public opinion on public policy are organized around a "should" and an "is." Almost everyone agrees that in a democracy public policy should be strongly affected by public opinion. "We often gauge the quality of democratic government," Erikson, Wright, and McIver (1993:1) write, "by the responsiveness of public policymakers to the preferences of the mass public" (see also Manza and Cook 2002a:630). But there is a lot of disagreement about how strong the effect is. Is it as strong as it should be, meaning that the democratic political process is working well? Or is it much weaker, meaning that the democratic political process is working badly?

The past couple of decades have favored the "strong effect" view. Most studies show opinion influencing policy; some show its impact to be extremely powerful (Burstein 2003; Erikson et al. 1993; Erikson, MacKuen, and Stimson 2002). But a counterargument has emerged. Benjamin Page (2002), long seen as a proponent of the strong effect view, has reversed course and now argues that key studies overestimate the impact of opinion on policy. One reason, he argues, is sampling bias. Public opinion polls focus on issues important to the public – the very issues on which the public is most likely to hold elected officials accountable, and on which, therefore, democratic governments are most likely to do what the public wants. Other scholars have begun to express the same concern (Jones and Jenkins-Smith 2009:54; Lax and Phillips 2012:150).

Two claims follow, one empirical and one interpretive. First, if survey organizations asked about less-important issues, we would find opinion having less impact on policy than extant work suggests. Second, if opinion does have less impact, democratic procedures and institutions must not be working as well as we thought.

This chapter addresses both claims, supporting the first but not the second. Those concerned about sampling bias have had no data to support their views. This chapter does, and it shows Page and others are right – sampling bias has indeed led us to overestimate the impact of public opinion on public policy.

What this means is another matter. The second claim rests on two assumptions: that the public has meaningful opinions on less-important issues, and that politics is zero-sum – either the public gets what it wants, or special interests do. This chapter questions both assumptions, contending that on many issues the public has no meaningful opinions, and that therefore successes by organized interests in winning the policies they want need not come at the public's expense.

I will begin by reviewing work on the impact of public opinion on public policy and arguments that sampling bias leads us to overestimate the impact. I then assess the impact in a data set designed to minimize such bias – the data set described in Chapter 2. My analysis shows that sampling bias very likely affected the conclusions of several classic studies (Domhoff 2002a; Monroe 1998; Page and Shapiro 1983; Erikson et al. 2002). The chapter then reconsiders how data on opinion and policy should be interpreted, and it delineates what the argument and findings imply for our understanding of democratic politics.

THE IMPACT OF PUBLIC OPINION ON PUBLIC POLICY

How strongly does public opinion affect public policy? It is extremely difficult to say. As noted in Chapter 2, policy is measured in so many different ways that statements about impacts on policy are inherently ambiguous – what is the "policy" being referred to, exactly?

The measurement of public opinion is problematic, too. Intuitively, it makes sense to analyze how action on *particular proposals* was affected by public opinion on *those proposals.* When the public wants the government to do something, does the government respond? We could gauge the overall impact of opinion on policy as a combination of how often the government responds, and how strongly.

Unfortunately, until quite recently, the public was seldom asked about specific policy proposals. Instead, they were asked only about general attitudes on issues. If research on the link between opinion and policy could proceed only when policy-specific opinion data were available, we could study very few issues indeed.

What did researchers do? In the absence of policy-specific opinion data, they developed two approaches to examining the relationship between opinion and policy. The first was to gauge the impact of the public's views on broad issues rather than specific policies.[1] For example, researchers who wanted to analyze how public opinion influenced congressional action on the Vietnam War found no good measure of what the public wanted Congress to do; they therefore considered how Congress was affected by the public's views about whether the United States had made a mistake in sending troops to Vietnam (McAdam and Su 2002:709). Similarly, public support for equal employment opportunity legislation was gauged, not by a question about

---

[1] This is not to say that there were explicit discussions about whether researchers should limit themselves to public opinion about specific policy proposals, or consider opinions on broad issues (as opposed to policies) as well. Instead, researchers seem to have proceeded in an ad hoc way, including in their analyses both opinions on specific policies and opinions about broad issues (e.g., Page and Shapiro 1982, 1983). This approach is perfectly understandable when a new research agenda is being developed, but it would have been desirable to follow up with discussions about the value of seeing whether government action on specific proposals was consistent with public opinion on those proposals. This didn't happen until quite recently (see the discussion below).

policy preferences, but rather by a question about support for blacks having "as good a chance" as whites to get jobs (Burstein 1998a:50). Perhaps surprisingly in light of the mismatch between the questions asked and the policies being considered, researchers often found public opinion affecting policy.

The second approach to linking opinion and policy using available data is what might be called the "big picture" approach, in which the public's global views on a wide range of policies are related to similarly global measures of policy. In some work, trends in the public's responses to many survey questions are carefully combined to produce a measure of "policy mood" (Stimson 1999:3) – the public's overall liberalism across a wide range of domestic policy domains, focusing on the size and scope of government and policies associated with the welfare state (health care, pensions, unemployment compensation, taxes, spending, etc.; Stimson 1999; Erikson et al. 2002:ch. 6; Ellis and Stimson 2012:ch. 3). In other work the focus is trends in the public's responses to many questions about government spending – should the government spend more, less, or the same? – in broad, important policy domains, including defense, welfare, health, the environment, and education (Soroka and Wlezien 2005, 2010; Wlezien 2004; Wlezien and Soroka 2012). The measures of policy are similarly aggregated – the overall liberalism of a large number of policies (Erikson et al. 2002:ch. 8) and of government spending in the policy domains for which opinion is measured. Much of this work focuses on the federal government in the United States, but there are also substantial bodies of research on American states and foreign countries (Erikson et al. 1993; Monogan, Gray, and Lowery 2009; Wlezien and Soroka 2012).

Research in this "big picture" tradition often shows public opinion strongly affecting policy. Stimson and his collaborators (1993:560), for example, contend that at the federal level in the United States, there is a "strong and resilient link between public and policy," and, in another study, "nearly a one-to-one translation of preferences into policy, where policy and preferences are measured in familiar percentage liberal terms" (2002:316). At the state level, according to Erikson, Wright, and McIver (1993:80), the impact of opinion on policy is "awesome."

Recently, some researchers have begun to argue that however valuable both approaches have been, it is nevertheless essential, if we want to understand the impact of opinion on policy, to examine the relationship between public opinion on specific policy proposals and the government's actions on those proposals, even if that requires creating entirely new data sets. Lax and Phillips (2009:369), for example, contend that conclusions about the impact of opinion on policy "cannot be considered determinative without good measures of policy-specific opinion" (see also Lax and Phillips 2012; Warshaw and Rodden 2012). Proponents of this view have collected data on the public's opinions about very specific policies being addressed by Congress and state legislatures – for example, about requiring a 24-hour waiting period for an abortion, limiting personal or corporate campaign contributions, allowing same-sex marriage, and changing the eligibility rules for Medicaid (Lax and Phillips 2012:150–51).[2] At this point there are few such studies, both because they represent a break with tradition and because of the expense involved in asking the public about the ever-changing specific policies on the legislative agenda. Nevertheless, their proponents see them as especially valuable, making it possible to "evaluate causality ... [in the relationship between opinion and policy] more cleanly" (Lax and Phillips 2009:369). These studies too, often, though not always find a strong relationship between opinion and policy (Lax and Phillips 2009:383; 2012:149, 160).

Thus, we find repeatedly that opinion influences policy, sometimes very strongly, regardless of whether the researches use measures of public opinion not closely matched to the relevant policies, aggregated measures, or policy-specific measures.

---

[2] The public is also asked about very specific policies in studies of other aspects of links between citizens and elected officials (Ansolabehere and Jones 2010; Jessee 2009; Jones 2011).

Not everyone agrees with this conclusion, however (e.g., Domhoff 1998:171; Monroe 1998), and others are cautious. Page and Shapiro (1983:189) conclude that public opinion "genuinely affects government policies" in the United States, but they are reluctant to make strong claims about democratic responsiveness. Manza and Cook (2002a) highlight these disagreements by contrasting "large effects" and "small effects" images of the impact of opinion on policy.

Why might our estimates of the impact of opinion on policy be too high? A key possibility is sampling bias. All three approaches focus on policies especially likely to be important to the public – and it is on such issues that the impact of opinion on policy is especially likely to be strong. Page (2002:332) emphasizes this point, and increasing numbers of researchers are expressing the same concern – there is a good chance our estimates of the impact of opinion on policy are too high "because research is too heavily directed toward high-salience issues," according to Jones and Jenkins-Smith (2009:54), while Lax and Phillips (2012:150) add that "Some caution must be taken in generalizing our findings" because they don't have a random sample of policies (see also Jacobs and Tope 2007:1486–87; Jessee 2009:63; Manza and Brooks 2012:105; Shapiro 2011:986).

How consequential is sampling bias? We don't know, but we have every reason to anticipate its being important. Every book on research methods emphasizes its importance, as do scholars pursuing qualitative, historical, and conventional quantitative research (e.g., Baumgartner et al. 2009; Becker 1998:ch.3; Gamson 1990; King, Keohane, and Verba 1994:ch. 4; Pierson 2004:140). This chapter considers whether those who have contributed so much to our understanding of the relationship between public opinion and public policy need to seriously confront an issue about which some are already expressing concern. I examine the relationship between public opinion and congressional action on the 60 policy proposals described in Chapter 2, and show how sampling affects the availability of public opinion data and our estimates of opinion's impact on policy.

RESEARCH DESIGN AND DATA

Twenty of the 60 policy proposals were enacted. Ideally, we would assess the importance of sampling bias by examining how congressional responsiveness to public opinion on a random sample of policy proposals compares to responsiveness in biased samples. But we can't do so because public opinion data are not available for most of the proposals in the random sample.

Instead, I will try to make the best use of available data to see whether sampling bias leads us to overestimate the impact of opinion on policy. If it does, we must reconsider our previous conclusions about the impact of opinion on policy, and direct our research toward getting policy-specific data on random samples of policy proposals.

I rely here on what is perhaps the most detailed discussion of matching opinion and policy – that provided by Stimson (1999). He argues that it is useful to distinguish between narrower measures – opinion on particular issues (albeit not specific policy proposals) – and broader ones, including his own global measure of the public's liberalism, which he calls "policy mood."

I use Stimson's two types of measures and add a third, based on data from the General Social Survey (GSS), the American National Election Studies, and the Roper Center at the University of Connecticut.

A question is categorized as measuring a "specific issue preference" if it addresses a topic fairly clearly related to a policy proposal. For example, a question asking whether the United States currently had enough oil reserves is seen as related to a proposal to increase domestic oil reserves; similarly, a question asking whether the United States should take the lead internationally in the fight against global warming is linked to a proposal to reduce greenhouse gases. Even these questions don't ask about specific policy proposals, but they're the best available.

A question measures a "general issue preference" if it describes preferences in the policy proposal's domain but does not address the proposal itself, even indirectly. For example, a proposal to provide more health information and counseling to Medicare recipients was matched with a GSS question on government spending on health care. The connection between question and policy is not close, but studies of the opinion–policy relationship are usually based on exactly these kinds of data.

Finally, when no measure of specific or general issue preference is available, Stimson's (1999:140–41) estimates of the public's mood in broad policy domains (education, health, race, and so on) – essentially measures of liberalism – are used when appropriate. Linking Stimson's measures to particular policy proposals may be problematic – Stimson never uses them this way – but doing so may be better than nothing.

The measure of issue importance is the Gallup "most important problem" question – "What do you think is the most important problem facing this country today?" Responses were matched to the 60 policy proposals by two independent raters. For instance, responses mentioning "polluting the environment" and "the Savings and Loan crisis" were matched with policy proposals to reduce greenhouse gases and bail out the savings and loan industry, respectively. Often policy proposals did not fit any Gallup response category. For example, no Gallup response option encompassed a policy proposal to change interstate highway weight limitations. A proposal was defined as salient when at least 1 percent of the respondents said the issue was important.[3]

DATA AVAILABILITY, SALIENCE, AND SAMPLING BIAS

The availability of public opinion data on each proposal along with information about salience and enactment are described in Table 3.1.

---

[3] "Importance" and "salience" are treated as being the same, though some authors see subtle distinctions between the two. There are multiple ways to gauge salience, including media coverage and using different cutoff points in the Gallup data. There are problems with both media and Gallup measures, but researchers feel driven to use them for lack of alternatives (Earl et al. 2004; Jennings and Wlezien 2011; Wlezien 2005). I tried using other Gallup cutoff points, issue coverage in the *New York Times*, and combinations of the two. The results were the same regardless.

TABLE 3.1. 60 Sampled Policy Proposals, 101st Congress (1989–1990), Salience, Availability of Public Opinion Data, and Enactment

Issue Salient to at Least 1% of Public		Issue Not Salient to at Least 1% of Public	
Bill No.	Subject	Bill No.	Subject
Specific Public Opinion Data Available			
1606	Expand boundaries of Rocky Mountain National Park*	3855	Establish a regional petroleum reserve
1928	Suspends duty on a chemical	4634	Vehicle weight limitations on highways
2419	Chattahoochee National Forest Land Exchange*		
3785	Compensation from pornographers for victims of sexual assault		
4328	Textile Trade Act		
4547	Suspend duty on C.I. Pigment Red 242		
4603	Amends Medicaid to cover personal care services		
5966	Reduce accumulation of greenhouse gases, etc.		
Only General Public Opinion Data Available			
376	Requires presidential reports on reforms in Nicaragua	0072	Requires consultants to register for defense contracts
499	IRS indexing and reduction of capital gains	0181	Social Security benefit computation formula
824	Conservation of coastal wetlands	1441	Labeling requirements for foods with cholesterol*
1278	Savings and loan bailout*	2791	Encourage reclamation of abandoned mined lands*
1433	Expands benefits for military infertility procedures	3324	Public interest considered in railroad bankruptcies
1454	Student Right-to-Know and Campus Security Act*	3847	Establishing a Department of Environmental Protection
2302	Reduce requirements for training for nursing aids	4520	Measuring foreign direct investment*

TABLE 3.1. (cont.)

	Issue Salient to at Least 1% of Public		Issue Not Salient to at Least 1% of Public
2344	Authorize transfer of two naval vessels to Philippines*	5389	Additional requirements for defense procurement system
2423	Improve responses to oil spills*	5598	Space patents*
2655	International Cooperation Act	5891	Resolution Trust Corporation Funding Act – second round*
3104	Adding Pemigewasset River to national status*		
3120	Establish permit requirements for sewer systems, etc.		
3264	Prohibit disposal of solid waste from one state in another state		
3643	Improving programs providing health insurance information		
5740	Expands veterans' health care programs*		
	Only Mood Data Available		
2136	Sets legal standards for incarceration in child custody cases*	178	Reduces federal funding for foster care and adoption
5472	Family violence prevention and services	336	Standardization of measurement of bolts
		337	Extends compensation for veterans' spouses that remarry
		1449	IRS construction rules
		2273	Americans with Disabilities Act*
		2408	Transfer programs to Rural Development Administration
		3077	Promote education of human rights and freedom

4025	Require use of child safety restraint systems on aircraft*
4266	Pay raises for District of Columbia federal employees
5753	Repeals rules concerning passive foreign investment company

No Public Opinion Data Available

601	Income tax refunds to trust fund for incurable diseases
895	Garnishment of federal pay treated like nonfederal pay
1605	Admission of more refugees from communist countries
2799	Allow planting of alternative crops in 1990*
2983	Designates clinic as "Gene Taylor Veterans' Outpatient Clinic"
3016	Include foreign service employees in census
3664	Agricultural Commodity Promotion and Research Act*
3927	Immigrant visas for people denied freedom of emigration
4552	Duke Ellington coin
5120	Prohibits gifts among federal employees
5322	Expands rights of senior executive service*
5771	Commemorative Olympic coins*

Notes: Salience gauged by responses to Gallup "most important problem" question. Asterisk means proposal was enacted; total is 20. Chi-squared for salience (yes vs. no) by availability of public opinion data (specific and general vs. mood only and none) = 19.9, $p < .001$.

If data were available at more than one level of specificity, the most specific are identified.

There are data on specific issue preferences for 10 policy proposals (17 percent) and on general issue preferences for 26 more (43 percent) – 60 percent altogether. For the other 40 percent, no issue preference data could be found; I will say such data do not exist, even though some may be found eventually. Thus, previous research that included only issues on which opinion had been measured (however indirectly) probably ignored at least 40 percent of the proposals Congress considers.

Stimson's measure of policy mood is potentially relevant for proposals that can be described as liberal or conservative – half the remaining proposals, 20 percent of the total. The final 20 percent could not be described as liberal or conservative, making the policy mood measure irrelevant.[4] Thus, data on issue preferences are available for 60 percent of the proposals, and mood data for 20 percent more, using a very loose definition of relevance; there are no measures of public opinion at all for 20 percent.

As we might expect, preference data are available only for a biased sample of proposals: for salient issues, nearly always (24 of 26 proposals; Table 3.1); for nonsalient issues, barely more than a third (12 of 34). This adds credibility to the claim that estimates of the impact of opinion on policy are too high.

HOW STRONGLY DOES OPINION AFFECT POLICY?

How much does it matter if we analyze data for a random sample of policy proposals instead of the usual biased sample? To get some sense of this, I analyzed the data for the 60 proposals in ways as similar as possible to two classic studies: Monroe's (1998) on the relationship between opinion and policy cross-sectionally, and Page and Shapiro's (1983) on the relationship over time. I also

---

[4] All proposals were coded independently by three coders, using Stimson's criteria; 29 (48%) did not fit a liberal–conservative dimension. This is in line with Page and Shapiro's (1983:183) finding that 40 percent of their issues "were not easily locatable on the liberal-conservative dimension."

found data that describe sampling bias in Erikson et al.'s (2002) work on the global relationship over time between mood and policy change. (Both Page [2002] and Manza and Cook [2002a] pay special attention to these studies in their reviews.) Some comparisons will also be made with Domhoff's (1998, 2002a, 2002b) work.

Cross-Sectional Analysis: Monroe

Monroe (1998) analyzes the relationship between public opinion and public policy, 1980–1993, by finding 566 survey questions on potential federal policies, ascertaining whether a majority of those with opinions wanted policy change, and then seeing whether policy changed. Opinion and policy are seen as consistent when the public preferred the status quo and policy remained unchanged, and when the public wanted policy change, and policy changed.

Monroe finds opinion and policy consistent for 55 percent of the issues (Table 3.2a, based on Monroe 1998). He also finds a substantial bias against change. When the public wants the status quo, policy remains unchanged 70 percent of the time, but when it wants change, policy changes only 45 percent of the time, producing a bias measure of 70–45, or 25.

Like Monroe, I consider proposals for which specific or general issue preference data are available, and I gauge consistency between opinion and policy. My approach differs a bit from his; instead of looking at preferences for or against change, I categorize opinion and policy as consistent when a proposal is enacted while a majority of the public favors it, or not enacted when a majority is opposed.[5]

For the 36 proposals for which specific or general issue preference data are available, opinion and policy are consistent for 18,

---

[5] The majority–minority criterion may seem arbitrary, given how sensitive distributions of responses are to question wording; analyses identical to those reported were conducted with a division between favorable and unfavorable at 62%, the mean of all the distributions, rather than 50%. The results were the same.

TABLE 3.2. *Public Opinion and Public Policy: Cross-Sectional Analysis*

A. *Consistency between Opinion and Policy 1980–1993, from Monroe (1998:13)*

| | Majority Preference | |
Policy Outcome	Status Quo	Change
Status Quo	*70%*	55
Change	30	*45*
N	230	336
Consistent 55%		

B. *Consistency between Opinion and Policy, Proposals with Opinion Data*

| | Majority Preference | | |
Policy Outcome	Favors Proposal	Opposes Proposal	Total
Proposal Enacted	*12 (41%)*	1 (14%)	13
Proposal Not Enacted	17 (59%)	*6 (86%)*	23
N	29	7	36
Consistent 50%			

C. *Consistency between Opinion and Policy, All Proposals*

| | Majority Preference | | | |
Policy Outcome	Favors Proposal	Opposes Proposal	None	Total
Proposal Enacted	*12 (41%)*	1 (14%)	5 (23%)	18
Proposal Not Enacted	17 (59%)	*6 (86%)*	*17 (77%)*	40
N	29	7	22	58[a]
Consistent 31%				

Note: Italics identify opinion consistent with policy.

[a] On two proposals, specific and general opinion data were available and contradicted each other; these have been left out of this analysis.

or 50 percent, a figure close to Monroe's (Table 3.2b). The bias against change in my data, however, seems greater; when the public opposed a proposal, it died 86 percent of the time (six proposals out of seven), but when the public wanted enactment, Congress acted only 41 percent of the time, producing a bias measure of 86–41, or 45.

Neither Monroe nor I find public opinion having much impact (he found the relationship between opinion and policy statistically significant at the 0.05 level; I did not, possibly because my sample was smaller). Nevertheless, it is important to consider what happens when the viewpoint is shifted, from considering the 36 proposals on which public opinion is known (the biased sample), to considering all 60 (the stratified random sample).

Imagine that members of Congress know what the public wants only if poll data exist. Then, when members of Congress know what the public wants (as it does on 36 proposals), it acts accordingly half the time.

If we consider all 60 proposals, however, our perspective changes. The 18 proposals on which the government responds to the public are no longer half the total, but only 31 percent (Table 3.2c). On the other 69 percent, sometimes the government is definitely unresponsive (when it ignores issue preferences), and sometimes (when there are no data on preferences) we can't say whether it is or not.

Of course, members of Congress have many other ways of getting information on what some people, if not the public as a whole, want done on particular issues – they talk to lobbyists, see or read about demonstrations, read newspaper editorials from their districts or states (the time period covered here was before electronic media became important), get letters from constituents, and so on. Unfortunately, there are very few studies of how much information they acquire altogether on specific policy proposals, and even on broader issues (such as civil rights or the Vietnam War). But the studies show quite consistently that with regard to data that are available publicly (through reports in print media) and from interviews with lobbyists, members of Congress hear very little from the public or lobbyists on the vast majority of policy proposals and broader issues (see, e.g., Baumgartner and Leech 2001:1200–1; Baumgartner et al. 2009; Burstein and Sausner 2005, and the chapters in this book). We have no way of knowing how much information they receive about the public's preferences completely out of the public eye. The more we can learn about this, the better, but in the meantime we have no reason to think they get a lot, particularly with regard to the very high proportion of issues not salient to the public.

Congruence over Time: Page and Shapiro

Like Monroe, Page and Shapiro (1983) analyze the relationship between opinion and policy for all the issues on which they could find public opinion data. Their focus, however, is change over time; by seeing whether public opinion changed before policy, or the reverse, they argue, they can make stronger inferences about causality than they could in cross-sectional analysis.

They found public opinion data documenting 357 instances of significant change in Americans' policy preferences between 1935 and 1979, and they focused on the 231 in which policy changed also. Opinion and policy were described as congruent when both moved in the same direction, and noncongruent otherwise. They found congruence in 66 percent of the 231 instances and noncongruence in the rest.

Data on trends in specific or general issue preferences are available for 19 of the 60 policy proposals considered here. I consider opinion and policy to be congruent if a proposal is enacted after the public becomes more favorable (percent favorable increasing by at least 5 percent), or not enacted if public support remains the same or declines. (Again, my approach is similar to Page and Shapiro's, but not identical; as noted, for example, they focus on instances of policy change; I consider all policy proposals for which data are available.)

For the 19 proposals, opinion and policy are congruent for 15, or 79 percent, a percentage a bit greater than Page and Shapiro's. This is a measure of what they would describe as the effect of opinion on policy.

If we step back, though, and ask what the data tell us about the determinants of policy for all 60 proposals, the results look quite different and highlight how little we can say about the impact of opinion on policy. The 15 proposals on which the government is definitely doing what the public wants (by conventional standards) are 79 percent of the proposals for which preference data exist, but only 25 percent of all 60. For the other 45 proposals, we know the government is not doing what the public wants on 4, or 7 percent of the total of 60. On the remaining 41, we have no way to know if the government is responsive. Public opinion data are available for so small a fraction of the policy proposals that the impact of sampling bias on the results could be very substantial.

Policy Mood and Policy Change: Erikson, MacKuen, and Stimson

Erikson et al. (2002:368) find the impact of opinion (measured in terms of policy mood) on policy so powerful that they are somewhat mystified. "How," they ask, "could the degree of popular control be so strong?"

Like Monroe (1998) and Page and Shapiro (1983), they begin with data on public opinion and then find data on relevant policies. Unlike Monroe, and Page and Shapiro, they describe how they selected some policies for analysis but not others; we can see if their sampling procedure is biased and, if so, how the bias might affect their conclusions.

Erikson et al. (2002:328) want to examine how the public's policy mood affects what they call "major shifts in American governmental policy" over time. Their focus is domestic policy, and their concern is whether opinion and policy are moving together along a liberal–conservative dimension. To decide whether a policy shift is "major," they begin with a list of 189 laws designated as especially important at the time of passage by David Mayhew (1991), updated through 1996.

Several types of laws don't match the concerns of Erikson et al. (2002:330), however, and are eliminated from the data set, including laws dealing with foreign, defense, or agriculture policy – for example, reorganizations of the Defense Department

(1958 and 1986), the nuclear test ban treaty (1963), the War Powers Act enacted at the end of the Vietnam War (1973), and major laws affecting foreign trade (e.g., the Trade Expansion Act of 1962) and subsidies to agriculture. Left out because they are (in Erikson et al.'s view) local rather than national in scope, or neither liberal nor conservative, are the 1956 law creating the interstate highway system; the laws that created NASA, the Arms Control and Disarmament Agency, and the Departments of Housing and Urban Development, and Transportation; some antidiscrimination laws, including the Age Discrimination Act of 1967, the Equal Pay Act of 1963, the Equal Rights Amendment (not ratified by the states), and the Equal Employment Opportunity Act of 1972; the National Environmental Policy Act of 1969; the 1986 Tax Reform Act; the "savings and loan bailout" (1989–1990); statehood for Alaska and Hawaii; and crime control laws, including the Omnibus Crime Control and Safe Streets Act of 1968, and the Organized Crime Control Act of 1970. Altogether Erikson et al. exclude from their data set 43 percent of the laws Mayhew describes as especially important.

Page (2002:329) suggests that Erikson et al. (2002) find opinion strongly affecting policy partly because policy mood is a measure of liberalism and they exclude policies that don't lie on the liberal–conservative dimension. And all the policies are important – that is, especially likely to be affected by public opinion. Had Erikson, MacKuen, and Stimson analyzed a random sample of policies, or even all the laws Mayhew considers important, they would have found opinion having much less impact on policy.

Small Effects: Domhoff

Up to this point, I have contended that the impact of opinion on policy has been overestimated by researchers generalizing from biased samples. Domhoff (1998, 2002a, 2002b), in contrast, could hardly have overestimated the impact of opinion, because he sees it having so little: almost none on policies that elites care about – especially foreign, defense, and economic policies – and a modest impact on others (cf. Erikson 1976).

Domhoff provides no quantitative evidence to support his claims, but Monroe and Page and Shapiro present some that is relevant. Monroe (1998:14) finds consistency on defense and foreign policy issues perhaps slightly greater than overall consistency (61 percent and 67 percent consistent, respectively, compared to the overall 55 percent), and "economic and labor" issues perhaps slightly less (51 percent). Page and Shapiro (1983:182) find congruence on foreign policy a bit less than the overall measure (62 percent vs. 66 percent overall), and "economic and welfare policies" the same.

Of the 60 policy proposals analyzed here, 34 have data on public opinion adequate to gauge consistency for the different types of issues (Table 3.3a). In this data set, consistency between opinion and policy is higher for foreign, defense, and economic policies than for others – the opposite of what Domhoff claims.[6] If we add the proposals for which no public opinion data are available (Table 3.3b), overall consistency between opinion and policy declines, as expected, but responsiveness on foreign, defense, and economic policies remains higher than on others.

Domhoff would have a number of responses to these conclusions, including an important one shared with Page (2002), namely, that without including other variables in the analysis, it is impossible to ascertain whether public opinion has an independent effect. This is true. Given how obvious this is, it is remarkable how few quantitative studies of the determinants of policy estimate the effects of elite activities and public opinion simultaneously (Burstein 2003:34–35). The little evidence there is, though, is that public opinion continues to affect policy even when elites' influence is taken into account.

---

[6] It should be noted that Domhoff, Monroe, and Page and Shapiro all treat the classification of issues as unproblematic, but they shouldn't have – much political debate is about how issues should be classified and framed (Baumgartner and Jones 1993). I classified the Americans with Disabilities Act as an economic policy, for example, because much of the testimony at hearings and the congressional debate revolved around the costs of accommodating the needs of the disabled; but many people view the act as a civil rights law.

TABLE 3.3. *Opinion and Policy by Issue*

A. *Consistency between Opinion and Policy, Proposals with Opinion Data*

Opinion and Policy	Foreign, Defense, Economic Policies	Other Policies	Total
Consistent	11(58%)	6 (40%)	50%
Inconsistent	8 (42%)	9 (60%)	
N	19	15	34

B. *Consistency between Opinion and Policy, All Proposals*

Opinion and Policy	Foreign, Defense, Economic Policies	Other Policies	Total
Consistent	11(42%)	6 (19%)	29%
Inconsistent	8 (31%)	9 (28%)	
No Opinion Data	7 (27%)	17 (53%)	
N	26	32	58

Note: Consistency is assessed by Monroe's (1998) criteria; see Table 3.2.

IMPLICATIONS FOR THE STUDY OF DEMOCRATIC POLITICS

Summing up a volume on public opinion and public policy, Page (2002) entitles his chapter "The Semi-Sovereign Public" to remind readers of Schattschneider's (1960) classic *The Semi-Sovereign People*. The reminder is important, Page (2002:325) argues, because the book "largely confirms, or is consistent with, Schattschneider's view of American politics. There is considerable evidence of government responsiveness to public opinion.... But the evidence also indicates that there is considerable room for interest groups, party activists, policymakers, and others to prevail against the public on many issues."

The quotation is accurate, but advances in the social sciences since Schattschneider wrote reduce the value of his framework for studying opinion and policy. Indeed, his framework (which is widely shared) may blind us to how those advances should affect current work.

Even by the time Schattschneider wrote, some social scientists had realized that: (1) sampling bias may affect our estimates of statistical relationships, (2) limits on individuals' cognitive capacities mean that on most policy issues the public has no meaningful opinions, and (3) power is not necessarily a zero sum phenomenon in which gains by one side must come at the expense of the other (Parsons 1960:ch. 6). The implications of each have become more apparent in the years since.

Sampling Bias and Cognitive Capacity

The likely consequences of sampling bias are being discussed by increasing numbers of social scientists. Until now, no one has drawn a random sample of policy proposals, matched legislative action on each one to a policy-specific measure of public opinion, and gauged the relationship between the two, but the path to doing so seems reasonably clear and the likely results predictable – we would find opinion having less impact on policy than we have in the biased samples used up to this point.

But this conclusion rests on a hidden assumption – that the public actually has opinions. When we say that the government will be less responsive to the public on issues that aren't salient, we nearly always mean that on such issues the public has opinions that legislators ignore. But legislators may not respond to public opinion for a second reason – there may be no public opinion to respond to.

Those who study the impact of opinion on policy know that many people have no opinion about most specific policies. But researchers can't very well analyze the impact of "no opinion" on policy – that just doesn't make sense. So over the years researchers have developed ways to measure opinion that allow them to focus on opinions people do have, while putting aside the public's likely lack of opinion on many policies. Mostly this is done by asking opinion questions that are easily answered, even by people who know very little about politics. Thus, for example, people are asked whether they are liberal or conservative (Ellis and Stimson 2012:ch.4); whether they think that government spending in broad issue domains should be increased, decreased, or kept the same (a type of question "not highly demanding of the public"; Soroka and Wlezien 2010:40–41); whether they would favor or oppose a policy proposal that has just been described to them (Jessee 2009:67; Ansolabehere and Jones 2010:585); and what their views are on issues highly salient in current political debates (Ansolabehere and Jones 2010:585; Jessee 2009:65; Jones 2011; Lax and Phillips 2009:367, 370; Lax and Phillips 2012:150).

Alternatively, people may be asked questions about many policies in broadly defined issue areas (Ansolabehere, Rodden, and Snyder 2008; Stimson 1999), and their answers carefully combined to produce measures of preferences that are stable and reliable. But the need to combine items undercuts any claim that people may be said to have meaningful opinions about most specific policy proposals.

All these efforts to create meaningful measures of public opinion on policy are vitally important; without them we wouldn't be able to say anything about the impact of opinion on policy. Yet they give us no reason to believe that most people have opinions on most policies (see also Luskin and Bullock 2011 on debates about the public's level of knowledge about politics; Converse 1964; Zaller 1992). As a practical matter, it is difficult to imagine most people having opinions on H.R. 5753, proposing to amend the Internal Revenue Code to exempt export trade corporations and foreign sales corporations from passive foreign investment company rules; H.R. 895, proposing to treat federal pay in the same manner as nonfederal pay with respect to garnishment; H.R. 2799, proposing to amend the Agricultural Act of 1949, with respect to the 1990 crop year, to permit up to 20 percent of program acreage to be planted with alternative crops, such as canola, rapeseed, milkweed, or meadowfoam; or H.R. 2136, proposing to limit the term of incarceration for civil contempt in child custody cases to 12 months. Some of these proposals may seem inconsequential at first glance but actually have important implications for many people. Rules on corporate taxation may affect the distribution of the tax burden by income group, garnishment the likelihood of divorced spouses being able to collect child support payments, and agriculture policy not only the income of farmers but also the openness of American markets to agricultural products from less-developed countries. Collectively the 40 percent of policy proposals for which no specific or general opinion data are available must influence a tremendous amount of government activity.

Thus, it's likely that public opinion affects public policy even less often than Page suggests – partly because the public is not asked its opinions on less-salient issues, and partly because if it were, most people would have no meaningful opinions.

Must Gains for Some Come at the Expense of Others?

But what does this imply about how well democracy is working? The conventional view is that a high correlation between opinion and policy (in analyses carefully trying to assess causality) means that democratic institutions are working well, giving the public what it wants, while a low correlation means democratic institutions are working poorly, enabling special interests to prevail (Erikson et al. 1993:81; Manza and Cook 2002b:23; Page 2002:325). This implicit zero-sum view of the political process partly explains why researchers hopeful about democratic government are so pleased when they find the correlation high. As Erikson et al. (1993:81) write, for example, "with an imputed correlation of about .91, state opinion explains over 80 percent of the variance in state policy liberalism. This leaves little variance to be accounted for by other variables. Thus, state opinion is virtually the *only* cause of the net ideological tendency of policy in the state" (emphasis in original). And the zero-sum view also explains why those who find special interests getting what they want so often assume that they have done so by defeating the public. Page seems to accept this logic when he weighs the impact of public opinion, on the one hand, against the ability of special interests to prevail, on the other.

But politics is not necessarily zero-sum. If we find that special interests often get what they want, that does not mean they have done so at the expense of the public. In fact, interest organizations were developed in part to strengthen the connection between the public and the government (Clemens 1997); interest organizations can communicate to policymakers the opinions of large numbers of constituents and inform the constituents how the policymakers have responded. When interest organizations support the same policies as a majority of the public – a possibility seldom considered in quantitative analyses of policy change (Burstein 2003) – both can win. And when the public has no opinion, organized interests can get what they want without having "to prevail against the public," to use Page's (2002:325) term.[7] A relatively low correlation between opinion and policy should not be interpreted to mean the public is being defeated. If we want to see how often other forces defeat the public, we must be sure to study actual struggles, with the public on one side and special interests on the other.

Once we agree that the very existence of public opinion on many issues cannot be taken for granted, we have to consider why it exists for some issues but not others. It is sometimes claimed that the public has no opinion on issues because education and public discourse are controlled by powerful institutions that keep many issues off the political agenda (see the review in Manza and Cook 2002b). This must be true sometimes, but surely on a great many issues people have no opinions because they have no reason to and lack the time and background knowledge needed to develop them (Jones 1994). Congress deals with so many proposals that not even its own members can form independent opinions about them all (Krehbiel 1991).

---

[7] There is the argument that the public may lose because it doesn't understand its true interests (e.g., Bartels 2005) – the public should have particular opinions, but doesn't because of ignorance and manipulation by the powerful. But to do research on a random sample of policy proposals, in which the analyst would try to attribute to the public opinions it should have, would be challenging indeed. The focus here is on actual opinions.

When the existence of public opinion on particular issues is taken to be uncertain, an additional problem must be addressed: if we are to consider the population of proposals for which public opinion exists, we need criteria for deciding whether it exists for each proposal. There is a considerable literature on when public opinion may be said to exist in some meaningful sense (Converse 1964; Shapiro 1998; Sinnott 2000; Zaller 1992), but it has never been used to decide whether opinion exists on particular issues. It would be necessary to figure out how to do so. And because salience is so critical to responsiveness, we need to understand the factors that affect it as well. Our attention must shift to the tremendous amount of political conflict over winning access to the public agenda (Hilgartner and Bosk 1988; Jones 1994; Jones and Baumgartner 2005).

CONCLUSIONS

This chapter examines two claims about the impact of public opinion on public policy – first, that sampling bias has led us to overestimate its impact, and, second, that if the true impact is less than we have thought, that means democratic institutions have not been working well.

Other scholars (Jones and Jenkins-Smith 2009:54; see also Jacobs and Tope 2007:1486–87; Lax and Phillips 2012:150; Manza and Brooks 2012:105; Page 2002; Shapiro 2011:986) have expressed concern that we have overestimated the impact of opinion on policy because we have analyzed only biased samples of policies – disproportionately the highly salient policies for which the impact is likely to be especially strong. Their concerns proved to be well warranted. Reconceptualizations of others' work (Erikson et al. 2002; Monroe 1998; Page and Shapiro 1983), together with data from my 60-policy proposal sample, indicated that past work indeed overestimated the impact of opinion on policy, sometimes dramatically so.

The second claim is another matter. Analyses that adopt a zero-sum view of the political process assume that when the correlation between opinion and policy is relatively low, special interests must be prevailing over the public and democratic institutions must be failing. But that is not necessarily true. The government may respond strongly to the public when the public has meaningful opinions, and to other forces otherwise. Zero-sum battles between the public and special interests are only a part of the political process. How large a part? How often does the public prevail over special interests, and how often the reverse? At this point, we don't know. What we do know is that current estimates of the impact of opinion on policy are probably too high, and that a more accurate, lower estimate, would *not* necessarily imply that democratic responsiveness is at risk.

4

Advocacy

How Americans Try to Influence Congress

Toward the end of the 18th century, Americans struggled with a question of potential world-historical significance: could the people of a large and diverse nation govern themselves?

The prospects were not especially bright. No one else had ever succeeded in creating such a government. The 13 states managed to cooperate in their struggle for independence from Great Britain, but just barely. It took the states four years to create their first national government, ratifying the Articles of Confederation in 1781, but within six years the Articles had come to be seen as so flawed, by so many important figures, that a convention was called to revise them. The convention decided the Articles were unworkable and proposed to replace them with a new national document, a constitution – in effect, proposing to overthrow one government and create another on a new basis. The new constitution was sent to the states for ratification in September 1787. It was ratified, but only after a difficult struggle – the critical state of New York ratified it by only three votes (Maier 2011).

A major objection to the proposed constitution was that although it organized the federal government and delineated its powers, the Constitution said little about the public's rights, including the right to make demands on the government itself. Some states made ratification of the Constitution implicitly conditional on the immediate enactment of a Bill of Rights, and it was the very first amendment (1791) that guaranteed the public the right to debate political issues and make demands on the federal government. The federal government was to "make no law . . . abridging the freedom of speech, or of the press, or the right of the people peaceably to assemble, and to petition the Government for a redress of grievances."

Thus, the right of the public to speak and write, to act as individuals and in groups, to try to influence the government has been enshrined in American law (though not always in practice) almost since the nation's establishment. And Americans have taken advantage of this right. They have created new types of organizations – political parties, interest groups, and others – to express their views. They have created and abandoned some forms of political action – torchlight parades, four-hour open-air debates – and gone on to develop others – protest demonstrations, press conferences, political action committees, Facebook pages. They have developed myriad ways of trying to influence policy, always trying to find the most effective ways to get the policies they want. Indeed, political advocacy and its impact are at the heart of democratic politics everywhere.[1]

This chapter focuses on a certain set of activities people engage in to influence policy – activities that make news, that is, activities reported in newspapers and magazines – and the next chapter examines their impact on policy.

This chapter asks four questions:

How much political advocacy do Americans engage in?
How is their advocacy distributed across policy proposals –
    which provoke a lot of advocacy and which only a little?
What do Americans do when they want to influence policy?
And who advocates – who participates more, and who less?

Of course, questions similar to these have been asked before. There are hundreds – perhaps thousands – of studies of political participation, of who participates and what they do. This chapter

---

[1] For developments in other countries, see Dahl 1989; Markoff 1999; Tilly 1976, 1997, 2005.

builds on many of these studies. What does it add? Let us considering the chapter's questions in turn.

How much advocacy? And how is it distributed across policy proposals? Decades ago, Mancur Olson (1971) argued very persuasively that economic organizations would seldom engage in collective action to influence policy, even when there appeared to be much to gain; his logic has been extended to other kinds of organizations and to individuals. Yet even he didn't quite believe the implications of his own argument. He predicted there would be little collective action, yet it seemed obvious that there's a great deal, so he spent much of his book *The Logic of Collective Action* describing the circumstances under which organizations would act collectively. Ever since, a vast amount of research has been devoted to explaining why, in the face of powerful reasons not to participate in politics, so many people and organizations do so anyway (Jenkins 1983; Knoke 1988; Oliver 1993).

But perhaps they don't. Even among social movements described as among "the most intense, large-scale, and divisive in American history" (the anti–Vietnam War movement, as described by McAdam and Su 2002:697), the level of protest does not seem especially high. During the Vietnam War's peak years, 1965–1973, McAdam and Su discovered the average number of protests per month, nationwide, to be just under 11, and the average number of large-scale protests, with more than 10,000 participants, 0.38 per month – arguably not a huge number in a nation of 200 million people. The story for the civil rights movement is similar – even during the peak years of the movement, the number of protests reported nationwide never reached an average of one per day (Jenkins, Jacobs, and Agnone 2003; Burstein and Sausner 2005:409–10). Even if we assume that protests are vastly underreported, that does not seem like a lot. And these are the most intense movements.

What of others? Baumgartner and Leech (2001) provide a hint. In their study of a random sample of issues on which there had been lobbying, the results were tremendously skewed; a handful of issues accounted for a very high proportion of all the lobbying, while on most issues there was hardly any. And their issues were those on which they already knew there had been some lobbying. What of advocacy on a random sample of policy proposals? Putting the logic of Olson's argument together with Baumgartner and Leech's findings, we might very well find that Olson's original view was correct – there really is very little advocacy.

What do Americans do to influence policy? We know a great deal about Americans' political participation as individuals – what proportion vote, contribute money to candidates, work for political parties or candidates, attend protests, contact government officials, and so on (Schlozman, Verba, and Brady 2012). But the dominant approach to this topic is based on surveys asking individuals about their political activities in general – whether they engage in particular activities, and how often. Survey respondents are not asked what they do to influence particular policies.

To learn what Americans do to influence policy, we must turn to studies of policy change. Such studies analyze how policy is affected by a wide variety of variables, including macrolevel characteristics of states, such as their economic development, ethnic and racial composition, urbanism, family composition (e.g., Amenta, Caren, and Olasky 2005; Jacobs and Carmichael 2002), the party balance (e.g., Hero and Preuhs 2007; Olzak and Soule 2009; Schickler, Pearson, and Feinstein 2010), and the resources of organizations trying to influence policy (e.g., Jenkins, Leicht, and Wendt 2006; Shipan and Volden 2006). Most studies focus on only one issue, however, and relatively few focus on what people actually do – protest, give speeches, sign petitions, etc. What McCammon (2012:4) has written about social movements – researchers "focus on a variety of circumstances *other than the actions of movement actors*" (emphasis in original) – is also true for the study of politics more generally.

Probably the most comprehensive account of what Americans do to influence policy is Walker, Martin, and McCarthy's (2008) description of the repertoires of those making claims on government in the United States between 1960 and 1990, on all issues, based on reports of events published in the *New York Times*.

What they are studying is advocacy – events that make news. The research they report on is by far the most comprehensive on advocacy by Americans, based on data collection carried out with great care over a long period of time, well documented and widely used by many researchers. The data set includes a very wide range of activities, including protest demonstrations, boycotts, leafletting, and press conferences – activities including both confrontational protests and conventional political activities. The authors find that of actions directed at governments (they also consider actions directed at corporations and educational institutions), 34 percent may be considered "conventional" (p. 53), while 36 percent involve rallies or demonstrations, 4 percent "symbolic displays," 10 percent civil disobedience, 11 percent "withholding obligations," and 5 percent "riots, conflicts, attacks."

Unfortunately, there are several reasons to think of these data as very problematic descriptions of what Americans do to influence policy. First, the authors of the article are themselves dubious. It seems inherently implausible that only a third of Americans' political activities are conventional – by definition most activities must be conventional. As Walker et al. (2008:48) put it, their data exhibit an "underrepresentation of conventional tactics."

Second, work in European countries often finds a much higher proportion of advocacy to be conventional – what advocates do very frequently is make speeches (e.g., Koopmans et al. 2005:137, 196, 223; della Porta 2008:284). The European findings are not entirely comparable to the American data; although a similarly wide range of activities is taken into account, only a few highly salient issues are examined, and the focus is often on extremists rather than ordinary citizens. Had the studies included more issues and fewer extremists, conventional activities would surely have been more common and the contrast with the American data greater.

Third, and perhaps most important, the American data tell us how Americans express their views on the environment, peace, women's issues, civil liberties, social policy, African American rights, and other broad policy domains (Walker et al. 2008:54), but not what their specific goals were. If we want to know how the public tried to get the government to do anything in particular, the data cannot tell us (cf. McCammon 2012).

Who advocates? Who is more prominent among Americans trying to affect policy, and who is less so? Here again we owe a great deal to the vision of those who created the "Dynamics of Collective Action" data set. They describe which sorts of groups initiated political claims and how often (Walker et al. 2008:60) – occupational groups, students, women, ethnic groups, religious groups, and so on. But because their initial focus was on protest by relatively powerless groups, and not on policy change per se, they left out of their data set activities initiated by the government, management, and "elites," excluding "conventional collective activity of businessmen's associations, political party officials, lobbyists, and government office holders" (Dynamics of Collective Protest 2009:2). Yet theoretical work tells us that those excluded from the data set are likely to strongly influence policy, and a great deal of empirical work shows them very active in the policy process (e.g., Baumgartner et al. 2009; Koopmans and Statham 1999; Koopmans et al. 2005; Leech 2010:544–45; Smith 2000; Soule and Olzak 2004; Statham and Geddes 2006). Thus, past attempts to identify who advocates are incomplete. If we want to discover who advocates, we must follow the agenda set forth by Koopmans and Statham (1999:206) and include in our data everyone trying to affect policy.

To discover how Americans try to influence Congress, it is essential to build on the accomplishments of others, to combine those accomplishments in new ways, and to move beyond past work into new territory. This will involve considering whether Olson (1971) might have been right when he concluded there should be very little collective action; taking Gamson's (1990) and Baumgartner et al.'s (2009) lessons about the importance of sampling and extending it to the study of advocacy on policy proposals; following up on the work of those who created the best data sets on advocacy (as described in Earl et al. 2004; Koopmans et al. 2005; Koopmans and Statham 2010b; McAdam and Su

2002; Walker et al. 2008) by focusing not only on advocacy in broad policy domains, but on efforts to influence congressional action on particular policy proposals as well; taking up the research agenda of Koopmans, Statham, and others (Harris and Gillion 2010; Koopmans and Statham 1999; Koopmans et al. 2005; Leech 2010; McAdam, Tarrow, and Tilly 1996) and including all types of advocacy and all types of advocates in the research; and searching much more widely than others have for evidence of advocacy.

QUESTIONS ABOUT ADVOCACY

1. How Much Advocacy?

Ever since Olson's *The Logic of Collective Action* appeared in 1965, it has been clear theoretically how much collective action intended to affect public policy there should be: not much. Organizations attempting to affect policy are seeking a collective good that will benefit every member of the organization. Because everyone will benefit, regardless of whether he or she devoted resources to help the organization win the collective good, it is rational for everyone to wait for others to do the necessary work. There will thus be little or no collective action, and therefore failure to acquire the collective good (Olson, 1971:21). As Olson writes about organizations in an economic context, "*A lobbying organization, or indeed a labor union or any other organization, working in the interest of a large group of firms of workers in some industry, would get no assistance from the rational, self-interested individuals in that industry*" (p. 11, italics in original; see also Lichbach 1995:chs. 1–2; Riker and Ordeshook 1968; Vasi and Macy 2003).

Before Olson wrote, it was generally assumed that individuals with shared interests would act together to achieve their goals. After Olson, it has generally been assumed they will not. So powerful was Olson's logic that it has arguably dominated work on collective action for 40 years, even though it seemed, even to Olson, so obviously contrary to fact. There seems to be a lot of collective action, and Olson devoted most of his book to considering the circumstances under which collective action would be rational.

Much the same arguments have been made for individuals' efforts to influence policy. The effort required is likely to be large, the chance of affecting policy small, and the benefit the same whether effort was made or not (Ansolabehere, de Figueiredo, and Snyder 2003; Downs 1957; Riker and Ordeshook 1968). Few people, therefore, will try to influence specific policies, and many of those who do will be motivated by nonpolitical concerns.

Yet there does seem to be a lot of advocacy by individuals and organizations – so much that it has hardly seemed worthwhile to test Olson's original hypothesis. There is a lot of research on how strongly advocacy affects policy, but little that asks how much advocacy there is. Researchers have data on how much advocacy there is – they must have such data to gauge advocacy's impact – but they often fail to present or analyze the data. Is there really a lot of advocacy? Perhaps not as much as we think.

As already noted, the two movements described as probably the most massive and intense of the second half of the 20th century – the anti–Vietnam War and civil rights movements – may not look quite so massive or intense once context is taken into account.[2]

McAdam and Su (2002:706) found an average of fewer than 11 "public protest events" per month nationwide during the period of the movement's peak activity.[3] This means that in the average month during this period of great movement activity, most cities and towns – indeed, most states – would have

---

[2] Other movements, sustained over a long period of time, such as the environmental movement, might involve more total collective action, but their peak intensity was not as high.

[3] No doubt their source of data, the *New York Times*, ignored many demonstrations, but it probably reported most of the largest (McCarthy et al. 1996; Oliver and Myers 1999), and the combination of size and coverage seems likely to make such events politically meaningful.

experienced no protests at all. And the average month would have seen *no* large-scale protests in the entire country.

What if we focus, not on the average months, but on the months of peak activity, early in 1970 and 1972? With 90 protests in a single month, there could have been protests all over the country (though McAdam and Su do not report on their location), and it is easy to imagine that four protests with at least 10,000 participants, the maximum in any single month, would gain considerable attention – which in fact they did.

Yet what does even this really amount to? In an entire month, there might have been one large demonstration in New York, one in Chicago, one in San Francisco, and one in Washington, D.C. And that's it – no large demonstrations in Texas, Florida, Michigan, Ohio, Pennsylvania, or any of the other more populous states, not to mention across the entire South and all the Plains states. And the months of peak protest were very unlike other months during the war – only 3 out of the 97 months studied had more than 40 protests (McAdam and Su 2002:711).

What about the civil rights movement? It lasted much longer than the antiwar movement, its period of peak activity was longer, and it encountered much more intense resistance. We might very well expect it to have stimulated far more collective action than the antiwar movement did. Yet in their study of incidents of "nonviolent protest by African Americans, including public demonstrations and marches, sit-ins, rallies, freedom rides, boycotts, and other protest actions" between 1948 and 1997, Jenkins et al. found the average number of protests per year to be 27.66 (Jenkins et al. 2003:285–86), just over one every two weeks for the entire country. This does not seem like a lot.

It may be argued that the average is misleading, because the incidence of African American protests was highly skewed. By far the greatest number occurred during the 1960s, approximately 40 percent during just three years, 1960, 1963, and 1965. Yet even the number of protests occurring in each of those years – roughly 160, 140, and 240 – never reached an average of one per day. Doubtless there were days with multiple protests, but there were also many days with none.

No doubt there were civil rights protests not reported by the *New York Times*. But protests are more likely to be covered than less-dramatic political activities, and, once such protests came to be seen as meaningful by northern papers like the *Times*, there were real efforts to cover those of any magnitude. Even if we imagine that the *Times* reported only 1 protest out of 20,[4] the average over the entire 50-year period would have been only 1.5 per day nationwide (552 per year), and, during the peak year, no more than 13 (4,800 protests over 365 days).

What about other social movements? It is difficult to catalog all potentially relevant data sets, but it may be instructive to look at protest pertaining to a third very important American movement, the women's movement. Using methods of data collection comparable to those of McAdam and Su (2002) and Jenkins et al. (2003), Rosenfeld and Ward (1996:63–64) found the number of "collective actions," both pro- and antifeminist, to be small, no greater than 25 together, in any year between 1955 and 1992. When Soule et al. (1999) used Rosenfeld and Ward's data to analyze the impact of the women's movement on congressional action, they reported a total of 101 "outsider events" (collective action outside the "institutional political arena") between 1956 and 1979, and 318 "insider" events.

Much broader in scope is the work of Walker et al. (2008). They describe all claims (or protests, or collective action – their terminology is not consistent, but they do include many kinds of

---

[4] Comparing newspaper reports of protest to local police reports, McCarthy et al. (1996:488) found that the media covered from 2.9% to 100% of demonstrations taking place in Washington, D.C., depending on the number of demonstrators and the year. Looking at coverage by the *New York Times* alone, they (1996:490) found it covering 4.1% of permitted demonstrations in 1982 and 1.8% in 1991; because the *Times* was more likely to report larger demonstrations, this amounted to coverage of 67% and 20.3% of demonstrators, respectively. Its coverage thus provided a much better sense of the number of demonstrators than the number of demonstrations. Oliver and Myers (1999:38) found local newspapers in Madison, Wisconsin, covering 32% of protest events of all types in 1994. On the whole, Earl et al. (2004:76) write, newspaper event data are no more problematic than other types of data used by social scientists, including survey data and data on crime rates.

activities, as described above, not just protest) reported in the *New York Times* between 1960 and 1990, covering "the entire range of issue areas and movement claims that enter the public sphere" (p. 45). Just under 10,000 were directed at governments, roughly 320 per year (p. 53), or less than one per day.

This is a remarkable number – it's impossible to believe that there was less than one protest per day against all governments in the entire country. No one argues that the *New York Times* reports all claims made on governments, but the *Times*' reportage is taken very seriously and the data described by Walker et al. (2008) are used as measures of claims in much research on policy change (e.g., Johnson, Agnone, and McCarthy 2010; King, Bentele, and Soule 2007; Larson and Soule 2009; Olzak and Soule 2009; Soule and Earl 2005). Yet even if the *Times* reports only one claim out of a thousand, the total number doesn't seem high – even 1,000 incidents a day in a nation of over 235 million adults totals about 4 per million. Walker et al. (2008) may have reported a finding of great importance without highlighting its significance – even the best research on political claims finds relatively few. Studies of other types of advocacy, including campaign contributions, PAC activity, and lobbying similarly find less advocacy than most people expect (Ansolabehere et al. 2003; Baumgartner and Leech 2001:1200–1; Hansen and Mitchell 2000; Wright 1996).[5]

Especially interesting is McAdam and Boudet's (2012:180–81) work on opposition to energy projects in the United States

---

[5] Some work on political participation by individuals seems to suggest that there is much more participation than reported here. Addressing this concern fully is impossible here, but, as with advocacy activity, it seems easy to overestimate the amount of participation. Some measures of total participation mix measures of activities taking place during a 12-month period with measures of other activities taking place over a longer period, or even a lifetime (see, e.g., Inglehart and Catterberg 2002:305; Verba, Schlozman, and Brady 1995:540–45). And some measures include activities that most people probably wouldn't think of as political participation at all; for example, Verba et al. (1995:541) seemingly count as participation any non–job-related contact with government about "problems or issues with which you were concerned"; this could include complaining to a public utility about a bill or calling the Department of Motor Vehicles to inquire about renewing a driver's license.

between 2000 and 2005. They found very little oppositional
activity in the 20 communities they studied – little conventional
political activity, few protests, and no disruptive protest at all.
They wind up concluding that past work (presumably including
McAdam's own) "has dramatically exaggerated the frequency
and causal significance of true social movements," partly because
of the "wildly nonrepresentative" nature of the studies "that
comprise much of the empirical work conducted to date"
(p. 181). It may be said that past work didn't so much exaggerate
the actual frequency of social movement activity, as misinterpret
what was found. Nevertheless, their new conclusions matter.

Olson's original argument that we should expect little collective
action may have been even more powerful than widely believed.

2. How Is Advocacy Distributed across Policy Proposals?

If there is little advocacy, necessarily there would be very little on
most policy proposals. Yet some proposals could provoke a lot of
advocacy if atypical incentives were available to potential advocates.

In the only study of a random sample of issues, Baumgartner
and Leech (2001:1200) found that the vast majority of their 137
issues generated very little lobbying, while a few "become the
object of veritable lobbying extravaganzas." Twenty-three issues
were addressed by only one organization, and 44 by fewer than
five, while the top 5 percent generated half the reports of lobbying
(Table 4.1).

Baumgartner and Leech's sample included only issues on which
there had been some advocacy – lobbying – on every issue. But the
policy proposals examined here need not have been the object of
advocacy at all beyond introduction of a relevant bill. If there is in
fact very little advocacy on most policy proposals, our view of the
policy process would differ greatly from the conventional one,
which emphasizes the intensity of conflict.[6]

---

[6] Amenta et al.'s (2009) study of how often "national advocacy organizations"
(p. 636) were mentioned (not necessarily in a political context) in the *New York
Times* during the 20th century finds similar skewness. Of the 1,247 such

3. How Is Advocacy Expressed?

Social scientists interested in systematically collecting data on publicly visible political activities were long interested primarily in protest. The focus was initially justified by the claim that protest, though an important part of American politics, had been ignored (Gamson 1990). That did not mean that protest should be studied alone. Indeed, it was essential to study all types of political activity together. Gamson (p. 138) emphasized that "the American Medical Association and Students for a Democratic Society are not different species but members of the same species faced with different political environments." "In place of the old duality of extremist politics and pluralist politics," he stated, "there is simply politics" (pp. 137–38). It would be a mistake to make sharp distinctions between protest and other types of political activity (Harris and Gillion 2010; McAdam, Tarrow, and Tilly 1996).

Nevertheless, major data collection efforts long focused on protest (e.g., Jenkins et al. 2003; Soule and Earl 2005) and paid little attention to what was often described as conventional political activity. Eventually, though, there were calls for taking a broader view and collecting data on all (or at least a great many) publicly visible efforts to influence policy (Koopmans and Statham 1999; Tilly 2008).

These calls were heeded. Both of the most widely used data sets, the "Dynamics of Collective Action" data at Stanford (http://www.stanford.edu/group/collectiveaction/cgi-bin/drupal/) and the Political Mobilisation data set at the Social Science Research Center Berlin (Koopmans 2002) now include a wide range of political activities – 68 in the former and 71 in the latter – among them press conferences, speeches, vigils, petitions, picketing, physical attacks, property damage, lawsuits, reports on the results of public opinion polls, the takeover of buildings, marches,

organizations they identified from a variety of sources, 300 were not mentioned in the *Times* at all. The most frequently mentioned organization, the AFL-CIO, got 14% of all mentions, and the top 10, 38% – almost two-fifths of mentions referring to 0.1% of all national advocacy organizations.

and a variety of types of demonstrations. Those who use those data sets (e.g., Koopmans et al. 2005; Walker et al. 2008) and those who develop their own (e.g., McCammon et al. 2007, 2008) often include lobbying and other forms of conventional political activity in their analyses.

Nevertheless, there are major disagreements among researchers about the relative frequency of different types of political activity. It is difficult to compare studies, because they differ in the political units studied (the United States, Canada, European countries, American states), the policy domains considered, aspects of data collection, and in other ways. Even so, the results are sometimes striking. As noted above, Walker et al. (2008:53) find conventional activities much less common than unconventional ones, while some European studies find the reverse – in a study of claims pertaining to unemployment in six European countries, for example, della Porta (2008:284) found 84 percent taking the form of verbal statements (categorized as conventional) and 9 percent taking the form of protests (typically seen as unconventional). Because most political activities must be conventional, by definition, the latter results seem more plausible. The apparent "underrepresentation of conventional tactics" in the United States has been attributed to news media's tendency to focus on dramatic events (Walker et al. 2008:47–48), but that wouldn't explain why the results differ so much between Europe and the United States.

This research takes a very broad view of advocacy, including all types of publicly reported activities supporting or opposing the 60 policy proposals (as detailed later in this chapter). But past research gives us much less guidance than we might like as to how advocacy will be distributed among types of activities.

4. Who Advocates?

The longtime focus on protest necessarily led to a focus on particular types of actors – protesters, or, stated more broadly, organizations that were somehow outside ordinary politics, often unable even to gain access to power holders to express their views. As the range of activities studied expands, so should the range of actors. If we analyze lobbying, we ought to find ourselves studying lobbyists, who by definition have access to power holders.[7]

But the range of actors studied has not expanded as logically as we might expect. The Political Mobilisation project includes all political claims "regardless of the nature of the actor" (Koopmans et al. 2005:254; see also della Porta 2008:284; Koopmans and Statham 1999). The Dynamics of Collective Action (2009) data set, however, excludes activities by elites, including elected and appointed government officials – even though such officials are widely seen as influencing policy (Barkey and Parikh 1991) – and activities by others if initiated by elites; for example, claims made by witnesses at congressional hearings are excluded because the hearings are initiated by members of Congress.

The differences in scope naturally produce very different findings; studies taking the broader view generally find that over half of reported activities are the work of "state and party actors" (Koopmans and Statham 1999:211; Koopmans et al. 2005:82). One might say that the difference between the approaches is that one is interested in what some kinds of people – disproportionately "outsiders" – do to influence policy, and the other in what everyone does.

SEEKING EVIDENCE

Data Sources

For more than 35 years, much of the data used to study public political activity has come from newspapers. Data collection has been strongly affected by technology and resources. Initially, American data were drawn from the *New York Times Index* – it was essentially the only compilation of events (including political activities) available for a long period, and researchers lacked the

---

[7] Of course there have long been studies of lobbying and lobbyists, as well as of PACs and other organizations and individuals with ready access to government officials. But these studies aren't based on reports in the press.

resources needed to read the paper itself. Gradually, more data became readily available; researchers began to gather information from selected entire issues of one newspaper per country (Kriesi et al. 1995) and moved on to skimming most sections in all issues of single newspaper (Larson and Soule 2009:297–98) and to using multiple newspapers per country (Koopmans 2007a). Many studies assess bias in the selection and description of events and other validity issues (e.g., Earl et al. 2004; Koopmans et al. 2005:24–27, 261; Olzak 1989:128–29); researchers have concluded that while such data must be interpreted cautiously, they are good enough to constitute a solid basis for analyzing protest, collective action, and claim making.

The cost of collecting data has been dramatically reduced by advances in information technology and the advent of the World Wide Web, and recently there has been some movement toward using electronic databases to search many newspapers and magazines (Koopmans and Rucht 2002; Nam 2006; Soule 1997; Woolley 2000). There are now databases (Proquest, LexisNexis, and others) that include hundreds of newspapers and magazines. In an early use of such a database to study protest, Soule (1997) used NEXIS to scan all the articles from 37 newspapers and news agencies pertaining to shantytowns, a tactic developed on American college campuses to protest South African apartheid, "allowing for a more thorough data collection than was ever before possible" (p. 864).

The data for this study were drawn from the Proquest database. At the moment, relatively few publications from before the early 1980s are included, but for more recent periods, hundreds are. Electronic databases not only increase the availability of data; they can also increase the transparency of research results and make data collection easier to replicate.

Gathering data from print media is a two-step process – finding articles describing relevant events and then coding them. For the data to be credible, both steps must be completed reliably – we must be confident that were the research done again, the results would be the same. There is an extensive literature on the reliability of coding (as described below), but much less has been written on reliability in the process of finding articles. When multiple coders are used, it is possible to determine how often they all select the same articles, but not how often they all fail to include articles describing advocacy. As Koopmans et al. (2005:264) wrote, "relevant articles that had been overlooked by the coders were lost forever from our view" (see also Soule and Earl 2005:349). This problem can be greatly mitigated by using electronic databases, and searching for articles using carefully selected key words (Soule 1997:864, 876). The search process is described in Appendix Table 2.[8]

Operationalizing Advocacy

The research reported here describes publicly visible advocacy – publicly visible in the sense of being described in widely available print media – for or against congressional action on 60 policy proposals. At this point it is necessary to operationalize advocacy. How relevant to a proposal must an activity be to count as advocacy and enter the data set?

H.R. (House of Representatives bill) 2423 dealt with reducing spills from oil tankers in Puget Sound. If a strict standard were adopted and only advocacy explicitly referring to that policy proposal were included in the data set – "I call on Congress to pass H.R. 2423 or an identical bill to reduce spills from oil tankers in Puget Sound" – the data set would include almost no advocacy. Rarely do people express themselves this way.

If, in contrast, a very loose standard were adopted and all advocacy pertaining to bills addressing oil tankers or Puget Sound were included, the data set would be huge but little advocacy would be related to oil spills from tankers in Puget Sound.

---

[8] The sources included in the database have changed over time, and during the data search I did not realize it would not be possible in retrospect to discover exactly which sources were available at which times. Because almost all the data were from the 1980s and 1990s, the number of sources was consistently large, and there do not seem to have been instances of sources being dropped from the data base once they were included.

The "Goldilocks" dilemma was thus how to focus searches for advocacy – not too broadly, not too narrowly, but just right. Advocacy pertaining to three types of policy proposals was included:

1. Advocacy that refers to the specific bill number, identifies the proposal in such detail that it clearly refers to the specific bill, or very plainly concerns a congressional bill with content identical, or very similar, to the original proposal (that is, 1 of the 60)

2. Advocacy that refers to federal (not necessarily congressional) action on the same general issue in a way consistent with the relevant policy proposal, but not included in the first category because (a) the action proposed is executive rather than congressional, (b) the proposal is very significantly stronger or weaker than the original proposal, (c) the proposal proposes a similar outcome for other targets, and/ or (d) the proposal broadens the proposed outcome for the same targets

3. Advocacy that refers to state-level action on the same general issue in a way consistent with the relevant policy proposal. Statements about state-level action are included because states often address proposals before the federal government does, and members of Congress may take state action into account as signifying the preferences of residents (e.g., Burstein 1998b:63–65; cf. King, Cornwall, and Dahlin 2005:1213; McCammon et al. 2001:65).

Thus, the first category includes advocacy closely linked to the 60 proposals, while the second and third refer to similar proposals and may provide information to elected officials about the general direction of the public's preferences. Included are both explicit statements for or against government action on a specific proposal and statements that are implicit but very clear.

By way of example: H.R. 4634 proposed that for safety reasons the weight of trucks traveling on interstate highways be limited to

70,000 pounds. The *Mississippi Business Journal* of February 29, 1990 (Rabb 1990:10), reported that Gil Carmichael, the newly appointed head of the Federal Railroad Administration, "wants a moratorium on truck weights, limiting all interstate highways to no more than 80,000 pounds." Pat McAdams, a transportation manager with Leaf River Forest Products in New Augusta, was reported to support Carmichael, saying that "as a citizen, I have to say 80,000 pounds is high enough." In the context of the article, it is clear they are referring to proposed congressional action on weight limits. Thus, both statements are coded 1 on specificity – they are concerned about proposed congressional action very similar to that in H.R. 4634, though the exact weight limits differ. Carmichael and McAdams clearly favored the bill, but they didn't say so explicitly; their statements are therefore coded as implicitly favoring federal action.

Another example: during a debate in the House of Representatives about funding the savings and loan bailout (H.R. 5891), the *New York Times* (Labaton, March 22, 1991, p. D1) reported that Rep. Bernie Sanders of Vermont was the only representative who rose to speak against the bill, saying, "It's a curious bill. . . . On one side, we have the President of the United States and the leadership of both parties. On the other side, I suspect we have the vast majority of the United States." Sanders was very clear about which bill he was referring to and his opposition to it. Rep. Chalmers P. Wylie of Ohio was quoted as saying, "Every day we delay results in throwing away additional money." He was clearly for the specific bill, but didn't say so explicitly. Speeches by members of Congress intended to persuade others are viewed as advocacy. Votes and bill sponsorship are not – they are the actions at which advocacy is directed.

Finding Evidence of Advocacy

The search for events began with standardized keyword searches of the Proquest database for each proposal. To find as many statements of preference as possible without making the number unmanageable, the searches (described in Appendix Table 2) were

fairly broad. The initial screening found 16,727 articles potentially including advocacy relevant to the policy proposals; the
number of articles per proposal ranged from zero (on H.R. 601,
H.R. 895, and H.R. 4547) to 3,771 (H.R. 3264). The unit of
analysis was the incident of advocacy, not the article; articles
could report more than one incident, but each incident was
included only once, even if reported in multiple articles. Only
contemporary events were coded; neither events that occurred in
the past nor events for which a date could not be ascertained were
included.

Advocacy was reported in 116 newspapers and periodicals,
including major newspapers such as the *New York Times* and
the *Los Angeles Times*; lesser papers such as the *Morning Call*
(Allentown, Pennsylvania), the *Journal Record* (Oklahoma City),
and the *Tri-State Defender* (Memphis, Tennessee); and publications directed at a variety of audiences, including *Billboard*, the
Chronicle of Higher Education, *Forbes*, *Italian Voice*, the
National Review, *Off Our Backs*, the *Progressive*, the *Village
Voice*, and *Waste Age* (see Appendix Table 3). The earliest advocacy occurred in 1971, the last in 2000.

Searching so widely produced far more evidence of political
activity than conventional searches would have. The *New York
Times*, the sole data source in many studies, included more instances of advocacy than any other publication, but just 10.3 percent
of the total.

Of course, no search finds all advocacy. Researchers doing
this kind of work take the numbers seriously nevertheless
(Burstein and Sausner 2005). Among events taking place in
public or semipublic settings, those reported in the media seem
especially likely to affect policy; Koopmans et al. (2005:25) go so
far as to say that when such events do not make it into the media,
they "may be considered not to have occurred at all." They may
be indulging in a bit of hyperbole; the point here is that this
research includes far more publicly visible advocacy than other
research has, but it makes no claim to include everything people
do to influence policy – no research does, and it is hard to see
how any research could.

Reliability

The second step in creating the data set was coding reports of advocacy; the coding manual is included as Appendix Table 4. Here reliability should be easier to address – there's no risk of material being overlooked and "lost forever."

To achieve high reliability, the data must be the product, to the greatest extent possible, of objective, replicable coding procedures. Coders work independently, following detailed instructions, and measures of reliability should correct for the likelihood that coders will agree by chance – a commonly used measure, percentage agreement among coders, will overestimate reliability. Some research follows these guidelines, but much does not. The collection of this kind of data, from so many sources, on so many policy proposals, in a closed-question format, is virtually unprecedented; attaining high levels of reliability was therefore very challenging. Reliability was measured using Scott's π. The conventional rule of thumb is that levels above .8 are very good, and levels between .67 and .80 can be used cautiously (Hayes and Krippendorff 2007; Scott 1955). Reliabilities are reported below, variable by variable, as relevant. A detailed discussion is provided in Appendix Table 4.

In sum, at an abstract level, the work reported here resembles earlier work, describing advocacy on public policy. But there are some very significant differences as well. The policies of interest are specific policy proposals. The advocacy is directed at those proposals. The goal is generalization. The search for evidence of advocacy is much broader. And the approach to reliability is more rigorous.

Of course, it's necessary to point out some limitations of these data as well. The focus on advocacy directed at specific policy proposals makes it impossible to reach the sorts of broad conclusions found in other studies – about advocacy concerning major policy domains, for example. It may not be possible to say as much about the social and political context as in some other studies. Analyzing 60 proposals makes it difficult to study each one as deeply as would be possible in a study of a single policy or policy domain. The approach presented here cannot replace the work of others, but it can certainly make its own unique contribution.

HOW MUCH AMERICANS ADVOCATE, WHAT THEY DO, AND WHO DOES WHAT

1. How Much Advocacy?

In one way, the search for data on advocacy reported here is narrower than other searches for data on publicly visible political activities: it includes only activities directed at specific policy proposals, rather than all the activities in broad policy domains. But in other crucial respects the search is broader: it includes all types of political activities, by all types of actors, included in a database encompassing hundreds of publications. The breadth of the search is important; if it is hypothesized that there will be little advocacy, evidence must be sought as widely and systematically as possible.

There were 1,614 instances of advocacy for or against the 60 policy proposals – 86 percent directed precisely at one of the 60, 11 percent at other federal action along similar lines, and 3 percent at comparable proposals at the state level. Since the average length of time a proposal was on the congressional agenda was around five years (2.6 congresses, as noted above), that amounts, very roughly, to around 300 per year. Is this a lot of advocacy or a little?

This question may be answered in comparative or absolute terms. Unfortunately, there are no closely comparable studies, and because researchers seldom focus on how much advocacy they discover (as opposed to describing trends or relative frequencies of different types of advocacy), there is no standard way to compare studies. Nevertheless, we can say something meaningful about orders of magnitude.

As noted above, Walker et al. (2008:45) find that from 1960 through 1990, roughly 320 collective action events per year were directed at governments on "the entire range of issue areas and movement claims that enter the public sphere." Compared to that, 300 instances of advocacy per year targeted at only 60 congressional policy proposals seems substantial. (No doubt searching hundreds of newspapers and magazines rather than just the *New York Times* makes a difference.)

What about studies focusing more narrowly on single major policy domains? The 1,614 instances of advocacy on the 60 policy proposals exceed the 130 or so protests taking place annually during the Vietnam War (McAdam and Su 2002:697), the 28 nonviolent protests by African Americans reported per year between 1948 and 1997 (Jenkins et al. 2003:285), and the total of 101 "outsider" events and 318 "insider" events pertaining to women's issues for a 24 year period, 1956–79 (Soule et al. 1999); the number reported here may be more comparable to the 160, 140, and 240 reported during the peak years of the civil rights movement, 1960, 1963, and 1965. Of course, some protests involve many participants, but probably not very many.

What about absolute numbers? Here Olson becomes more relevant. Calculations are necessarily very crude, but if we put Walker et al.'s (2008) numbers in the context of the population of the United States, roughly 115 million adults age 18 and over in 1960 and 185 million in 1990, the number of claims per million adults per year must be very small. They don't provide annual numbers, but if we say the average number of adults was 150 million and the average number of claims against government 320 per year, that amounts to about two claims per million adults per year. Other studies find similar numbers (Burstein and Sausner 2005).

The amount of advocacy per million adults per policy proposal is less – hardly surprising considering that the comparison is between "the entire range of issue areas and movement claims that enter the public sphere" and just 60 policy proposals, even though advocacy includes more types of activities and actors than the claims analyzed in other studies. But what if we tried to estimate the total amount of advocacy? The 60 were about a hundredth of the 5,977 in the sampling frame. If we estimated

(without worrying about sample size, confidence intervals, dupli-
cate bills, etc.) that the total number of claims directed at Congress
on all the policy proposals was 1,614 times 100, or 161,400,
that's a bit less than one instance of advocacy per 1,000 adults
in 1990 – much larger than two per million, but arguably still very
small.

The numbers of claims and amount of advocacy described here
necessarily underestimate the actual level of political activity.
Much is not reported (Earl et al. 2004; McCarthy, McPhail, and
Smith 1996; Oliver and Myers 1999), and single claims or instances of advocacy may represent the desires of many people. What's
more, very large numbers of political demands are made in private. Even so, though the amount of political activity directed at
Congress is not necessarily close to zero, it doesn't seem especially
large, either. Certainly the magnitude should be discussed more
than it has been.[9]

2. How Is Advocacy Distributed across Policy Proposals?

Baumgartner and Leech (2001) found very little lobbying on most
issues in their sample, and a very high proportion of all lobbying
focusing on a handful of issues. The findings for policy proposals
are similar. Thirty-one proposals generated no advocacy at all,
and 48 (80 percent of the proposals) just 5.2 percent of the total,
while three proposals – H.R. 2273, the Americans with
Disabilities Act; H.R. 4328, the Textile Trade Act; and H.R.
181, Social Security benefit computation formula – produced 52
percent.

The amount of advocacy could be related to the apparent
public importance of policy proposals, but that's not obvious
here. Almost 13 percent of all advocacy was directed at a Social

---

[9] Some social scientists are very skeptical of analyses that take seriously the
reported levels of advocacy, perhaps because such data are rarely described in
per capita terms, and the totals seem, to some readers, disconcertingly low. Yet
the very same data are taken very seriously when it is their impact being
calculated rather than their incidence. It is difficult to justify treating the numbers
as accurate for purposes of causal analysis if they are not accurate descriptively.

TABLE 4.1. *Distribution of Collective Action and Lobbying across Policy Proposals and Issues*

Percentage of Policy Proposals or Issues	Cumulative Percentage of: Statements of: Preference	Lobbying Reports
Lowest 50% (of 60 Policy Proposals, 137 Issues)	0.0	2.3
Through 70%	1.5	8.1
Through 80%	5.2	15.3
Through 90%	22.6	33.4
Through 95%	48.0	50.3

Note: Data on lobbying reports are from Baumgartner and Leech 2001:1202.

Security benefit computation formula affecting only recipients born between 1917 and 1922, whereas advocacy focusing on three proposals of much greater likely impact – carbon dioxide emissions, the creation of a federal Department of Environmental Protection, and environmental impact statements – made up just 1.4 percent of the total.

3. How Is Advocacy Expressed?

As noted above, recent work on protest and claims takes many forms of action into account. Researchers have not yet agreed, however, on how the forms of action should be categorized. Koopmans and others (Koopmans 2002:37–39) have adopted the most inclusive approach and describe 10 broad forms of action. This study describes 12; Table 4.2 compares the two approaches.

The categorization schemes differ in two major ways. Because this study focuses on advocacy for or against particular policy proposals, it does not include political decisions or executive action – not so much advocacy as the consequences of advocacy – or judicial decisions, which in the United States do not pertain to pending legislation.

In addition, the very broad category of verbal statements in Koopmans (2002:38) is subdivided here into categories based on

TABLE 4.2. *Forms of Collective Action, Koopmans et al. and This Study*

Koopmans et al.	This Study
Political decisions	
Executive action	
Judicial action	
Verbal statements (including press conferences, speeches, interviews, newspaper articles, nonspecified statements)	Speech (one-way communication in front of an audience)
	Two-way communication (e.g., press conference)
	Editorial
	Letter to the editor
	Congressional testimony
	Substantive article
	Interview
	Other message events (including statements attributed to particular actors without the form being specified)
Meetings	
Direct-democratic action (pertaining to initiatives and referenda)	
Petitioning	
	Delegation
Demonstrative protest (including public assemblies, marches, legal nonviolent demonstrations, vigils/pickets)	Protest events
Confrontational protests (including strikes, boycotts disturbance of meetings, symbolic confrontations)	Strikes, boycotts (with or without violence)
Violent protests (including symbolic protest, such as burning flags)	Riots (with or without violence)

type of communication and venue. We don't know if these differences matter, but they might, and verbal statements constitute so high a proportion of advocacy that it seems wrong to treat them as an undifferentiated mass.

Koopmans's "meetings" are broken down here by type – press conferences, speeches, and delegations. The "direct-democratic action" category is irrelevant because the United States has neither referenda nor initiatives at the federal level.

The distribution of instances of advocacy by type is reported in Table 4.3 (reliability coefficient of .69). The most common, by far – 59 percent of the total – is "other." Normally, finding so high a proportion of units of analysis categorized as "other" would mean there is something wrong with the set of categories. Here, though, the "other" category reflects something real about the conventions of news reporting. Newspaper articles very frequently report that someone "said" something but provide no information about the type of utterance – whether it was in an interview, speech, press conference, or whatever. In the absence of previous work, there was no way to anticipate this, nor is it obvious what could be done about it.[10] It makes sense to consider these reports as oral statements, type unspecified, but to take note of the lack of detail by categorizing them as "other."

Next-most common are editorials (almost all in newspapers) and substantive articles (in newspapers and other periodicals), with letters to the editor not far behind. The print media do not simply report advocacy by others; they are often where advocacy occurs.

Almost all the collective action takes the form of discourse, including speeches, interviews, letters to the editor, and so on. The amount of protest – demonstrations, strikes, boycotts, and riots – is minuscule. Not a single event involved violence by participants, bystanders, or the police. Studies of European collective action on especially contentious issues find a bit more protest, but not that much; della Porta (2008:284, 292), not quite sure how to summarize her findings, describes the frequency of protest on unemployment as both rare and "not necessarily" rare (see also Koopmans and Statham 1999).

---

[10] Such claims must be found in other studies based on newspaper stories, but they are not mentioned in published reports, so we don't know how they are counted.

TABLE 4.3. *Event Type*

	Frequency	Percentage	Cumulative Percentage
Other Message Event	952	59.0	59.0
Editorial	161	10.0	69.0
Substantive Article	140	8.7	77.6
Speech	85	5.3	82.9
Letter to Editor	79	4.9	87.8
Congressional Testimony	72	4.5	92.3
Two-Way Communication	49	3.0	95.3
Interview	41	2.5	97.8
Protest Event	26	1.6	99.4
Delegation	9	.6	100.0
Strike or Boycott	0	.0	100.0
Riot	0	.0	100.0
Total	1,614	100.0	

It may be objected that little protest is found because the proposals are a stratified random sample. But that is precisely the point. If we want to describe a few dramatic political struggles, that's one thing; if we want to understand politics generally, that's another.

Why should elected officials respond to protest or to other forms of advocacy? Studies of the impact of advocacy (or protest or claim making) on policy change ask *whether* elected officials respond, but have little specific to say about *why*.[11]

For example, Tilly and Tarrow (2007:126–28) briefly discuss why members of Congress might respond to public opinion about women's issues (out of "electoral motivations"; p. 127), but not why they respond to protest. Walker et al. (2008:40–41) emphasize that protesters are especially likely to target democratic governments (as opposed to corporations or educational

---

[11] See, e.g., McAdam and Su 2002; Agnone 2007; Meyer and Minkoff 2004; Olzak and Ryo 2007; Santoro 2002, 2008; Soule and Olzak 2004; McCammon et al. 2001, 2007; and Amenta et al. 2005; for a review, see Burstein and Linton 2002.

institutions) because governments are more "open" to influence, but they don't define openness or say why it matters (see also Meyer and Minkoff 2004). McAdam and Su (2002:711–12) contend that "social movements derive their effectiveness by posing a disruptive threat to the established order" and argue that "the spur to increased and more favorable state action comes not from disruption per se but from the apparent victimization of demonstrators." But they don't show that members of Congress saw antiwar activity as a disruptive threat or why they would be affected by threats or apparent victimization. Similarly, Soule and Olzak (2004:478) contend that "social movement organizations ... influence policy makers because they strategically use institutionalized tactics, such as litigation and lobbying." That may be true, but why?

Why might elected officials respond to advocacy? Empirical work on advocacy and policy change usually assumes that responsiveness is simply a function of the resources or level of activity of those making claims (Burstein and Linton 2002).

Theoretical work, though, increasingly asks what elected officials' most important needs are as they consider legislation, and examines how advocates might win influence by addressing those needs. Elected officials' most important goal is reelection. To win, they need information that will help them enact policies likely to be popular. They seem especially interested in three types of information – about the importance of problems they are asked to address, so they can establish priorities among issues; about the likely impact of policies proposed to address the problems; and about the likely impact of their actions on their reelection chances (Arnold 1990:ch. 4; Baumgartner and Leech 1998:137; Hansen 1991:12; Hirsch and Shotts 2012; Kingdon 1981:172; Krehbiel, 1991:ch. 7; Mayhew 1974). The concept of information is a broad one, including not only facts, but the context that gives meaning to those facts as well. What some social scientists call information, others would characterize as causal arguments or claims – attempts to present information in a convincing way (see, e.g., Stone 1989; cf. Andrews 2001:75; McCammon et al. 2001:57).

Political actors often work hard to provide this information –
often slanted to their own point of view – in the hope it will
influence those in office. Very little is known about whether
individuals and organizations provide elected officials with the
information they want or if the information affects policy. But
McCammon and her colleagues (McCammon et al. 2001, 2007,
2008) demonstrated the importance of interactions between activists and legislators, highlighting the importance of framing (or
reframing) issues in ways that change legislators' minds about
where their electoral advantage lies. Burstein and Hirsh
(2007:187) found that of nearly 1,000 witnesses testifying before
congressional committees on 27 policy proposals, almost two-
thirds provided information on the importance of the problem,
three-fifths on the likely effectiveness of the proposed policy, and
over a third on the possible electoral consequences of voting for or
against a proposal (see Chapter 6).

The data set, therefore, includes some measures of information
provided by advocates to see if advocacy reported in print media
resembles congressional testimony.[12] It does not record whether
advocates argued for the importance of the problem, but there are
data on statements about the likely effectiveness of the proposed
policy, the number and likely political activities of people represented by witnesses, and the categories of people likely to benefit.
The information had to be fairly specific and linked reasonably
closely to the particular policy proposals. Thus, statements along
the lines of "I oppose this bill attacking pornography because all
attempts to regulate morality fail" would be excluded because the
claim about consequences is generic and does not refer to the
particular bill. Similarly, claims that an agricultural bill would
benefit farmers or the residents of farm states would be included,
but claims that the bill would affect every American would not be.

Those making statements reported in the print media are much
less likely than those giving testimony to show why elected

---

[12] The print media occasionally reported on congressional hearings, but most such
accounts were brief, and need not have included information provided by
witnesses.

TABLE 4.4. *Information Presented by Political Actors: Percentage of Actors Providing Information about Importance of Problem, Effectiveness of Proposed Solution, and Electoral Consequences of Action for Members of Congress*

	Reported in Print Media	Testimony at Congressional Hearings
Importance of Problem[a]		64
Effectiveness of Proposed Solution[b]	7.6	58
Electoral Consequences – Mention Number of People Represented or Political Activities[c]	2.0	15
Electoral Consequences – Mention Number of People Affected, or How Widely Dispersed[d]	2.7	3

Note: Political actors can provide more than one kind of information, so percentages can add up to more than 100; or no relevant information so the percentages may add up to much less than 100. Data on congressional testimony are from Burstein and Hirsh (2007:187).

[a]Does the political actor present an explicit argument that the problem addressed by the policy proposal is important?

[b]Does the political actor make explicit predictions that the proposal will have the intended consequences if enacted?

[c]Does the political actor mention the number of members in the organization he or she represents (if any), or anything about the political activities by the organization, its members as individuals, or other similar individuals? (Percentage of events initiated by interest organizations only.)

[d]Does the political actor mention the number of people likely to be affected by the proposal, in terms of demographic categories, or how widely dispersed the people potentially affected by the proposal are?

officials should support the policy proposal (Table 4.4).[13] I have argued (Burstein 1998a) that collective action in one venue may complement that in another. Public statements may express

---

[13] Agreement between coders on the questions reported in Table 4 ranged from 91% to 99%. However, because the distribution of responses was extremely skewed, the expected rate of agreement was very high, and a handful of disagreements produces very low reliability. It seems fair to say, though, that the descriptive finding here – that very little information is being conveyed – can be taken as accurate.

demands for action, while congressional testimony provides the more detailed information legislators want about the likely benefits and costs of doing so.

4. Who Tries to Influence Congress?

Following Olson's logic in a general way, few people or organizations will try to influence Congress, and the total amount of advocacy directed at the 60 policy proposals seems consistent with this view. So who would the advocates be? For whom would the balance of costs and potential benefits make advocacy worthwhile? Olson delineates many hypothetical examples, including circumstances in which organizations created for one purpose can also lobby at almost no marginal cost, and in which members of small groups are able to monitor each other to mitigate the free rider problem. There are four circumstances potentially affecting cost-benefit calculations for advocates whose activities are reported here.

The first is when advocacy on particular proposals costs very little because it is incidental to some other activity (Olson 1971: ch. 6). Members of Congress and their staffs frequently take positions on proposed legislation (Mayhew 1974) – indeed, they account for a third of the advocacy events (Table 4.5, reliability = .74). Sometimes they do so to impress constituents, but often they are attempting to sway congressional colleagues – a finding consistent with the work of others highlighting the importance of state actors (elected officials and government employees) in the policy process (e.g., Baumgartner et al. 2009:9; Burstein and Hirsh 2007; della Porta 2008:284; Koopmans and Statham 1999:211; Koopmans et al. 2005:102). For them, the marginal cost of stating preferences on a particular proposal is virtually nil (there are electoral consequences to worry about, but that is not a cost in the relevant sense). Executive agencies report regularly to Congress and are asked about the problems they face and the likely effectiveness of proposed solutions. Because the resources needed to make and support their statements of preferences are built into their budgets, it might even be said that the executive agencies are paid for expressing their

TABLE 4.5. *Actor Type*

	Frequency	Percentage	Cumulative Percentage
Interest Organization	573	35.5	35.5
Member of Congress, Staff	528	32.7	68.2
Unaffiliated Individual	326	20.2	88.4
U.S. Executive Branch	93	5.8	94.2
State or Local Government	66	4.1	98.3
President	22	1.4	99.6
Multiple Interest Organizations	5	.3	99.9
Multiple State, Local Governments	1	.1	100.0
Political Party (Not Elected Official)	0	.0	100.0
U.S. Judiciary	0	.0	100.0
Total	1,614	100.0	

preferences. Just under 6 percent of the 1,614 claims of preference were made by executive agencies. In sum, a very substantial proportion of advocacy is the work of "state actors." (There were no statements by political parties or the judiciary.) This is somewhat less than found by Koopmans (2007a:192) for statements about European institutions and by Statham and Geddes (2006) for Europeans' statements about immigration, but still a very substantial proportion.

In addition, newspapers and periodicals publish many articles that state preferences for or against policy change, including editorials, syndicated columns, and substantive articles written by individuals who are not lobbyists. The authors of these articles are paid to write them, but not by organizations with an interest in the policy proposals. Instead, they are paid by the publications to write about policy; stating preferences about specific policies is simply part of their jobs. Twenty-eight percent of claims by interest organizations consists of editorials (a total of 161), and 26 percent of claims by unaffiliated individuals take the form of substantive articles (86).

It is striking how much advocacy is the work of people paid to express their opinions – not paid in the way lobbyists are, to express particular opinions (the focus of Olson's inquiry), but rather paid (at least in part) the way editorial writers, syndicated columnists, and politicians are, to express opinions broadly, with the expression of opinions on specific issues being particular manifestations of the more general task.

The second circumstance potentially affecting cost-benefit calculations concerns the likelihood that advocacy will influence policy. A key element of the collective action problem is that potential actors believe that their actions will have no impact on the legislative process. But individuals and organizations invited to testify at congressional hearings may legitimately feel that their testimony will have an impact (Burstein and Hirsh 2007). Four percent of the claims made by interest organizations, and 5 percent by unaffiliated individuals, are made in testimony reported in the press.

Third, advocacy may occur when the number of potential actors on an issue is small, so that they can monitor each other's involvement and pressure each other to act (Olson 1971:ch. 2). The number of states is small; state and local governments together contribute just over 4 percent of the statements of preferences.

Finally, advocacy may occur when low marginal cost is combined with emotional satisfaction stemming from the action itself (Ansolabehere, de Figueiredo, and Snyder 2003). Many people who donate to campaigns, for example, know their contributions won't affect the outcome. A case in point in this data set concerns the so-called Notch Act, a proposal to change Social Security benefit levels for individuals born during a brief period early in the 20th century (the "notch" between those born earlier and those born later). Elderly individuals wrote so many letters to financial columnists that the columnists began to express irritation about the number of letters based on the false belief (widely rebutted in the press) that their age group was getting lower Social Security payments than anyone else (for example, Quinn 1999). But 41 percent of all letters to the editor (32 of 79) were devoted to this issue, written by retired individuals who probably enjoyed expressing themselves in their free time.

It's not possible to say with any certainty what proportion of advocacy occurred because of these circumstances, but a good argument could be made that the proportion is not small.

RETHINKING ADVOCACY

If we want to understand policy change, we need to know what people do to bring it about. How do they express themselves? How often? Who is involved?

These questions are not easy to answer. Researchers have not agreed on how to define advocacy or policy; they collectively study biased samples of issues and seek data in only a narrow range of sources; they have paid a great deal of attention to protest but much less to other forms of advocacy; they have shown little interest in testing hypotheses about how much advocacy there is; and they have not focused on advocacy directed at Congress.

This chapter has focused on advocacy, broadly defined, directed at a stratified random sample of 60 policy proposals being considered by Congress, using data sought more widely than ever before to find out how much advocacy there is.

The picture of American politics that emerges is both unsurprising and challenging.

Most policy proposals provoke little or no advocacy once the bills are introduced. Most people can't be expected to have opinions on most issues and therefore can't be expected to advocate. From the congressional point of view, the workload, including the number of requests (public and private) for action, seems immense. But out among the public, on most issues, there is quiet.

Most advocacy consists of verbal statements of policy preferences, editorials, and substantive articles; there are very few protests, none of them violent.

Publicly reported advocacy is much less likely than congressional testimony to provide elected officials with specific types of information relevant to their decision making. The public may make broad demands; lobbyists and government officials work out the details.

Advocacy is dominated by people for whom advocacy is part of their jobs – the work of individuals and organizations for whom the marginal cost of advocacy is close to zero.

None of these conclusions should *seem* very surprising. It's not worthwhile for people to get involved in politics, most of the time (Olson 1971). People mostly express themselves in conventional ways. Important work, in politics as elsewhere, is often done by professionals (McCarthy and Zald 1977).

Yet the conclusions actually *are* surprising. They're new. They're not part of widely held views of advocacy and the policy process. They're not found in past work on advocacy directed at the U.S. Congress.

These conclusions are the product of rethinking some key aspects of the study of advocacy in democratic countries. I focused on advocacy linked closely to specific proposals and not on general claims in broad policy areas. In order to make generalization possible, I analyzed a stratified random sample of policy proposals. And I searched for data especially widely; though more advocacy was reported in the *New York Times* than anywhere else, the *Times* reports amount to only a tenth of the total.

Of course, the research reported here complements what others have done, and it is easy to imagine each aspect being criticized. Perhaps the policy proposal will not be seen as an especially useful way to conceptualize and measure congressional action. Perhaps those who focus on especially important issues will not be persuaded of the significance of efforts to sample and generalize. Perhaps the suggestion that it is important to study efforts to change specific policies will not win many adherents. But I think it vital in the study of politics to examine what people do to affect specific policies that matter to them, and to do so in a way that enables us to generalize about policy change.

The next step is an obvious one – to determine how claims affects policy change.

5

The Impact of Advocacy on Congressional Action

How strongly does advocacy affect policy change? Very strongly, say some. That interest groups strongly affect policy is conventional wisdom, and it is now seemingly taken for granted that social movement organizations, formerly seen as powerless because they represent political outsiders, often have substantial policy impact as well (e.g., McAdam and Su 2002:716). There are many reasons for this: interest organizations control resources useful to politicians; their members care intensely about their issues, in contrast to the generally indifferent public; they are often able to manipulate the information available to politicians; and so on (see, e.g., Dahl 1956; Jones 1994; Kollman 1998; Lohmann 1993; Wright 1996). The image of lobbyists dominating the legislative process is a staple of American political discourse (Leech 2010).

Not strongly at all, argue others. We wouldn't expect advocacy to have much impact because in key approaches to democratic theory, the most important determinant of policy change will be public opinion.[1] Politicians need votes to win elections, so the public has the ultimate authority over policy. Making this point

[1] See, e.g., Ansolabehere and Jones 2010:583; Downs 1957; Erikson, MacKuen, and Stimson 2002:447–48; Erikson et al. 1993:1; Jones 2011:764; Lax and Phillips 2009:382–83; Shapiro 2011; Soroka and Wlezien 2010:2–3; Wlezien and Soroka 2012:1407–8.

especially strongly, Lohmann (1993:319) has written that "it is puzzling that rational political leaders with majoritarian incentives would ever respond to political action" by interest organizations.

In line with the "strong impact" view, studies of interest organizations almost always hypothesize that they will affect policy. Often, however, they actually have little or no impact. Linton and I (Burstein and Linton 2002:394), for example, reviewed more than 100 estimates of the impact of interest organizations on policy (as presented in major journals) and found that half the estimates showed no impact, and another 6 percent were unclear about whether there was any impact. Andrews and Edwards (2004:498) note that "current scholarship indicates a modest role at best for advocacy organizations on congressional voting patterns," while other review articles (Baumgartner and Leech 1998:187; Smith 1995:123) find the evidence of organizational impact "inconclusive" (see also Ansolabehere, de Figeuiredo, and Snyder 2003; Potters and Sloof 1996; Wright 1996). As Leech (2010:534) writes, "Almost everyone believes that interest groups are influential, and yet systematic studies have as often pointed to the limits on interest group influence as have concluded that strong influence exists." The evidence, in total, is decidedly mixed.[2]

This chapter presents two hypotheses about the impact of advocacy on policy change. The first is that advocacy affects policy change *more strongly* than past research suggests. As described in Chapters 2 and 4, in many studies there has been a mismatch between the measures of advocacy and the measures of policy: either the advocacy is not directed at changing specific policies, or the measures of policy are so broad they cannot be the result of any particular advocacy, or both. If research were to

---

[2] The literature being reviewed often defines itself as focusing on particular types of activities, such as lobbying, contributing to campaigns, protesting, etc., and no terms are used consistently to cover all these activities. Here as above they're all called advocacy even if the authors of the works cited wouldn't use that term themselves.

gauge the impact on specific policies of advocacy aimed *at those policies*, the impact should be especially powerful.

The second hypothesis is that advocacy affects policy change *less strongly* than past research suggests. Past research focuses on issues evoking especially intense advocacy and rarely asks if the impact of advocacy depends on how much there is. Chapter 4 concluded that there is little advocacy on most policy proposals. Might there be too little to have much impact?

To see if the impact of advocacy on policy is stronger than past research suggests, this chapter builds on the previous ones by conceptualizing and measuring both advocacy and policy in ways linking the former especially tightly to the latter. The approach developed here weaves together several threads in recent work – on defining and measuring policy and collective action, and trying to generalize about policy change – to modify our current image of the policy process. To see if the impact is weaker, we return to a consideration of how little advocacy there is.

COMPETING EXPECTATIONS ABOUT THE IMPACT OF ADVOCACY

How much effect does advocacy actually have on policy? Probably the fairest summary of research findings would be that there is a reasonable probability that the effect is not zero.

This may not seem like much of a conclusion, after decades of increasingly elaborate and sophisticated research. Yet the conclusion isn't unreasonable. Many studies find that the null hypothesis of no impact can't be rejected at conventional levels of probability – or, in everyday terms, that advocacy almost surely has no impact. Many other studies find advocacy having an impact that probably isn't zero, using the same criteria. Some of the latter studies find the effect large enough to be politically meaningful (Burstein and Linton 2002), but many others present their findings only in terms of statistical significance and make no attempt to say how strongly advocacy affects policy. Advocacy could be having a substantial impact on policy, but many studies that find some impact avoid reaching conclusions about how much.

It's not especially surprising that many researchers fail to discuss how much impact advocacy has. In many areas in the social sciences, it is simply a convention to discuss statistical significance but not the substantive meaning of coefficients; the study of policy change is one of those areas. What's more, researchers who try to interpret their coefficients might very well find the results difficult to interpret. Sometimes measures of policy are not politically meaningful, in the sense that advocates won't care about them – the number of laws enacted on a topic would be an example. Sometimes measures – welfare state effort, for example – are the product of so many policy choices that it is hard to imagine describing the advocacy activities directed at them all. Sometimes measures of advocacy are not linked closely to the measures of policy – how might protest against state governments and private corporations be expected to influence Congress? And even if specific studies are unproblematic, attempts to compile their findings would be impeded by the lack of standardization among studies – measures of policy and advocacy vary so much from study to study that trying to compare them would be a hopeless task. Leech (2010:549) concludes that asking whether interest groups are influential is "an extraordinarily frustrating question" partly because "it is so difficult to answer," and her statement may readily be applied to the study of advocacy generally.

In the face of poor measures, limited interest in moving beyond statistical significance, and lack of standardization, those who do develop good measures and try to interpret their coefficients substantively often find themselves with little guidance. A good example of the consequences is provided by Fording's (2001) work. He gauged the impact of what he called "insurgency" – "any act of violence on behalf of blacks or minorities, either spontaneous or planned, which is either framed as or can be construed as politically motivated" (p. 119) – during the peak period of civil rights activity, 1962–80.

Fording hypothesized that insurgency would affect Aid to Families with Dependent Children (AFDC) growth (welfare recipients per million population) and rates of incarceration (prisoners per million population), and he found the impact of insurgency to be substantial. Each incident of insurgency was associated with growth in the AFDC rolls of approximately 250–300 recipients per million (an increase of approximately 1 percent per incident) and with an increase in the number of prisoners of 23 per million (an increase of approximately 1.5 percent per incident).

These findings suggest a political system exquisitely attuned to its environment, with single incidents producing (as Fording interprets his results) large effects, in percentage terms. Does this seem likely? Because so few studies report data this way, we have no basis for comparison. We do know, however, that members of Congress are normally extremely busy, too busy to even be aware of the levels of insurgency Fording described, much less organize so as to respond strongly and consistently (Arnold 1990; Jones and Baumgartner 2005; Jones, Larsen-Price, and Wilkerson 2009; Krehbiel, 1991; Lohmann 1994). The findings seem a bit implausible, yet without other researchers taking the initiative and producing comparable results, it's difficult to know what to make of them.

How strongly might advocacy, as described in Chapter 4, affect congressional action on the policy proposals described in Chapter 2?

Why the Impact Could Be Greater than Often Believed

It seems obvious that attempts to estimate the impact of advocacy on policy change should carefully link potential causes to effects; the focus should be on whether actions intended to influence particular policies actually do so. A good example is the work by McCammon et al. (2007; McCammon 2012) showing how enactment of state laws allowing women to serve on juries was affected by activists' efforts to influence elected officials on that issue, through letter-writing campaigns, speeches, and lobbying.

Yet that is not how most studies proceed. Many gauge the impact, not of advocates' activities, but of their resources (such as organizations' budgets or number of members; Burstein and Linton 2002:397) or of the density or diversity of organized interests (Monogan, Gray, and Lowery 2009). As described in Chapter 4, many studies that do gauge the impact of activities focus, not on activities directed at particular policies, but on activities in broad policy domains; many focus, not on specific policies, but on measures that sum up a great many policies.[3]

Thus, many studies attempting to estimate the impact of advocacy on policy change do *not* carefully link potential causes – advocacy on specific policy proposals – to effects – legislative action on the same proposals. Because they are considering the impact of advocacy on something the advocates are not actually trying to influence, or the impact of something other than advocacy (such as resources) on policy, their estimates of impact are bound to be low and underestimate the impact of advocacy on policy.

Even studies that analyze targeted activities may underestimate the impact of advocacy, if they neglect the activities most likely to influence elected officials. Hirsh and I (Burstein and Hirsh 2007) argued that those trying to influence policy will be especially effective when they provide legislators with information potentially relevant to their reelection – information about the importance of the problem they are being asked to address, the likely success of a proposed policy change, and the activities of groups favoring or opposing the change (cf. Baumgartner et al. 2009:123–27; Jones and Baumgartner 2005:ch. 2). Some types of information do indeed have an impact when conveyed in testimony to congressional committees (see Chapter 6). But studies of advocacy seldom consider information (Chalmers 2013).

And there is an additional reason why past work may very well have underestimated the impact of advocacy on policy: it has

---

[3] Some advocates do favor policy change along very broad lines – they want social welfare expenditures to be generous, or the United States move in a more conservative direction, for example. But to get what they want, they must influence legislative action on many specific policies, sometimes repeatedly over long periods of time. As noted in Chapter 2, those who try to explain change in complex, multipolicy measures often neglect advocacy – it would be extremely difficult to show how advocacy directed at single policies influences a whole set of policies incorporated into one measure (Erikson et al. 1993; Erikson et al. 2002; Gray et al. 2004).

focused on policies most likely to be influenced by public opinion (Chapter 3), and therefore less likely, in the conventional view, to be influenced by advocacy.

Thus, there are three aspects of past work that may lead researchers to underestimate the impact of advocacy on policy: failing to carefully link causes and effects, paying insufficient attention to forms of advocacy especially likely to be effective, and analyzing policies especially unlikely to be affected by advocacy. The research described here attacks all these problems and should therefore find advocacy having a substantially greater impact on policy than we would normally expect.[4]

Why the Impact Could Be Less than Often Believed

Thus, there are good reasons to believe that the impact of advocacy on policy has been underestimated in past work. But there are also good reasons to believe the impact has been overestimated.

As noted above, researchers tend to focus on policies that are especially controversial and on the legislative agenda for an especially long time. If such controversies provoke an unusually high level of advocacy, we would expect the impact of advocacy to be especially strong. If advocacy on less-controversial issues is less frequent, then sampling bias would have led to exaggerated estimates of the impact of advocacy (just as it did for public opinion).[5]

In fact, we have found from both a careful reading of past work and the new data presented in Chapter 4 that there is little advocacy even on some very controversial issues. We often find protest having no impact (e.g., Burstein 1998b:84–85; McAdam and Su 2002; Soule et al. 1999:251–52) – not surprising given how little there is.

As already noted, studies of interest organizations almost always hypothesize that they will affect policy – quite a minimalist

---

[4] Jessee (2009) makes a similar point on the relationship between voter ideology and candidate positions on specific policy proposals.

[5] Chapter 4 might seem to contradict the assumption that there is a relationship between how controversial an issue is and how much advocacy it provokes, but it focuses on an informal sense of how important issues were, not on how controversial.

standard, arguing only that there will be some impact, not that the impact will be large enough to be politically meaningful. The fact that they often have no impact seems to have no effect on the ubiquity of the hypothesis, but perhaps it should.

No doubt there are circumstances in which a very small number of events could have a dramatic impact on congressional action, if they win the attention of legislators and provide them with information that is new and disturbing. As Jones and Baumgartner (2005:55) write, "New information carries with it the potential to shock, to disrupt, and to destabilize as it intrudes into the policy process." An anti–Vietnam War protest in San Francisco in 1972 likely had no impact on members of Congress because it provided no new information – everyone already knew San Franciscans opposed the war. A first major demonstration in Topeka, Kansas, might have been an entirely different matter – if substantial numbers of people believed to be pro-war make it known that they are opposed, that is new information, and the impact on members of Congress is much more likely to be substantial (Burstein and Linton 2002; Lohmann 1993; Santoro 2002). But such events must by definition be rare – they attract attention because there is something exceptional about them – and it is difficult to imagine what kind of event would have a dramatic impact with regard to most of the issues Congress addresses – any event, not just advocacy. Even when dramatic events win attention to an issue, their impact on policy may depend on other circumstances – had the most dramatic events of the civil rights movement occurred when public opinion favored racial discrimination rather than opposing it, the result might very well have been new policies oppressing minorities rather than aiding them (Burstein 1998b:ch. 4).

Thus, thinking about the likely impact on policy change of activities targeting those policies, in a random sample of policies, leads to two opposing hypotheses:

1. With a research design focusing on tight linkages between advocacy and the policies at which it is directed, the impact of advocacy on policy should be especially strong, relative to what is found in other research but

2. With a research design focusing on a sample of policies, many of which are likely to stimulate little advocacy, there may be too little advocacy to have much impact.

First, it is necessary to describe which types of actors engage in which types of advocacy for and against enactment of the policy proposals. Then the impact of their advocacy is assessed.

ADVOCACY AND ADVOCATES

The events and political actors are described in Tables 5.1 through 5.3. Most events – 86 percent – are targeted at the 60 proposals, 11 percent at similar proposals at the federal level, and 3 percent at the state level (Table 5.1). Political conflict in Congress focuses on specific proposals; it is not dispersed among a set of similar proposals. Sometimes political conflict in Congress is preceded by conflict at the state level on similar issues (Burstein 1998b:ch. 3; Gray, Lowery, and Godwin 2007), but that is not the case here. The focus of conflict is very clear.

Supporters outnumber opponents – a bit more than 60 percent of the advocacy events favored the proposals – and use somewhat different tactics. Opposition is twice as likely as support to be expressed in editorials; supporters are a bit more likely to be writing letters to the editor and engaging in protest. But although the differences between the distributions are statistically significant, most of the differences between supporters and opponents are small. Including the statements directed at similar proposals has little effect on the distribution.

Most of those supporting and opposing proposals are interest organizations and members of Congress and their staffs (Table 5.2), with unaffiliated individuals also playing a substantial role; the U.S. executive branch, state and local governments, and the president are much less important. Members of Congress and their staffs, unaffiliated individuals, and state and local governments weigh more heavily among supporters, while interest organizations are especially important among opponents.

TABLE 5.1. *Advocacy Events for and against Policy Proposals, Targeted at Specific Proposals and Overall*

Events	Total		Favor Proposal		Oppose Proposal	
	Targeted at Proposal, %	All Events, %	Targeted at Proposal, %	All Events, %	Targeted at Proposal, %	All Events, %
Other	58.2	59.0	58.9	60.0	57.1	57.0
Editorial	10.6	10.0	7.5	7.2	15.9	15.2
Substantive Article	9.2	8.7	9.1	8.3	9.4	9.3
Speech	5.4	5.3	5.7	5.1	4.9	5.6
Delegation, Testimony	4.3	5.0	4.6	5.5	3.9	4.1
Letter	5.0	4.9	5.7	5.6	3.7	3.6
Two-Way Communication	3.0	3.0	3.1	3.0	2.9	3.0
Interview	2.5	2.5	2.7	2.7	2.2	2.2
Protest	1.7	1.6	2.7	2.5	0	0
Total	1,389	1,614	879	1,056	510	558

Note: Rows ordered by the percentage each type of event, of total. Chi-square, difference in distribution of types of events between those favoring proposal and those opposing, all events, 43.4, $p < .001$. Chi-square, difference in distribution of types of events between those for proposal and against, events targeted at specific proposal only, 39.1, $p < .001$

TABLE 5.2. *Advocates for and against Policy Proposals, Targeted at Specific Proposals and Overall*

Advocate	Total		Favor Proposal		Oppose Proposal	
	Targeted at Proposal, %	All Events, %	Targeted at Proposal, %	All Events, %	Targeted at Proposal, %	All Events, %
Interest Organization	36.0	35.8	32.8	33.0	41.6	41.2
Congress	35.7	32.7	37.2	33.5	33.1	31.2
Unaffiliated Individuals	19.4	20.2	22.3	23.3	14.3	14.3
U.S. Executive Branch	4.9	5.8	2.8	3.4	8.4	10.2
State, Local Governments	2.9	4.2	4.1	5.9	.8	.9
President	1.2	1.4	.8	.9	1.8	2.2
Total	1,389	1,614	879	1,056	510	558

Note: Rows ordered by the percentage each type of actor, of total events. Chi-square, difference in distribution of types of actors between those favoring proposal and those opposing, all events, $77.1, p < .001$. Chi-square, difference in distribution of types of actors between those favoring proposal and those opposing, events targeted at specific proposal only, $54.6, p < .001$

Those with official public roles – members of Congress and their staffs, the U.S. executive branch, state and local governments, and the president – are especially likely to try to get what they want by talking (Table 5.3). Including the "other" category of events, which consist of oral statements of unspecified type, 95 percent of the advocacy by members of Congress and their staffs, for example, involves talk – other events, speeches, testimony, interviews, etc. – as opposed to articles, letters, and protests. Private parties, in contrast, are much more likely to make use of the written word. Interest organizations editorialize – 29 percent of what they do – and unaffiliated individuals write articles and letters to the editor – almost half of what they do. Unaffiliated individuals are more likely than anyone else to protest, but do so very seldom.

Often it is easy to see the link between type of actor and type of activity. Focusing on the 1,389 events targeting the 60 policy proposals (as opposed to similar proposals at the federal or state levels), we find that so much advocacy by interest organizations consisted of editorials because the organizations were newspapers (or occasionally, magazines) acting on their own behalf. Members of Congress give speeches. Unaffiliated individuals are very often syndicated columnists or individuals writing letters to the editor. Representatives of the U.S. executive branch and state and local governments often make their views known when testifying before congressional committees.

ADVOCACY AND CONGRESSIONAL ACTION

Now we come to the key question: How much impact does advocacy have on congressional action?

The impact of advocacy is estimated for two measures of congressional action – first, simply whether the proposal was enacted; and second, how far the proposal got in the legislative process, in six stages: (1) introduced and referred to committee only, (2) subject of committee hearing, (3) reported out of committee, (4) passed one house, (5) passed both houses, and (6) enacted into law.

What should the unit of analysis be? The obvious one is the proposal; we want to know how far each of them got. But it also

TABLE 5.3. *What Advocates Do*

Event	Interest Organizations, %	Congress, %	Unaffiliated Individuals, %	U.S. Executive Branch, %	State, Local Governments, %	President, %	Number
Other	51.2	76.4	33.8	69.1	62.5	68.8	809
Editorial	29.4	0	0	0	0	0	147
Substantive Article	5.6	3.4	29.7	2.9	2.5	0	128
Speech	1.2	10.7	3.3	2.9	2.5	25.0	75
Delegation, Testimony	3.6	2.6	4.1	13.2	22.5	0	60
Letter	3.0	1.0	17.5	1.5	2.5	0	69
Two-Way Communication	2.2	4.2	1.9	2.9	5.0	6.2	42
Interview	2.4	1.6	3.3	7.4	2.5	0	35
Protest	1.4	0	6.3	0	0	0	24
Number	500	496	269	68	40	16	1,389

Note: Chi-square differences among advocates in type of activity, 748.0, $p < .001$.

TABLE 5.4. *Congressional Action on Proposals and Congress-Proposals*

Congressional Action	60 Proposals	155 Congress-Proposals
Referred to Committee	22	90
Hearing Held	5	16
Reported Out	4	8
Passes One House	7	15
Passes Both Houses	2	6
Enacted into Law	20	20

Note: Each stage includes the previous ones – "hearing held" means hearing held, but not reported out; "reported out" means hearing held and proposal was reported out, etc.

makes sense to consider the impact of advocacy during each congress each proposal was on the agenda. If a proposal is on the agenda for multiple congresses, does it get farther in congresses in which it wins more support, whatever happens to it ultimately? Here the unit of analysis is the "congress-proposal" – one proposal on the agenda for one congress (Burstein, Einwohner, and Hollander 2005:299). With 60 proposals on the agenda for an average of 2.6 congresses, the number of congress proposals is 155. A third of the proposals were enacted eventually, but the likelihood of enactment during any particular congress was just 13 percent (20 out of 155; Table 5.4). Just over a third of the proposals, but 58 percent of congress-proposals, got no further than referral to committee. Thirty-one proposals were the target of no reported advocacy, and 101 – 65 percent – of the congress-proposals.

Thus, the effect of advocacy will be estimated for four dependent variables: (1) the farthest each of the 60 proposals got into the legislative process during the entire time it was on the congressional agenda, (2) whether it was ultimately enacted, (3) how far each proposal got during each congress it was on the agenda, and (4) whether it was enacted during any particular congress.

Unfortunately, it is not possible to analyze how or why proposals were amended, if they were, at each stage of the legislative process. We simply don't know how to do so. A very small number of studies describe substantive policy change in ways that are both politically meaningful and quantitative, but the amount of work is huge even in only one policy domain (Steinberg 1982). There are a few studies that describe policy change quantitatively in a number of policy domains, but the measures are simple and not politically meaningful (e.g., Boli-Bennett and Meyer 1978). There are many histories that describe policy change in detail, but not in ways that can be included in statistical analysis (for an attempt to combine quantitative and qualitative approaches, but only for a single policy, see Burstein 1998b). At current levels of conceptualization and measurement, it is possible only to see what happens to the policy proposals, ignoring any changes that might occur as they move through the policy process. None of the proposals was altered so dramatically that its final content shifted in direction from what the proposal was originally, but that is all that can be said. Future work must address this problem.

The research reported here defines advocacy especially broadly, samples policy proposals in a new way, and seeks data especially widely. With all these new elements in the research design, it seems prudent to keep the data analysis very simple. Thus, most analyses consider the impact of each advocacy measure, for and against the proposal, one at a time.

For the equations in which the dependent variable is enactment, binary logistic regression was used, and for equations in which the dependent variable is how far the proposal got, ordinal logistic regression. When the unit of analysis is the congress-proposal, arguably not all the units of analysis are independent – the same proposal appears in more than one congress – so robust standard errors are calculated (Long and Freese 2001:69–70 and chs. 4–5).

The research design essentially pits two arguments, and two sets of forces, against each other. On the one hand, carefully linking the measures of advocacy action and policy change, along with improved measurement of both, should produce findings showing an especially strong relationship between the two. On the other hand, there could be so little advocacy that its impact on policy change would almost necessarily be very limited.

The effect of advocacy on the 60 proposals for the entire time each is on the agenda is described in Table 5.5. The magnitude of the impact is easy to summarize: zero. Not a single type of advocacy, nor scales summing all types, for or against proposals, has a statistically significant impact on either how far each proposal got

TABLE 5.5. *Effect of Advocacy on Congressional Action, 60 Policy Proposals*

Variable	How Far Proposal Got, Referral through Enactment		Proposal Enacted?	
	Ordinal Logistic Regression Coefficient	Standard Error	Binary Logistic Regression Coefficient	Standard Error
Single-Variable Models				
Article for	-.02	.04	-.01	.05
Article against	.03	.08	.00	.10
Delegation, Testimony for	.27	.16	.16	.16
Delegation, Testimony against	.08	.17	-.18	.31
Editorial for	.10	.08	.11	.08
Editorial against	.03	.05	-.03	.07
Interview for	.09	.20	.08	.20
Interview against	-.06	.28	-17	.32
Letter for	.03	.06	-.01	.08
Letter against	.22	.21	.14	.23
Other for	.01	.01	.01	.01
Other against	.01	.01	-.003	.02
Press Conference for	.08	.12	-.02	.16
Press Conference against	.06	.18	.00	.25

TABLE 5.5. *(cont.)*

Variable	How Far Proposal Got, Referral through Enactment		Proposal Enacted?	
	Ordinal Logistic Regression Coefficient	Standard Error	Binary Logistic Regression Coefficient	Standard Error
Protest for	.10	.13	−.07	.19
Protest against			No protests	
Speech for	.05	.06	−.01	.09
Speech against	.06	.09	−.08	.18
Total Statements for	.01	.01	.004	.007
Total Statements against	.01	.01	−.003	.01
Number of Congresses on Agenda	.06	.10	−.12	.14
Last Congress on Agenda	−.05	.17	−.60	.35
Multivariate Model				
Total Statements for	.01	.01	.02	.01
Total Statements against	−.01	.01	−.02	.02

Note: The Brant test of the parallel regression assumption was not significant for most of the ordinal logistic regression equations, meaning that the assumption could not be said to have been violated. For two variables, interview against and protest for, the test could not be calculated because for some categories of the dependent variable, there were no cases.

or on enactment alone.[6] A very simple multivariate model, including total advocacy for and against, produces the same result. To consider very simply whether persistence or timing matter, the impact of the number of congresses each proposal was on the agenda was estimated, as was the impact of having final consideration more or less recently (in terms of which congress each proposal was last on the agenda). Neither mattered.

The effect of advocacy within congresses is described in Table 5.6. Here there is some evidence of impact, especially with regard to how far each proposal got within each congress. Of the 18 independent variables (articles, editorials, etc., for and against), eight had a statistically significant impact on how far each proposal got. With regard to enactment alone, advocacy was more likely to have an impact within congresses than overall, but still not very much – 3 of the 18 variables had an impact. Total advocacy events for and against had a statistically significant impact on how far proposals got, but not on enactment. In the multivariate models, neither advocacy for nor against influenced how far proposals got, but total advocacy for proposals did increase the likelihood of enactment.

It is noteworthy that almost all the coefficients are positive. It may very well be, as Baumgartner et al. (2009:75) suggest, that active opposition to policy proposals is stimulated by mobilization for the proposals, but the data do not address this possibility.

Has better conceptualization and measurement of advocacy, policy change, and the relationship between them improved our ability to estimate how strongly advocacy affects policy change? Other researchers' findings are not presented in ways consistent enough to permit estimation of a baseline expectation (Burstein and Linton 2002). Nevertheless, it seems difficult to argue that the relationships found here are strong, and easy to argue that they are weak – with regard to results for the 60 policy proposals for the entire time they're on the agenda, they couldn't be any weaker.

---

[6] Cronbach's standardized α for all types of collective action favoring enactment is .888; for all types of action in opposition, .892.

TABLE 5.6. *Effect of Advocacy on Congressional Action, Policy Proposals within Congresses*

Variable	How Far Proposal Got, Referral through Enactment		Proposal Enacted?	
	Ordinal Logistic Regression Coefficient	Robust Standard Error	Binary Logistic Regression Coefficient	Robust Standard Error
Single-Variable models				
Article for	.01	.13	.07	.09
Article against	.16	.12	.16	.13
Delegation, Testimony for	.68**	.27	.58*	.25
Delegation, Testimony against	.45	.27	.20	.32
Editorial for	.30	.21	.37*	.17
Editorial against	.17*	.08	.09	.10
Interview for	.46	.31	.55*	.25
Interview against	.33	.46	Cannot be calculated	
Letter for	.24	.21	.24	.19
Letter against	.50	.31	.43	.28
Other for	See note	.02	.04	.03
Other against	.05**	.02	.03	.03
Press Conference for	.30**	.13	.13	.32
Press Conference against	.25	.44	.58	.51
Protest for	.51**	.20	.24	.29
Protest against			No protests	
Speech for	.23**	.07	.14	.13
Speech against	.42**	.10	.13	.26
Total Statements for	.03**	.01	.03	.01
Total Statements against	.03**	.01	.02	.02

TABLE 5.6. (*cont.*)

| Variable | How Far Proposal Got, Referral through Enactment | | Proposal Enacted? | |
	Ordinal Logistic Regression Coefficient	Robust Standard Error	Binary Logistic Regression Coefficient	Robust Standard Error
Multivariate model				
Total Statements for	.03	.02	.05*	.03
Total Statements against	.005	.01	-.05	.04

Note: The coefficient estimating the relationship between interviews against proposals and enactment could not be calculated. For the binary logistic regressions: for total statements for, the coefficient is .0257, standard error is .0138, significant at .068; for total statements for in the multivariate model, the coefficient is .0545, standard error is .0279, significant at .051. The Brant test of the parallel regression assumption was not significant for most of the equations, meaning that the assumption could not be said to have been violated. The Brant test of the parallel regression assumption could not be calculated for the relationship between interviews against a proposal and how far the proposal got, because several outcome categories had no such interviews. For "other" statements favoring the proposal, the Brant test was consistent with the parallel regression assumption having been violated at the .05 level; multinomial logistic regression with "referral to committee" as the base category showed the impact of a hearing to be statistically significant at the .05 level (coefficient 1.1, robust standard error .06), the impact on passing both houses significant at the .01 level (coefficient 1.2, robust standard error .06), and the impact on enactment likewise (coefficient also 1.2, robust standard error also .06).
* $p < .05$.
** $p < .01$.

This does not necessarily mean that the advocacy described here has minimal impact because there is so little of it. Perhaps other forces are much more powerful (Erikson, Wright, and McIver 1993:81). But this seems unlikely with regard to either public opinion or other variables often included in studies of policy change. Perhaps institutional biases favoring the status quo reduce the impact of advocacy (Baumgartner et al. 2009: 202–14, ch. 12). Perhaps advocacy for a proposal would have a strong effect were it not negated by advocacy against; if that were the case, though, the coefficients could be substantial but of opposite sign.

Nevertheless, most policy proposals were associated with so little advocacy that it is difficult to imagine the events having much impact on Congress. How plausible is it that Congress would be so exquisitely attuned to advocacy that a few events – a couple of editorials, a handful of letters to the editor, some public statements – in the entire country, over several years, could have a substantial effect? The findings of little or no impact are consistent with everything we know about how little attention Congress can pay to most issues (Jones and Baumgartner 2005; Workman, Jones, and Jochim 2009).

IMAGES OF DEMOCRATIC POLITICS

Research on how advocacy affects policy change has improved tremendously since the first consequential quantitative work was published in the 1960s. In some ways, though, the research has gotten stuck, both theoretically and methodologically, with important elements almost unexamined for long periods of time. Neither advocacy nor policy has been defined and operationalized consistently. Though it is widely understood that causal analyses should link specific causes to specific effects, in fact poor measures of advocacy are often used to explain change in poor measures of policy to which they have little logical connection. The importance of random sampling for generalization is well known, yet researchers persistently study one issue at a time – usually an issue of especially great popular concern – and try to generalize about what they find. Olson's *Logic of Collective Action* (1971) has been taken very seriously, but its potential implications for the impact of advocacy on policy change have not been considered.

The research reported here tried to address these problems. An especially striking finding is that despite defining advocacy broadly and making unprecedented efforts to find evidence of its occurrence, most policy proposals stimulated little or none (as reported in print media). The lack of advocacy potentially constrained its impact on policy change, and, indeed, there proved to be little impact. Of course, some types of advocacy have been ignored here, and it is always possible to say that no matter how refined one's research, more advocacy remains undiscovered. But this research has gone very far in its search for evidence.

Methodological and theoretical concerns have led to two competing hypotheses about the impact of advocacy on policy. Methodologically, I suggested that we often find advocacy having little impact because the advocacy is not linked closely to the policies studied; either the advocacy is not directed at any policy in particular, or the measures of policy are so complex that it would be incredibly difficult to examine how they are affected by advocacy. By focusing on advocacy directed at the 60 specific policy proposals, I hypothesized, we should find advocacy having more impact than in previous work.

Theoretically, I proposed that if we follow up on the implications of Olson's (1971) argument that there should be little collective action, applied to individuals' advocacy as well, we might discover that there is so little advocacy that it can't have much impact; I hypothesized, that is, that we should find advocacy having less impact than in previous work.

As it turns out, there is more support for the second hypothesis than the first. Advocacy has very little impact on policy – when analyzing its impact on policy proposals over the entire time they are on the congressional agenda, no impact at all. And it is very plausible that this is because there is too little advocacy to matter.

These conclusions may call for something of a rethinking of democratic policymaking. Among social scientists, the conventional image of democratic politics is one of ceaseless, almost overwhelming activity by interest groups and social movement organizations. Thousands of lobbyists besiege members of Congress, thousands of political action committees contribute hundreds of millions of dollars to candidates' campaigns, and public protests on issues like the Vietnam War, civil rights, and globalization galvanize the attention of the nation (Baumgartner and Leech 2001; Burstein 1998a; Tarrow 1994:ch. 11; Wright 1996). So tremendous is the flow of information and demands directed at Congress and state legislatures that they must work hard to avoid being overwhelmed (Jones 1994; Krehbiel 1991).

Yet there is evidence that runs counter to this image, some of it well known but perhaps not adequately appreciated, some of it hidden in plain sight. Experts on Congress know that nothing happens to the vast majority of bills introduced, and careful consideration of data on advocacy shows how little of it there is on most issues; indeed, most policy proposals disappear without a trace, having stimulated almost no visible advocacy. McAdam and Boudet (2012:181) suggest that past work on social movements has dramatically exaggerated their frequency and causal significance. On most issues important enough to be the subject of bills introduced into Congress, nothing much happens.

These views are not entirely contradictory. In a nation of hundreds of millions of people and very numerous, complex sets of interests, political activities that are uncommon, even rare, on a per capita basis can add up to enough to seem overwhelming to a Congress of only 535 members. Nevertheless, I would argue that our ability to understand democratic politics would be enhanced by striking a better balance between the "ceaseless activity" and "nothing much is happening" points of view.

Some key findings are similar to those of Baumgartner et al. (2009). Though the differences between the studies are substantial, in focus (lobbying versus collective action more generally), definition of the population (issues subjectively defined versus policy proposals), primary data source (interviews versus media reports), etc., both attempt to improve our understanding of the policy process in comparable ways; the differences between them may be seen as alternative views as how best to proceed. Both are also based on rather small samples (the one used here somewhat smaller than theirs), so the approaches and findings must be viewed with some caution. Future research will provide more information about which decisions about research design are likely to be most fruitful.

The previous chapters have moved from the desires of the public at large, manifested in public opinion, to those of the much narrower segment of the public that visibly advocates for or against specific policy proposals. The next step is to move farther into the policy process and examine what happens when people are given the opportunity to express themselves directly to members of Congress, presenting arguments in as much detail as they would like, at committee hearings.

6

Advocacy, Information, and Policy Innovation

Interest organizations consistently affect public policy – that's the conventional wisdom. As discussed in Chapter 5, however, the evidence for such influence is decidedly mixed, and my effort to find an especially strong relationship by carefully linking advocacy to policy change was unsuccessful. Indeed, advocacy had virtually no impact on policy change.

But perhaps it's just publicly visible advocacy – advocacy reported in print – that has little or no impact. Perhaps advocacy closer to the policymaking process itself could be important, especially advocacy sought by policymakers themselves.

Many theorists hypothesize that advocates influence legislators by providing them with information that will, according to the advocates themselves, enhance the legislators' effectiveness and help them win reelection.[1] Congressional committee and subcommittee hearings may be especially important venues for communicating information. Witnesses – often expert witnesses – are called upon to give testimony; they may buttress their oral testimony with written reports providing additional information; and

---

[1] Arnold 1990:38; Bradley 1980; Chalmers 2013; Hansen 1991:12; Heitshusen 2000; Hirsch and Schotts 2012; Kingdon 1981:210; Krehbiel 1991:20, 62; Leyden 1995; Smith 1995:98, 101; on information and policy generally, see Austen-Smith 1993; Diermeier and Feddersen 2000; Knoke et al. 1996:ch. 7; Lohmann 1993, 1994, 1998; Workman, Jones, and Jochim 2009; Wright 1996.

they are questioned by members of Congress who want the witnesses to clarify or supplement what they have said. Perhaps information provided by advocates at hearings affects policy change.

Unfortunately, we do not know whether such information influences policy. General ideas about information have not been used as the basis for practical research designs, data on the information provided has not been systematically gathered or analyzed, and hypotheses about such information have not been tested.

This chapter attempts to advance our understanding of what is said at committee and subcommittee hearings and how it affects policy change. My focus will be on the 27 policy proposals on which committee hearings were held and the nearly one thousand witnesses who testified at those hearings. The chapter describes the information the witnesses provide – who presents the information, the arguments they make, the evidence they provide – and the impact of the information on the likelihood that a proposal will be enacted into law.

The first step is to consider what types of information seem most likely to affect congressional action. The chapter continues by suggesting that members of Congress are especially likely to receive such information in committee and subcommittee hearings, presents hypotheses about the impact of information on congressional action, develops methods for measuring information and gauging its impact, describes the information presented by witnesses at hearings, shows what kinds of information affect congressional action, and outlines what additional steps would further our understanding of the impact of information on congressional action.

INFORMATION AND INFLUENCE

Research on interest organizations suggests that they have less influence on policy change than most people believe. Why do we find so little impact? Perhaps organizations (and individual advocates) actually have little influence, particularly on issues salient to the public. Competition for votes may force politicians to respond more to public opinion than to advocacy (Burstein 1999; Lohmann 1993). Here I consider an alternative possibility: that we underestimate the impact of advocacy on policy change because of an important flaw in our research (Baumgartner and Leech 1998; Potters and Sloof 1996; Smith 1995). In particular, researchers may have focused on modes of influence unlikely to have much impact, while neglecting one likely to be consequential.

Analyses of how interest organizations affect policy should consider precisely how influence is exerted on political institutions (Andrews 2001:73; Hansen 1991; Krehbiel 1991). Why might elected officials respond to interest organizations and other advocates? Work on policy change at the aggregate level seldom addresses this question explicitly; there is just a general sense that advocates who have more resources or are more active must have more influence (Burstein and Linton 2002). Some research on legislatures has this quality as well; the more resources an advocate has, the more influential it will be. More and more, though, theoretical work asks what elected officials' most important needs are as they consider legislation and examines how advocates might win influence by addressing those needs.

One such need is for information. Office holders work in complex environments, they are constantly pressured to act (or not act) on a myriad of issues, and they know their actions may have important consequences. To decide what to do, they engage in a constant search for information (Hansen 1991; Krehbiel 1991; Rucht 1999:212; on the centrality of information to relations between legislators and lobbyists, see Baumgartner et al. 2009:54–57).

Legislators seem especially interested in three types of information. First, they want information about the importance of problems they are asked to address. Legislators are constantly pressured to deal with more issues than they can manage. They must establish priorities and want information that will help them do so. Indeed, advocates work hard at getting Congress to pay attention to their concerns (Baumgartner and Leech 1998:137; Kingdon 1981:172; cf. Hilgartner and Bosk 1988).

Second, legislators want information about the likely impact of policies proposed to address the problems. Usually this means information about the probable effectiveness of those policies (Krehbiel 1991:ch. 7; for an example, see Amenta, Carruthers, and Zylan 1992:315). As Hirsch and Shotts (2012:67–68) write, "legislatures are uncertain about the link between policies and outcomes, and committees can acquire information about that link." They "exert considerable effort to craft complex legislation ... [that] must be coherently designed, appropriate to local circumstances, cost-effective, and practical to implement." Sometimes legislators receive information that introduces a new dimension into a policy debate and attempts to reframe the issue (Burstein and Bricher 1997; Gamson and Modigliani 1987; Riker 1986; for similar arguments in the European context, see Chalmers 2013). Often this involves a claim that a policy will have unintended consequences. Federal support of tobacco farmers, for example, long viewed in terms of economic benefits, has been reframed as exacerbating health problems caused by smoking (Baumgartner and Jones 1993:114–17, 209–10).

Third, legislators want to know the likely impact of their votes on their reelection chances. They want to know their constituents' policy preferences, how much particular issues matter to them, and whether their own actions are likely to affect constituents' votes at the next election (Arnold, 1990:ch. 4; Hansen 1991:12; McCammon et al. 2001:55).

Thus, advocates may influence legislators through the information they provide, particularly information about the importance of problems, effectiveness of proposed solutions, and likely electoral impact of decisions. For those who study legislatures, the concept of information is a broad one, including not only facts, but the context that gives meaning to those facts as well. What some social scientists call information, others would characterize as causal arguments or claims – attempts to organize and present information in a convincing way (see, e.g., Stone 1989; cf. Andrews 2001:75; McCammon et al. 2001:57).

How much evidence is there that advocates influence legislators by providing information? Very little. Theorists who highlight information provide enough evidence to make their hypotheses plausible (e.g., Hansen 1991; Krehbiel 1991), but no more. What about past research on organizational influence? If one thinks of information very broadly, as anything in the political environment that politicians might see as relevant to their activities, then organizational resources and activities could be seen as conveying information. For example, membership in labor unions could be seen as signifying the power of the working class; similarly, the number of organizations demanding action on a problem or the number of protest demonstrations could be seen as indicating the problem's importance and potential electoral consequences.

The information conveyed by most indicators of organizational resources and activities is unlikely to be of much use to elected officials, however, because it is too vague (Rucht 1999:216). Measures of organizational resources or protest activities say something about the importance of an issue, but nothing about the likely impact of specific policies or about how legislators' votes may affect their chances of reelection. How might elected officials get additional information, better suited to their needs?

COMMITTEE HEARINGS AS A SOURCE OF INFORMATION

Legislators acquire information in many ways – through talking to constituents and lobbyists, reading newspapers, and so forth – and it would be exceedingly difficult to study them all. But it may be possible to investigate what Arnold (1990:85) calls "the principal vehicle for gathering and analyzing information" in the U.S. Congress: the committee system (see also Jones 1994:151; Krehbiel 1991). Committees gather and organize information for their own members, for other members of Congress, and, quite often, for the executive branch as well.[2]

---

[2] See, e.g., Bradley 1980; Heitshusen 2000; Hirsch and Shotts 2012; Jones and Baumgartner 2005:chs. 1, 3; Jones and Jenkins-Smith 2009; Leech 2010:542; Workman et al. 2009.

A particularly important source of information is committee hearings. Members of Congress believe that hearings provide an efficient way to gather information and exert influence (Gormley 1998:183; Kingdon 1981:212–13; Mattei 1998:445; on the more general use of policy committees to acquire information cheaply, see Leifeld and Schneider 2012:732). They often testify before committees they are not on. Their colleagues take the time to listen to them. The content of bills is often affected by conflicts among witnesses about how issues should be framed (see, e.g., Baumgartner and Jones 1993; Johnson 1995:169; Weeks et al. 1986). Because committee resources are limited, simply holding a hearing on an issue communicates a committee's belief that an issue is important (Diermeier and Feddersen 2000; Edwards and Wood 1999:331).

Interest organizations, too, see hearings as important venues for conveying information. They see being called to testify as an indicator of influence (Laumann and Knoke 1987:96–97, 164–66) and believe their arguments affect members of Congress (Kingdon 1981:133; Smith 1995:99). Hearings are the first occasion for providing information publicly, so the information may be especially influential (Baumgartner and Leech 1998:38). And the mass media are often affected by conflicts among witnesses about how issues should be framed (see, e.g., Gamson and Modigliani 1989:8, 23; Weeks et al. 1986).

Though researchers almost never test hypotheses about the impact of information on policy change, numerous case studies claim that information provided at committee hearings affected congressional action. For example, evidence presented at congressional hearings on the Equal Pay Act of 1963 helped proponents of gender equality win support for prohibiting sex discrimination in employment, in Title VII of the Civil Rights Act of 1964 (Burstein 1998b:22–23). Congressional hearings on hate crimes were an important locus of debate, and information gathered at the hearings had a significant impact on the content and enactment of federal hate crime legislation (Jenness 1999:548, 559). Human rights organizations have seen congressional hearings as a critical forum for communicating information to members of

Congress and the public (Cmiel 1999:1235–36). Testimony by organizations concerned about federal funding of research on specific diseases seems to have affected the framing of debates, stimulating arguments about how harm caused by different diseases should be assessed (Best 2012).

Thus, it seems likely that information presented at hearings affects congressional action. Yet not everyone would agree. A key objection is that hearings do not provide much information. Some say they are stage-managed spectacles – theater, really – in which witnesses are chosen for political reasons, and what they will say is known in advance. In addition, for issues that are especially important, or that have been on the agenda for a long time, members of Congress may already be well informed, meaning they will already be familiar with the information provided at hearings.

There is no way to learn how much new information, if any, is acquired from testimony by any particular member of Congress, but several aspects of the research design and the congressional policy process increase the likelihood that at least some of the information provided at hearings is new to those who pay attention to it. First, bear in mind that the focus here is on enactment, an outcome potentially involving all members of Congress. While those who select the witnesses often know what they will say, the information they provide may be new to other members of Congress. Jury trials may be a useful analogy. Good lawyers are supposed to know in advance what their witnesses will say, and they make every effort to stage-manage their trials. Juries, however, do not know what the witnesses will say, and the lawyers, judge, and jury members themselves believe that the information provided by witnesses affects the verdict.

Second, the nature of both the policy proposals and the legislative process make it likely that information provided at hearings is new to many members of Congress. Members of Congress may have much information and well-formed opinions about critical issues that have been on the agenda for a long time, but most policy proposals in the dataset are neither critical nor on the agenda for long. Almost necessarily, therefore, most of the policy proposals will not have been very important in conventional terms; while some of the 60 proposals were important (such as the savings and loan bailout), most were little-known (such as proposals on campus security, patents in outer space, and solid waste disposal).

Not only were most proposals relatively obscure, but they were on the congressional agenda for only a short time – an average of 2.6 congresses. Of the 27 proposals that were the subject of hearings, for 20 there were hearings during only one Congress (Appendix Table 5). This is true even for very important proposals. For example, hearings pertaining to the savings and loan bailout all took place during a single congress; for members of Congress facing a critically important and very complex issue that had to be dealt with quickly, it is hard to believe that the hearings did not provide a great deal of new information.

We should also keep in mind that hearings provide information that is relevant to a particular policy proposal, not to an issue more generally; even if members of Congress know something about an issue, they may want information about how it is being addressed by the particular policy proposal. Thus, it seems reasonably likely that for most members of Congress, if not those who organize the hearings, much of the information provided is new.[3]

Two examples may be helpful. The "Crime Awareness and Campus Security Act of 1990" (enacted as part of Public Law 101-542) required institutions of higher education receiving certain forms of federal assistance to publish an annual report on campus security policies and crime statistics. Yet before the 101st Congress, the issue of campus crime hadn't been on the congressional agenda at all. How did it get there?

In April 1986, a student at Lehigh University, Jeanne Clery, was raped and murdered in her dormitory room by a fellow student. Her parents blamed Lehigh for its lax security procedures and, among other steps, created an organization, Security on Campus Inc., that requested state legislatures to require colleges

---

[3] In preliminary analyses, there was an attempt to focus specifically on information most likely to be new (e.g., information presented at the first hearing on a proposal, and information of very recent vintage, such as new census data), but doing so had no effect on the results.

and universities in their states to collect and disseminate information on crime on their campuses; such information could enable parents to take campus safety issues into account when deciding where to send their sons and daughters to school. By 1989, they had convinced Pennsylvania (where Lehigh was located) and 3 other states to enact such laws, and similar laws were pending in 12 other states. They also went to see their own U.S. representative, William F. Goodling, and asked him to introduce such a bill in the House; he did so (United States House of Representatives, Committee on Education and Labor, Subcommittee on Postsecondary Education 1990:59). Several hearings were held, and the bill was enacted into law in 1990.

It would be very difficult to argue that the hearings on campus crime and security were merely theater, providing no new information to members of Congress. The issue was simply not part of public discourse before the Clerys began their campaign. They, along with other members of their organization, some of them other parents whose sons or daughters had also been the victims of horrible crimes on campus, managed to win congressional attention to an issue that surely would not have been on the agenda had it not been for their efforts. There was some media coverage of their state campaigns (e.g., Randolph 1989), but it was through congressional hearings that members of Congress heard of the issue and became convinced that it deserved congressional attention.

H.R. 1278, the bill that became the "Financial Institutions Reform, Recovery, and Enforcement Act of 1989" – often referred to as the "savings and loan bailout" – was another matter. There was no need to convince members of Congress that the issues it addressed were important. The failure of over a fifth of the savings and loan associations in the United States, accompanied by headlines like "Can the U.S. Bail Out Thrifts without Sinking Real Estate?" (Nash 1989a) and "The Savings and Loan Crisis; 'Arizona Is Lost, Next Is San Francisco'" (Nash 1989b), made the financial crisis impossible to ignore and the need for congressional action imperative. But what to do? That was not at all obvious; few members of Congress were experts on the intricacies of the savings and loan industry, and experts disagreed among themselves. House committees held multiple hearings and compiled thousands of pages of testimony and supplemental materials. A report from the Mid-America Institute Task Force on the Thrift Crisis, incorporated in one of the hearings, was just one of many that defined the problems, proposed solutions, provided detailed financial analyses, and made arguments about how best to handle the crisis, including its conclusion:

The current crisis is at least in part the consequence of a flawed deposit insurance system. The deposit insurance contract provides incentives for thrifts to bear risk, especially when they are thinly capitalized, because insurance premiums do not vary with risk.

Unless the underlying problem with the pricing of deposit insurance is dealt with as part of the solution to the current crisis, there will undoubtedly be future economic shocks that create future crises. (U.S. House of Representatives, Committee on Banking, Finance, and Urban Affairs. Subcommittee on Financial Institutions Supervision, Regulation, and Insurance 1989:421)

No one would argue that most members of Congress or their staffs read all the hearings, or that they didn't have other sources of information. But there can't be any doubt that for many members the hearings provided critical information about what options were available to deal with the crisis, along with arguments and evidence as to which might be most effective.

Here it makes sense to draw attention to Schumaker's (1975) discussion of how we may divide government's responsiveness to interest organizations into five stages: access responsiveness, that is, the willingness of a government to hear interest organizations' concerns (similar to Gamson's [1990:28–29] "acceptance"), agenda responsiveness (placing organizations' demands on the political agenda), policy responsiveness, output responsiveness (effective implementation), and impact responsiveness (alleviation of the problems that led to the organizations' original demands). Success at each stage is necessary for success at the next, but not sufficient. Burstein, Einwohner, and Hollander (1995:284) point to testimony at congressional hearings as an indicator of access responsiveness. Does such testimony affect the likelihood that policy proposals will be enacted? That is the empirical question.

The focus is on testimony not because it is the only factor shaping congressional action or even the most influential. Many factors other than the information provided through testimonies affect congressional action. But information has been overlooked in previous research, and considering it may help us discover why theoretical expectations regarding organizational influence are at odds with much of the evidence.

HYPOTHESES

I hypothesize that among proposals subject to congressional hearings, the more information presented that a proposal (1) addresses an important problem, (2) will provide an effective solution, and (3) aid the reelection of members of Congress if enacted, the more likely it is to be enacted.

Conversely, the impact of information favorable to the proposal can be counteracted by information that is unfavorable, including claims that (1) the problem is not important, (2) the proposed solution will not work or will have harmful, unintended consequences, or (3) enactment will harm the reelection chances of members of Congress.

So far as I know, these hypotheses have never been tested.

RESEARCH DESIGN

To generalize about the impact on congressional action of information provided at hearings, it is necessary to define the unit of analysis, define the population, and draw a sample – already done – and, very crucially, systematically describe or measure the information presented by witnesses. Unfortunately, past work is of little help – studies of hearings do not systematically describe what witnesses say.[4]

---

[4] For examples and discussions of the state of the art, see Baumgartner and Leech 1998; Burstein 1998a; Jenkins-Smith, St. Clair, and Woods 1991; Potters and Sloof 1996; Segal, Cameron, and Cover 1992; Segal and Hansen 1992.

The initial units of analysis were the 60 policy proposals. Twenty-seven were the subject of at least one public hearing, on either the original bill or others of identical content; the total number of hearings was 66, listed in Appendix Table 5 (for a description of how hearings are run, see Johnson 2003). These were the source of the data.

Most research on the way organizations affect policy focuses on interest groups, which are seen as independent of both government and political parties. From a theoretical perspective, however, if what matters to legislators is the relevance, cost, and credibility of information (Hansen 1991), then all available information should be taken into account, regardless of source (DeGregorio 1998:143). For hearings, this means all witnesses, and our analysis takes them all into account – unaffiliated individuals and representatives of government agencies as well as private organizations – just as all advocates were included in Chapters 4 and 5.

Although scholars and those involved take congressional hearings seriously as sources of information, there have been very few attempts to analyze what all the witnesses say, beyond their favoring or opposing a policy proposal, and none, so far as I know, that try to measure theoretically relevant information provided by the witnesses. That is what is done here. For each hearing, what every witness said in initial oral statements, responses to questions, and written statements was content analyzed (including written statements from those who did not testify in person; cf. Laumann and Knoke 1987:97). Each organization and unaffiliated individual was counted once for testifying at a particular hearing; appearances at different hearings on the same policy proposal were counted separately. The total number of witnesses was 957. Five aspects of each appearance were coded:

1. *The witness's organizational affiliation:* (1) private interest organization, (2) state or local government, (3) federal executive branch, (4) U.S. Congress (members not on the committee holding the hearing), and (5) none – individuals testifying on their own behalf or as experts.

2. *The witness's position on the bill*: (1) favors enactment, (2) opposes enactment, and (3) neutral or ambiguous.

3. *Whether the witness communicated information (or made arguments or claims) pertaining to*: (1) the importance of the problem addressed by the bill, (2) whether the bill, if enacted, would have (a) the effect intended by its proponents, (b) no effect, or (c) the opposite effect, (3) the possibility that the bill, if enacted, would have consequences along a dimension not emphasized by the bill's supporters (an attempt to reframe the debate), and (4) the likely electoral consequences of action (or inaction) on the bill.

4. *The type of evidence used* to support claims concerning the importance of the problem and the effectiveness of the proposed solution: (1) findings from systematic research, meaning quantitative or qualitative research that might be presented in an academic or scientific context, even if purely descriptive, (2) comparisons to putatively similar problems or policies, meaning policies implemented in comparable political units (U.S. states, other democratic countries, or the federal government itself), and (3) anecdotes, meaning either personal stories or claims about public opinion not based on research.

To check on coding reliability, testimonies by approximately one-seventh of the witnesses were coded independently by two coders. The rate of agreement was 95 percent; most disagreements were due to one coder overlooking a statement rather than to substantive disputes.[5]

FINDINGS

Here, for a sample of 27 policy proposals, involving 66 hearings and 957 witnesses, is the first description of (1) how many witnesses testify on each side and the types of organizations they

---

[5] This way of calculating reliability is not ideal, but it was what seemed best when the research was being conducted.

represent, (2) how often they provide information about the importance of the problem addressed by the committee, the effectiveness of the proposed solution, and the potential electoral consequences of committee action, (3) how supporters and opponents of policy proposals compare with regard to the types of information they provide and the arguments they make, and (4) the types of evidence witnesses provide to back up their arguments.

Winning a hearing hardly ensures enactment. Of the 27 proposals, nine were not even reported out of committee, one was reported out of committee but got no further, three were passed by one house, two were passed by both houses but did not become law, 12 were enacted. This argues against the claim that hearings are only theater. It is not at all clear why members of Congress, their staffs, and the witnesses would devote so much effort to hearings when the outcome is far from certain, if they did not hope to affect the result.

Supporters, Opponents, and Neutrals

More supporters than opponents of policy change express their views at every stage of the policy process – they must, if they are to overcome the many obstacles to policy change (Baumgartner et al. 2009:ch. 4). Publicly visible advocacy events supporting the 60 policy proposals outnumbered events opposing change almost two to one (Table 5.2), and the imbalance is greater – almost three to one – in congressional hearings (Table 6.1). Nevertheless, hearings do provide a forum for competing views; one-fifth of the witnesses oppose the proposals, and almost as many take no stand (either stating no opinion or balancing pros and cons in their testimony).

Private interest organizations play an important role in congressional hearings, but they are hardly alone (Table 6.2). They provide far more witnesses than any other type of organization, but less than half the total. State and local governments contribute 7 percent; if we think of them as interest organizations vis-à-vis the federal government, then half the total witnesses represent interest organizations. One-fifth of the witnesses are members of Congress

TABLE 6.1. *Mean Number of Witnesses for Each Proposal, Opposed, and Neutral or Unclear*

Witness Position	Mean Number	Percentage
Supporters	21.6	61
Neutral or Ambiguous	6.3	18
Opponents	7.6	21
Total	35.5	100
Total Witnesses, All Hearings	957	

TABLE 6.2. *Witnesses' Organizational Affiliations*

Affiliation	N	Percentage
Private Interest Organization	418	44
State or Local Government	71	7
U.S. Executive Branch	109	11
U.S. Congress[a]	190	20
Unaffiliated	169	18
Total	957	100

[a] Almost all these witnesses were members of Congress not on the committee holding the hearing; if the hearing was being held by a subcommittee, this excludes members not only on the subcommittee, but on the committee itself as well. Statements by members of the committee were not included. A handful of these witnesses represented the GAO or Congressional Budget Office.

who are not on the committee holding the hearing, which suggests that they see hearings as an effective way to communicate with their colleagues.[6]

Witnesses from the executive branch most often represent the agencies that would implement the proposed legislation, but sometimes officials from the Office of Management and Budget

---

[6] DeGregorio (1998:143) notes that most studies of interest groups focus only on private organizations, but she says this is a mistake, given how often public-sector actors try to influence policy. The findings presented here buttress her claim. A disproportionate number of members of Congress testified on Social Security (see Appendix A, H781-5, 1993, 90 members) and on textile imports (Appendix A, H781-8, 1988, 23 members).

or other agencies discuss proposals' budgetary or tax implications. Almost one-fifth of the witnesses are unaffiliated – typically either technical experts or people describing personal experiences relevant to the issue at hand.

The movement from publicly visible advocacy to advocacy at hearings produces some change in the balance among those expressing their views, but not all that much.[7] Perhaps not surprisingly, members of Congress were more often involved as advocates in congressional hearings than in the events reported publicly in newspapers and magazines – a third of the witnesses were members of Congress, as compared to 20 percent of the advocates whose activities were reported (Table 5.2). Approximately a fifth of both witnesses and advocates whose activities were reported in the print media were unaffiliated individuals; represented slightly less often in congressional hearings were private interest organizations, state and local governments, and the U.S. executive branch.

The Arguments Witnesses Make

How often do witnesses provide the information that Congress is believed to want about the importance of the problem, the effectiveness of the proposed solution, and the electoral consequences of whatever action is taken? It is clear that hearings are part of an ongoing struggle for attention on the part of those involved. Although the mere fact of holding a hearing shows that the policy proposal is being taken seriously, almost two-thirds of the witnesses argue for the importance of the problem being addressed (Table 6.3). This includes just over half the representatives of private interest organizations and, most notably, more than four-fifths of the members of Congress. They have many

---

[7] Congressional hearings are publicly visible, in that they are part of the public record, and anyone can find out who said what. But they are not often reported in the print media that served as the source of data in earlier chapters; only a very small percentage of the advocacy events reported above were of hearings, and those reports provided little detail. Thus, the distinction between publicly visible advocacy and testimony at hearings is clear.

opportunities to convince their colleagues that particular problems are important; that they try to do so by testifying at hearings provides more evidence that they see hearings as an especially effective way to make their case.

Witnesses also emphasize the likely effectiveness of the solution being proposed; 58 percent make claims about what effect the bill would have if enacted. Effectiveness is a special concern of federal agencies, perhaps because of their experience with current policies and expertise in assessing how changes would affect their agencies. Witnesses sometimes argue that the proposed policy would lead to consequences along a dimension that the proposal's supporters do not emphasize – that is, they attempt to reframe the debate – but that is much less common than addressing the proposal on its own terms. A quarter of the witnesses make such arguments.

We might expect members of Congress to use hearings to acquire information relevant to their concerns about reelection. Four types of information relevant to electoral concerns were coded. Two speak relatively directly to such concerns – witnesses mentioning their organization's size or its political activities – and two indirectly – witnesses estimating how many people the proposed legislation would affect, or how widely dispersed they would be (implicitly, in how many states or congressional districts).

Mentions of organization's size or political activities were expected mostly from witnesses testifying for private interest organizations, but anyone could present information about the number or geographical distribution of those potentially affected. As it turns out, almost one-third of the witnesses representing private interest organizations mentioned their organizations' size, but very few – just 2 percent – explicitly discussed potential political action by members in response to congressional action. Three percent of witnesses from state and local governments discussed potential political activity, and 2 percent of witnesses overall.

Are these percentages high or low? Without clear theoretical predictions or other studies to provide a basis for comparison, interpretation is difficult. From one perspective, they seem low. Members of Congress are interested in the electoral consequences of their actions, yet the organizations seldom address their

TABLE 6.3. *Percentage of Witnesses Providing Information about Importance of Problem, Effectiveness of Proposed Solution, Reframing, Electoral Consequences of Action*

Witness Affiliation	Importance of Problem[a]	Effectiveness of Proposed Policy[b]	Reframe Problem[c]	Electoral Consequences		
				Organization Potential[d]	Political Action[e]	Number Affected[f]
Interest Organization	56	65	37	30	2	34
State or Local Government	59	45	20	11	3	30
U.S. Executive Branch	65	70	26	3	0	21
U.S. Congress	83	51	10	0	0	43
Unaffiliated	64	40	16	2	3	13
All Witnesses	64	58	25	15	2	30

Note: Witnesses can provide more than one type of information, so percentages can add up to more than 100. Chi-square = 92.31; $p < .001$.
[a] "Does the witness present an explicit argument that the problem addressed by the policy proposal is important?"
[b] "Does the witness make explicit predictions about whether the bill will have the intended consequences if enacted?"
[c] "Does the witness predict that the bill, if enacted, will have consequences along some dimension other than that emphasized by the bill's supporters?"
[d] "Does the witness mention the number of members in the organization he or she represents? [or] . . . anything about political activities by the organization he or she represents, its members as individuals, or other similar individuals?"
[e] Mention of political activities specifically.
[f] "Does the witness mention the number of people likely to be affected by the bill, not describing them as members of organizations, but rather as demographic categories or types of people? [or] . . . how widely dispersed the people potentially affected by the bill are?"

concerns. From another perspective, though, we might expect such a result – organizations that are neither large nor politically active have no interest in bringing up those facts. It is also possible that there are norms against publicly describing political activities.

Witnesses other than private interest organizations are considerably more likely to mention how many people might be affected by the proposed legislation, or how dispersed they might be, than to mention their organizations' size or its members' political activities. Almost one-third of those from state or local governments and more than two-fifths of the members of Congress described how many people would be affected or where they lived.

Supporters and opponents make their cases very differently. Supporters emphasize how important the problem is (Table 6.4) and argue that the proposed solution will be effective (Table 6.5); fairly often, they mention how many people will be affected. Opponents seem to concede the problem's importance – only 20 percent mention it. What they attack is the proposed solution; close to four-fifths claim it would be ineffective or have an effect that would be the opposite of that claimed by supporters, and a similar proportion try to reframe the debate, claiming that the policy would have consequences along a dimension that supporters do not discuss.

The Evidence Used to Support Arguments

We might expect witnesses to back up their arguments with evidence, but past research says little about how much or what kind. Here we find that witnesses seldom back up their testimony with systematic research. Only 16 percent making claims about the importance of the problem rely on research – supporters of the proposals more often than opponents – and only 12 percent of those discussing the effectiveness of the proposed solution – opponents more often than supporters (Tables 6.6 and 6.7). Comparisons to similar instances are infrequent, and only a handful of witnesses drew on scientific or social-scientific theories. Most often, witnesses tell stories – that is, provide anecdotes – especially when trying to show that a problem is important.

TABLE 6.4. *Issues Addressed by Supporters, Opponents, and Neutrals*

| | Percentage Addressing: | | | Electoral Consequences | |
| | | | | | |
Position of Witness on Bill	Importance of Problem	Effectiveness of Proposed Policy	Reframing Problem	Organizational	Number Affected
In Favor ($N = 582$)	82	60	5	14	35
Neutral or Unclear ($N = 171$)	57	22	29	12	23
Opposed ($n = 204$)	20	77	82	18	22

Chi-square = 125.5; $p < .001$.

TABLE 6.5. *Positions of Supporters, Opponents, and Neutrals on Effect of Proposed Policy*

Witness Position	Percentage Predicting That Bill, If Enacted, Would Have:			
	Intended Consequences	Opposite Consequences	Neither Intended Consequence nor the Opposite	No Predictions
In Favor	58	0	1	40
Neutral or Unclear	7	4	12	78
Opposed	0	14	63	23

Chi-square = 230.5; $p < .001$.

TABLE 6.6. *Evidence in Support of Witnesses' Statements Referring to the Importance of the Problem*

Witness Position	Percentage of Witnesses Referring to Issue, Using Particular Types of Evidence		
	Systematic Research[a]	Comparisons to Similar Instances[b]	Anecdotes[c]
In Favor	20	9	46
Neutral or Unclear	14	2	31
Opposed	5	1	5
Chi-square	25.45*	25.90*	117.03*

*$p < .05$.
[a] Systematic research includes quantitative and qualitative research that might be presented in an academic or scientific context, even if purely descriptive.
[b] Similar instances refer to similar policies implemented in comparable political units (e.g., U.S. states, other democratic countries, or the federal government itself).
[c] Anecdotes are personal stories or summaries of public opinion that are not based on formal research.

Who provides evidence based on systematic research? Most often witnesses from the federal government, perhaps because witnesses from the executive branch are sometimes invited because they have professional expertise based on such research (Table 6.8). Anecdotes

TABLE 6.7. *Evidence in Support of Witnesses' Statements Referring to Predicted Outcomes*

Witness Position	Percentage of Witnesses Referring to Issue, Using Particular Types of Evidence		
	Systematic Research[a]	Comparisons to Similar Instances[b]	Anecdotes[c]
In Favor	7	10	10
Neutral or Unclear	5	4	6
Opposed	23	9	29
Chi-square	47.72*	5.02	55.27*

*$p < .05$.
[a,b,c] See Table 6.6.

TABLE 6.8. *Supporting Evidence Provided, by Witnesses' Organizational Affiliation*

Witness Affiliation	Percentage of Witnesses Using Particular Types of Evidence[a]		
	Systematic Research	Comparisons to Similar Instances	Anecdotes
Interest Organization	22	15	40
State or Local Government	16	21	38
U.S. Executive Branch	33	15	33
U.S. Congress	27	7	58
Unaffiliated	12	10	44
Chi-square	21.00*	14.00*	24.19*

*$p < .05$.
[a] See Table 6.6.

are provided most often by members of Congress and unaffiliated individuals – indeed, it is easy to imagine the latter being invited to testify because their personal stories are seen as especially likely to convince others of the importance of the problem.

Supporters' and opponents' use of evidence is consistent with their arguments. Supporters most often emphasize the importance of the problem and back their claims with evidence 75 percent of the time (the total across row 1 of Table 6.6). They are much less likely to make claims about the effectiveness of their proposed solution, and also much less likely to back up those claims with evidence – only 27 percent do so (the total across row 1, Table 6.7). Opponents, in contrast, emphasize the ineffectiveness of proposed solutions and back up their claims with evidence (61 percent, across row 3 of Table 6.7), while neither downplaying the importance of the problem very often nor often providing evidence to strengthen their claim (11 percent across row 3 of Table 6.6).

THE INFLUENCE OF INFORMATION ON POLICY OUTCOMES

Hearings do serve, as some have hypothesized, as a way of communicating a great deal of information to members of Congress. Does the information influence congressional action on policy proposals? Testimony that the problem being addressed is important and the proposed solution effective have been hypothesized to increase the likelihood of enactment; so has scientific, comparative, and anecdotal evidence supporting such claims. And counterclaims – that the problem is not important or the proposed solution ineffective, or that the issue should be reframed – along with supporting evidence will make enactment less likely.

Measures and Methods

The dependent variable is a dichotomous measure of whether the policy proposal was enacted into law, coded 1 if the proposal was enacted and 0 otherwise. Given that only committee members are directly exposed to witness testimony, some might suggest that a more plausible dependent variable would be whether the bill was voted out of committee. The focus is enactment for both theoretical and methodological reasons. The central theoretical question is how interest organizations affect policy, which is changed only by enactment. Moreover, focusing on the committee vote would mean focusing on people whom some see as not getting much new information from the hearing, since committee chairs and ranking minority members (and their staffs) choose the witnesses and know what they will say. Enactment requires the votes of members not on the committee and hence not involved in choosing the witnesses; for them, the information provided at hearings is much more likely to be new.

The independent variables measure the core information provided by supporters and opponents of the policy proposal at the hearings. Because supporters and opponents make different arguments, different measures conveyed the information provided by each. For proponents of the proposed policy, there were dummy variables indicating whether the witness argued that the problem was important, suggested that the proposed policy would be effective, or attempted to reframe the issue. Also included was a measure gauging how many types of evidence – scientific, comparative, or anecdotal – each witness provided to support the claims. No measures of electoral concerns were included because so few witnesses mention them. For opponents, dummy variables indicated whether the witness argued that the problem was important, suggested that the policy would result in neither the intended consequence nor the opposite, or attempted to reframe the issue.[8] Again, a measure gauging how many types of evidence were used to support the claims was included.

A mixed-effects logistic regression model (Snijders and Bosker 1999) was fitted to estimate the influence of the information on enactment. The method used was adapted from demographic research to assess the effect of individual-level covariates on an aggregate outcome. In that literature, researchers use individuals' characteristics to predict attributes of the neighborhoods in which they reside (Adelman et al. 2001; Alba and Logan 1992; Tolnay,

---

[8] Although opponents frequently argued that proposed policies would have consequences opposite those suggested by proponents, this measure was not included in the analyses because it was collinear with measures suggesting unintended consequences.

Crowder, and Adelman 2000). Using similar methodology, information presented in individuals' testimonies is used to predict the likelihood that the policy being addressed will be enacted. The analyses are based on the 786 witness testimonies favoring or opposing the 27 policy proposals included in the sample, excluding the 171 testimonies in which witnesses were neutral.

Due to the nested structure of the data – with multiple testimonies grouped within each policy proposal – a mixed-effects model was used. Fixed effects were estimated for the informational variables, but the intercept was allowed to vary across policy proposals. The random intercept term accounts for the variation between policy proposals and reflects the assumption that some policy proposals are, on average, more likely to be enacted than others. The model is written as follows:

$$enactment = \gamma_{0j} + \gamma' x_{ij} + u_{0j} + \varepsilon$$

where γ_{0j} is the average policy intercept, γ' is a vector of parameters to be estimated from the model, x'_{ij} is a vector of covariates measuring the information provided at testimony I addressing policy j, u_{0j} is a random intercept term for policy proposal j, and ε is the residual error term.

Three equations predicting enactment were estimated. First, to isolate the effect of information supporting the policy proposal, enactment was modeled as a function of the information provided by supporters alone ($N = 582$). Next, to examine the impact of negative claims, a parallel model was estimated including testimony only from opponents ($N = 204$). Finally, to assess to the extent to which information provided by one side is offset by information provided by the other, a combined model including testimonies from both supporters and opponents was estimated.

Results

Information provided by supporters does increase the likelihood of enactment, as predicted (Table 6.9, model 1). Claims that the proposed policy will be effective make enactment significantly

TABLE 6.9. *The Effect of Information on Policy Enactment: Logit Coefficients and Standard Errors*

	Model 1	Model 2	Model 3
Testimony in Support:			
Argue Problem Is Important	−0.29		−0.48
	(0.32)		(0.29)
Argue Policy Will Be Effective	1.32**		1.17**
	(0.30)		(0.28)
Reframe the Issue	0.22		0.09
	(0.43)		(0.41)
Evidence to Support Claims	−0.93**		−0.98**
(Index)	(0.16)		(0.16)
Testimony against:			
Argue Problem Is Important		0.20 (0.74)	0.99
			(0.68)
Argue Policy Will Have neither		−5.47**	−2.33**
Intended Effect nor the Opposite		(1.02)	(0.62)
Reframe the Issue		−10.17**	−0.72
		(1.62)	(0.47)
Evidence to Support Claims		−1.09**	−0.76*
(Index)		0.38)	(0.37)
Intercept	−1.87	1.01 (2.56)	−1.71
	(1.03)		(1.09)
τ_{u0}^2	21.27**	92.06**	24.84**
	(7.14)	(38.43)	(8.22)
σ^2	0.34	0.07 (0.01)	0.31
	(0.02)		(0.02)
−2 log Likelihood	4,021.6	3,334.1	5,982.2
N	582	204	786

Note: Standard errors in parentheses.
* $p < .05$.
** $p < .01$.

more likely; testimonies making such claims are associated with a 274 percent increase in the odds of enactment [exp(1.32) = 3.74] compared to testimonies that do not. Neither arguments about the importance of the problem nor attempts to reframe the issue have any impact, however. Unexpected is the impact of evidence provided by proponents: the more they provide, the less likely the proposal is to be enacted.

The information provided by opponents has the effect they intend (model 2), significantly reducing the likelihood of enactment. Arguments that the proposed policy will have neither the intended consequences nor their opposite reduce the odds of enactment by 96 percent compared to testimonies that do not provide such information. Attempts to reframe the argument reduce the odds of enactment, and so does evidence presented by opponents to bolster their claims; the latter reduces the odds of enactment by 67 percent compared to testimonies without such evidence. Only claims about the importance of the problem make no difference.

When testimonies by supporters and opponents are analyzed together (model 3), we find the results from the first two models to be quite robust. The likelihood of enactment is increased by proponents' arguments that the proposed policy would be effective and reduced by opponents' claims that the policy would be ineffective and by the amount of evidence provided by both supporters and opponents. The sole contrast with previous models is opponents' attempts to reframe the issue, which are significant in model 2 but not in model 3.

What do these results tell us about what happens at hearings as supporters and opponents of policy proposals try to influence the legislative outcome by providing information potentially useful to members of Congress? As we have shown above, Congress gets much more information from supporters (61 percent of witnesses) than from opponents (21 percent), and supporters provide different kinds of information than do opponents. Supporters devote their greatest efforts to demonstrating the importance of the problem being addressed – more than four-fifths try to do so.

Opponents seem willing to concede this point; they address it relatively seldom. Instead, they focus overwhelmingly on the likely impact of the proposed policy; almost four-fifths say it would have no impact or the opposite of that predicted by supporters, and an equal proportion try to reframe the issue, claiming there would be consequences along dimensions not discussed by supporters. Effectiveness is not neglected by supporters – three-fifths of them address it – but they do not focus on it the way opponents do.

As noted above, witnesses' use of evidence is consistent with the emphases in their arguments. Much of the information they provide has no impact on enactment, however. Supporters' emphasis on the importance of the problems, in particular, seems misplaced. Testimony claiming the problem is important has no impact, and the evidence supporters provide actually seems to work against their interests. Because this is the first systematic analysis of information provided at hearings, we can only speculate about the reasons for this. Some have claimed that the very fact of holding a hearing on an issue manifests legislators' belief that the problem is important (Diermeier and Feddersen 2000); perhaps testimony on this point is simply redundant. And members of Congress may be especially likely to back up their claims about importance when their case appears to be relatively weak; perhaps that is why supporters' use of evidence is negatively related to enactment.

Much more consequential is information about effectiveness. Supporters' and opponents' claims about effectiveness both affect enactment, as does opponents' evidence. It could well be that once a hearing has been called for, members of Congress are especially concerned about effectiveness, and it is information about effectiveness that matters most to them.

CONCLUSIONS

This chapter began with a puzzle in the study of democratic politics: the contrast between the widespread belief that interest organizations and other advocates strongly affect public policy, and the lack of convincing evidence that they do. One possible reason for the paucity of evidence is our failing to test theories contending that legislators are affected by information provided by those hoping to influence policy.

I have aimed to bridge this gap between theory and research by describing the information provided to members of Congress at committee and subcommittee hearings, and by gauging its impact on the enactment of policy proposals. Doing this required a number of methodological innovations. Because such information had not been measured previously, it was necessary to identify what types of information have been seen as important in theories of legislative behavior, and to develop ways to measure them. This chapter thus makes methodological and substantive contributions to work on how organizations affect Congress.

Because this is the first study of information provided at hearings, what we learn is necessarily new. Some findings may not surprise experts on the legislative process, but they now may have objective evidence to support their beliefs. Less than half the witnesses at the hearings represented private interest organizations, while many were members of Congress not on the committee holding the hearing; presumably, those who testify believe that hearings are an especially effective way of providing information to colleagues. Supporters and opponents make different kinds of arguments as they attempt to influence legislative outcomes; supporters are much more likely to highlight the importance of the problem, opponents tend to emphasize the probable ineffectiveness of the proposed solution. Very few witnesses refer to possible electoral consequences for members of Congress who support or oppose the policy proposal. Witnesses make little use of evidence based on research to support their arguments, and even less use of comparisons to other issues or political units; anecdotes are by far the favorite kind of evidence.

Information does indeed affect enactment. Not all types of information matter, but several do, and their effects can be substantial. Information about the likely effectiveness of proposed policies is especially important.

This research is, of course, only a first step. Hypotheses about the importance of information in the policy process must be tested in a broader context. First, we need to learn more about how legislators acquire information – when they get a great deal from hearings and when they rely on other sources – and what types of information matter most. In addition, we need to determine whether assessing organizational impact in terms of information flow produces better results and more understanding of the policy process than assessing impact in more conventional ways – in terms of numbers of members, budgets, and the like. We must find out if organizational impact remains substantial when considered in the context of other forces affecting policy change, including public opinion, shifts in the party balance, and the more public expressions of views examined in previous chapters.

Given the many factors that can influence congressional action, this chapter may be seen as the first step in specifying how information affects the legislative process. The results reported here warrant additional research – research that will enable us to continue closing the gap between theories about the role of information in policy change, and the research needed to test them.

7

Conclusions

It has been 365 years since the struggle for representative democracy began during the English Revolution. It was then that the Levellers first articulated many ideas still central to democratic thought: that government should be subject to the people, that the rights of citizens should be protected by a written constitution, and that among these rights should be the right to vote, equality before the law, freedom of speech, legal representation, and the right to remain silent during judicial proceedings (Wootton 1992).

Close to 150 years passed before the establishment of the first representative government incorporating many of these ideas – the U.S. government under its current Constitution and Bill of Rights. During the next 150 years, however, demands for representative government became central to politics in much of the West, and since World War II to politics in much of the rest of the world.

The struggle for representative democracy has been predicated upon the belief that if the people of a country win the right to vote and to freedom of speech and association, they can influence their government – the government will pay attention to their demands. For a long time, this belief had to be sustained by argument and faith. There were few (or no) democratic countries whose experience could be used as evidence, and before the rise of modern social science, rigorous analysis of popular control over government was not possible.

Now, however, as our experience with democracy has increased and our capacity for analysis has improved, we can see whether the belief is correct. Indeed, for many of those devoted to understanding democratic politics, we *must* see whether it is correct. As Soroka and Wlezien (2010:2–3) write, the "opinion-policy relationship is central not just in everyday politics, but in the theoretical literature on democracy and representation as well, from Jean-Jacques Rousseau, to John Stuart Mill, to Robert A. Dahl. Indeed, for each of these theorists the connection between public preferences and public policy is one of the most critical components of representative democracy." "The capacity of a political system to respond to the preferences of its citizens," write Manza and Cook (2002a:630), "is central to democratic theory and practice." A close connection between opinion and policy not only enhances the credibility of democratic theory, it supports the hopes of the framers of the U.S. Constitution as well (Stimson, MacKuen, and Erikson 1995:560). Significant divergences between opinion and policy, however, challenge our beliefs about the possibility of public control of public policy (e.g., Hacker and Pierson 2005). Who wins struggles over public policy: the public itself, or organized interests whose goals differ from those of the public?

The number of studies gauging the impact of public opinion and organized interests on public policy is vast. Some studies of public opinion find its impact consistently powerful (e.g., Erikson, MacKuen and Stimson 2002; Erikson, Wright, and McIver 1993); others find it powerful on some issues or in some circumstances but not others (e.g., Smith 2000; Soroka and Wlezien 2010); some are doubtful about the magnitude of its impact (e.g., Page 2002; for the most comprehensive recent review, see Shapiro 2011). Similarly, some studies of organized interests find them having a very (and possibly increasingly) powerful impact on policy (e.g., Hacker 2004; Jacobs and Page 2005); others find their impact regularly meaningful but hardly uniform or overwhelming (Burstein and Linton 2002); and some find, like Baumgartner et al. (2009:259), that with regard to the policy advocates they studied, "none of them typically has much control over the collective outcome" of the policy debates they were involved in (also see Gray and Lowery 2000; Leech 2010). As to studies that consider both public opinion *and* organized interests – there aren't very many (see the reviews Burstein 2003, 2011; Burstein and Linton 2002). Some suggest that politics is indeed a zero-sum game, with more involvement by organized interests weakening the impact of the public, but others suggest the reverse, that organizations may enhance the connections between public opinion and public policy (Burstein 2003:35; Burstein and Linton 2002:396) – not a new idea by any means (see, e.g., Clemens 1997; Gray and Lowery 2004; Smith 2000), but one that gets relatively little attention.

It may be argued that it is frustrating but not surprising for answers to critical questions to vary so widely – there are always controversies about major issues, and it's not at all uncommon for findings to vary widely among studies. We could hope that debates among proponents of different views would lead to a sharpening of arguments and advances in theory and methods, so that the range of disagreements could be narrowed. Many recent studies do indeed advance our understanding of the opinion–policy linkage, but there are a number of problems not being addressed as well as they might be. I hope that by drawing attention to some of them and proposing new ways to address them, this book will enhance our understanding of democratic politics.

WHAT'S NEW HERE

Much of social science (though by no means all) sees generalization as a key goal. We want to understand not just this or that set of people, activities, organizations, or achievements, but how social processes work in general. That is certainly how many of those studying policy view what they're doing – they want to understand not just how public opinion on some issues affects policy on those issues, but also how public opinion affects policy overall in democratic political systems. Even when researchers are very well aware of the limitations of their own research, their goal is to expand our range of knowledge – to more issues (Erikson et al. 2002; Soroka and Wlezien 2010), more countries (Horne 2012; Soroka and Wlezien 2010), and over longer periods of time (Erikson et al. 2002). They want to understand the impact of some types of activity not just on some issues, but on as wide a range of issues as possible (Amenta and Caren 2004; Amenta et al. 2010; Baumgartner et al. 2009) – not the activities of just some of those involved in politics, but of everyone (Koopmans and Statham 1999; Koopmans and Statham 2010b:57; McAdam and Boudet 2012:24). Even when writing in great detail about a single social movement, they want to develop principles that can aid our understanding of social movements in general (McCammon 2012).

But however much those analyzing policy want to generalize, they rarely try to do so in a formal way – identifying a population of units to analyze, selecting a random (or close to random) sample, analyzing the sample, and generalizing back to the population. So far as I know, up to this point only Gamson (1990), in his research on SMOs, and Baumgartner et al. (2009), in their work on lobbying, have tried to do so. No doubt there are many reasons for this, but one has received special mention recently: it is very, very difficult. McAdam and Boudet (2012:24) argue for the importance of random sampling and, in fact, study a random sample of communities, but they also say that Gamson's approach to studying SMOs has never been emulated because, essentially, it's too difficult (p. 30); Nicholson-Crotty (2009:196) writes that gathering a random sample of policies is "effectively impossible."

In this book I have taken up McAdam and Boudet's (2012) and Nicholson-Crotty's (2009) implicit challenge and tried to generalize about legislative action on a (stratified) random sample of policy proposals – admittedly only for only one legislature during a very limited period of time, but generalize nevertheless. To do so I had to take on precisely what Nicholson-Crotty (2009:196) identified as a critical barrier to conducting research on policy with the goal of generalizing: the "difficulty of identifying a universe of observations." It is not possible to study a sample of policies without there being an identifiable population (or universe) of policies from which to sample.

Nicholson-Crotty (2009) was writing at the same time as Baumgartner et al. (2009), and may not have been aware of their efforts, or perhaps he thought that they were not really sampling policies – Baumgartner et al. were studying issues defined subjectively by lobbyists rather than policies defined objectively. But if we think of policies as something Congress might actually vote on, Nicholson-Crotty was right. He doesn't discuss why there is no identifiable population of policies, but I propose a reason: though a great deal of attention has been devoted to measuring public opinion and some types of advocacy, not very much has been devoted to measuring policy. Researchers may take great care in developing measures in their own work, but there has been little effort to think about how to measure policy more generally. As a result, policy is measured in such a wide variety of ways that it is indeed difficult to imagine how studies of policy might be brought together in a way that would make generalization possible.

I suggested a way to identify a population of policies – bills introduced into Congress – and have drawn a sample from the 101st Congress. I also recognized the disadvantages of focusing only on particular bills, and so developed the concept of a "policy proposal," the content of a bill or set of identical (or nearly identical) bills introduced into Congress over the course of however many congresses the bills could win sponsors. This made it possible to study congressional action (or inaction) on the content of a particular policy, and to do so for the entire history of the particular proposal. I make no claim that this will prove the best way to sample policies, but, together with the work of Baumgartner et al. (2009), it is a start – we now have two approaches to sampling and generalizing about policy, and have in effect issued an invitation for others to do better.

This approach to sampling and measurement has made it possible to address another significant problem in our studies of policy: causality. Some researchers are very careful to link hypothetical causes of policy to the policies they are concerned about –

linking, for example, public opinion about spending in particular policy domains to actual expenditures in those domains (e.g., Soroka and Wlezien 2010), and lobbying on specific bills or issues to legislative action on those bills or issues (e.g., McCammon 2012). But often the link between hypothetical cause and effect is logically weak – for example, when all protest on the environment, regardless at whom it is directed at or on what specific topic, is correlated with the number of bills on the environment passed by Congress; when public opinion on a broad issue (such as racial integration) – not on policy preferences – is correlated with congressional action on a particular policy proposal; or when public opinion on a couple of issues during relatively brief periods of time is correlated with total expenditures on many policies adopted over a much longer period.

Again, there are often many reasons for this, including the availability of data – if there are no data on public opinion about a particular policy, it may be better to use available data on related topics than to do no research at all on public opinion and that policy. But convention and lack of concern about sampling and measurement of policy probably play important roles. If there is relatively little concern about sampling and the measurement of policy, and a habit of using data collected for one purpose (such as describing trends in public opinion or protest on broad issues) for another (attempting to ascertain the causes of policy change), then concerns about tightly linking potential causes to effects may play a relatively small role in academic discourse on policy, other than in the technicalities of statistical analysis.

This problem is being recognized in the study of public opinion, as researchers (e.g., Lax and Phillips 2009, 2012; Warshaw and Rodden 2012) argue that our understanding of the link between opinion and policy depends on having data on opinions about the specific policies under consideration, and Baumgartner et al. (2009) make a similar point with regard to lobbying. I extend this logic to publicly reported advocacy, contending that if we want to understand how policy is affected by both public opinion and advocacy, it is important to focus on opinion and advocacy directed at the specific policy proposals being considered. The broad political context – elections, general trends in policy mood (Stimson 1999) – may of course influence congressional action, but there's no way to understand what Congress does without taking into account activities intended to influence its actions on specific policies.

It's important as well to assess what it is about advocacy that makes it effective. For the most part, work on advocacy is based on a very broad logic, that the more advocacy, of whatever type, the better, in terms of likely impact. Some types of advocacy – demonstrations that are especially large or that provoke a violent response from the authorities, for example – may be hypothesized to be especially effective, but the logic behind such claims often seems ad hoc. It has often been unclear just why legislators should respond to particular types of advocacy.

There is an argument about responsiveness, however, that has a great deal of potential – that what matters to legislators is information, particularly information about the importance of the problem they're being asked to address, the potential effectiveness of proposed solutions, and the likely impact of action on legislators' chances of reelection (see, e.g., Arnold 1990; Baumgartner 2009:54–57; Hirsch and Shotts 2012; Krehbiel 1991; Lohmann 1993, 1998; Workman, Jones, and Jochim 2009). I have focused here on a source of information often said to be especially important to members of Congress, namely, testimony at committee hearings. No one has analyzed the impact of this kind of information before, and it turns out to have a noteworthy impact on congressional action.

I have also analyzed the role in the democratic political process of two forces that are widely recognized but whose impact in the study of policy is not highlighted as it might be, possibly because both forces involve things that are absent rather than present: knowledge and political activity.

Everyone who studies politics knows that the public pays very little attention to politics most of the time, and most people know little or nothing about most issues. Often this is presented as a problem for democratic governance about which nothing can be done – it is very difficult to get people to take more interest in politics because on their own scale of priorities, people have more important things to do, and, indeed, things over which they can exert more influence than they can over policy. Sometimes the level of ignorance is acknowledged, but researchers suggest it is something that simply cannot be dealt with when examining government responsiveness to the public – as Soroka and Wlezien (2010:182) say, "expecting representative democracy to represent preferences that do not exist, in domains about which people do not care, is unreasonable." This makes sense, but it raises questions, as they acknowledge, about what it means to say that "democracy works."

As to political activity, it has long been understood that there is a powerful, logical argument as to why organizations and individuals should not try to influence policy – any sensible cost-benefit analysis (Olson 1971) shows that the cost of participation exceeds any likely benefit, especially considering how little impact action by any particular individual or organization is likely to have. But there has seemed to be a problem with the argument – not with the logic, but with its apparent conflict with reality. The most casual observation seems to show that rather than there being very little political activity, there is a lot, and therefore a great deal of effort has been devoted to explaining the circumstances under which the basic argument about participation will not apply.

I have argued that the observations finding a lot of political activity should not have been so casual. There does indeed seem to be a lot of political activity, but that is because observers adopt the point of view of those who feel overwhelmed by the amount or have an interest in seeing a lot. Many studies focus on members of Congress and their staffs and the tremendous amount of political activity directed at them. But in a nation of hundreds of millions of people, even a tiny, barely detectable amount of political activity on the part of individuals may seem overwhelming when focused on what is actually a very small number of members of Congress and their staffs. News reporters (these days, bloggers and tweeters as well those working for newspapers, television stations, and radio) want to report on what's happening, not on what's not happening, so naturally visible political activity by a few gets far more attention than inactivity by the masses. And many academics who write about social movements and interest groups also have an interest – however unconscious – in their generating a lot of activity. Sometimes the academics were participants in the movements they write about, or at least were very sympathetic observers (McAdam and Boudet 2012:ch. 1), and from their perspective, the intensity of activity seems self-evident. From a more professional perspective, there are entire academic subfields organized around particular types of political activity or organizations – social movements, interest groups, and the like; no one in those fields has an interest in discovering that there is really very little activity. And their continuing focus on the biggest, most visible, most important issues (much like journalists) only enhances the sense that the level of activity is very high. I have taken less for granted than most observers and, considering a sample of policy proposals and focusing on advocacy on those proposals, have discovered that theorists expecting little political activity may have been more correct than they themselves believed.

SOME INFLUENCES ON POLICY AND THEIR IMPLICATIONS

Sampling and measurement can seem like small, technical issues – matters of concern primarily to those tidying up after thinkers with real vision have addressed a problem. But sampling and measurement are not small technical issues. My findings about congressional action on policy have depended heavily on sampling and measurement, and so did Baumgartner et al.'s (2009) on lobbying. Some of the findings are not surprising, but some are, and so are some of the implications for our understanding of democratic politics.

I began with the belief that in order to generalize about the policy process, it is essential to study a random sample of policies. That belief in turn led to the realization that the study of such a sample would be very difficult because we had no adequate objective definition of policy that would allow us to define a population of policies and draw a sample.

Getting started this way led to some new findings, the reinterpretation of some old ones, and a reconsideration of some major theoretical works on democracy.

First, the concept of a policy proposal proved to be very useful. When addressing particular problems, members of Congress do not seem to develop lots of ideas and introduce a variety of bills at any one time; they neither begin with variations on a particular approach and winnow them down to one that will win the support of a majority, nor begin with a single approach and elaborate on it until they discover the variation that will win acceptance. Instead, they sponsor bills manifesting a particular approach and stick with that approach until it is either enacted into law or disappears from the congressional agenda. Usually this does not take very long; whether or not legislators introduce policy proposals when they think they have spotted a window of opportunity (Kingdon 1995), they usually introduce a proposal in no more than a handful of congresses before winning adoption or giving up. Seldom does a policy proposal become law through a process in which a few members of Congress slowly win support from their colleagues over an extended period of time (though there are important instances of this, including major civil rights laws and the Americans with Disabilities Act).

There is no doubt that public opinion plays a key role in American politics. When the public considers an issue important and clearly indicates what it wants, the government is very likely to respond. Indeed, it may respond even more strongly than we generally find, because the public is usually asked, not about whether it wants specific policies, but simply what its broad views are on a political topic.

Yet studying a sample of policy proposals shows the limits of public opinion, by forcing us to consider the implications for democratic responsiveness of something that social scientists already know – namely, that on most policies, the public has no opinions. On those policies – most policies – the government cannot possibly respond to public opinion. Yet that does not mean that democracy isn't working, at least not in the sense usually discussed. The public is not losing in a struggle with special interests because there is no struggle.

Those who assess the impact of advocacy – the publicly reported advocacy focused on here, or less-visible lobbying – often confront a disconcerting result: activities intended to influence policy very often fail to do so. The world of those who study policy change is filled with negative findings.

I suggested two ways of confronting such findings. First, past work often focuses on hypothetical determinants of policy that are not closely linked, even potentially, to the policies they are supposed to affect – for example, studies of attempts to influence environmental legislation consider the impact of protest not directed at the legislation being considered. By focusing on activities directed at particular policy proposals, we might very well discover that such activities have a stronger impact than we have generally found before.

Yet there is a competing point of view. There are powerful theoretical arguments that there will be little advocacy on most issues. If that is true, there may be too little to influence policy, and we may find that advocacy has less impact than we have found before. To discover how much advocacy there is, I searched both more narrowly and more broadly than others have – more narrowly in the sense of focusing on advocacy directed at the 60 policy proposals, and more broadly in the sense of using a major electronic database to gather data from far more sources than others have.

It turns out that there is very little publicly reported advocacy – sometimes none – on many issues. This finding is consistent with that of Baumgartner et al. (2009) in their analysis of lobbying on a sample of issues, and it is also in line with other recent work suggesting that past estimates of the level of political activity may have been too high (Burstein and Sausner 2005; Caren, Ghoshal, and Ribas 2011; McAdam and Boudet 2012). And it turns out, as we might expect if there is very little advocacy, that advocacy has very little impact on policy.[1]

---

[1] Work on advocacy in Europe (e.g., Kriesi et al. 1995; Koopmans 2007b) and on individual-level political participation in the United States (e.g., Inglehart and Catterberg 2002:305; Verba, Schlozman, and Brady 1995:540–45) seems to find

If on most issues the public has no opinion and there is little advocacy, what are the implications for policy change? If we assume that Congress will not adopt new policies unless fairly strongly pressured to do so, the lack of public opinion and advocacy suggests that there will be little policy change – and that is exactly what we see. Only a small proportion of the thousands of bills introduced into every congress are enacted into law, and, as Baumgartner et al. (2009:247–50) write, there is what they call a strong "status quo bias" – when there actually is a conflict between competing views, those supporting the status quo are considerably more likely to get their way than those supporting change (though they have their own explanation for this, to be discussed shortly).

What does affect policy? Public opinion when it exists, and probably publicly visible advocacy likewise. Increasingly, though, scholars seeking a principle to explain the impact of a variety of forces are turning to the concept of information, particularly information about the importance of problems government is asked to address, the likely effectiveness of solutions, and the potential impact of supporting a proposal on legislators' chance for reelection. I developed a way to systematically code information provided in congressional hearings and found that it does have a significant impact on Congress, suggesting this is a line of work well worth pursuing.

WHAT'S NEXT?

When I began this project, I shared one goal with most researchers studying policy, and, indeed, with most researchers studying the determinants of almost any social phenomenon – finding that the explanatory factors had a powerful impact on what they're hypothesized to explain. But what I found was very different – public opinion arguably has little impact on policy when the entire

considerably higher levels of participation than that reported here and in other work on advocacy in the United States. There are certainly different approaches to measurement involved (Burstein and Sausner 2005:413), but no one has tried seriously to reconcile the different approaches and findings.

range of policies is considered, and publicly visible advocacy has very little, often none.

This should be upsetting. No one really likes negative findings; they don't seem interesting, and they challenge the theories being tested – often widely admired theories with long histories.

The findings here may be even more challenging than they seem, because they help to draw attention to a phenomenon that is noted with some regularity but seldom discussed in depth: the impact of hypothetically important determinants of policy change is often found to be zero – far more often, really, for researchers and theorists to remain comfortable with their conventional approaches to policy change. Most studies of campaign contributions and roll call voting find that contributions have little or no impact (Ansolabehere et al. 2003). In half the attempts to gauge the impact of interest organizations on policy, there isn't any impact, and the impact may be substantial enough to matter in policy terms no more than a third of the time (Burstein and Linton 2002:394). Lobbying has very little measurable impact (Baumgartner et al. 2009; Leech 2010); the same is true of populations of interest organizations (Gray and Lowery 2000). Other work reaches similar conclusions (Andrews and Edwards 2004; Potters and Sloof 1996; Smith 1995; Wright 1996).

How do researchers respond to these findings? Not, for the most part, by abandoning their hypotheses and theories. This is perfectly sensible. When theoretical arguments seem sound and have wide support in the community of researchers, it doesn't make sense to abandon them on the basis of one, or even a few, negative findings.

Yet at some point it becomes difficult not to notice how common such findings are. How do researchers respond? Here it may be instructive to focus on the work of Gray and Lowery (2000) and Baumgartner et al. (2009), because it's reasonable to expect a lot from them. Their studies of populations of interest organizations and issues, respectively, are theoretically sophisticated, methodologically innovative, and very carefully and thoughtfully done. They expected to find interest organizations and lobbyists influencing policy, perhaps quite strongly, but found the actual influence minimal.

Gray and Lowery (2000:241) present their conclusions in a conventional way, saying that although they find the variables they're studying to have minimal impact, other studies on similar, if not identical, sets of forces will produce different findings. "This leaves us with two important questions," they write:

First, does this mean that interest organizations have little influence on public policy? The answer is almost certainly that they do matter.... [S]pecific interests clearly can have an important influence on legislative and executive actions in certain circumstances....

Second, does this mean that the population properties of density and diversity do not matter? Despite the limited evidence of impact reported here, we think that they do matter.

It's hard to argue with what they say. Interest organizations certainly do affect policy sometimes. Nevertheless, I think they should have taken their own findings more seriously and tried to explain them at greater length.

Baumgartner et al. (2009) produce similarly disappointing findings, but do go on to consider why in more detail. After noting (p. 237) that "it is difficult to find reliable predictors of policy change," they suggest that the reason may be found by considering the history of the policies they're studying. Groups seem to be having no impact on policy now because they had an impact in the past – their influence "is *already reflected in the status quo policy.* . . . The equilibrium policy, reflecting the relative balance of forces, was presumably already attained in previous rounds of the policy process" (p. 240, emphasis in original).

This is a very creative and plausible suggestion, but the key word is "presumably" – Baumgartner et al. have no evidence this occurred. Were they to get comparable data on the same issues for some period in the past – five years previously, ten years previously – and find similar results, they could propose the same explanation, all the way back to the first entry of the issue onto the legislative agenda. They could be right, but they need evidence. How might we start to rethink our approach to policy change? Or, putting it another way, if so many of the factors believed to determine policy actually have little effect, what does?

The most likely possibility, with some significant qualifications, is that the factors believed to determine policy actually do so, but flaws in our research have led us to underestimate their impact. Many aspects of conventional research designs seem bound to produce seemingly weak relationships between the hypothetical determinants of policy and policy itself. Policy is often measured poorly, frequently in ways that are not politically meaningful. Public opinion and advocacy are measured in ways that don't match up with policy – the public is asked its views about something other than the policy being analyzed, and the advocacy hypothetically influencing a particular policy is actually not directed at that policy at all. The types of advocacy activities taken into account aren't necessarily those likely to matter to elected officials.

Thus, we could improve our understanding of policy change by improving the way we design our research. A key first step would involve the reconceptualization and measurement of policy. Whatever the reasons might be for our failure to get beyond an ad hoc approach to such conceptualization and measurement, it's astonishing that not only is there no standard approach to doing so, there aren't even systematic efforts, or debates about how best to proceed. However much care goes into the measurement of particular policies (or sets of policies), our advance in understanding policy will be greatly impeded unless much more attention is paid to conceptualizing and measuring policy in general, so that policies and the forces affecting them can be compared. The approach described in Chapter 2 represents a useful advance, but it no more than scratches the surface – for one thing, it provides no way to trace the amendment process. We must find a way to take the qualitative – the words that constitute bills and amendments – and transform them into the quantitative.

The next challenge would be sampling and generalization. Once we have a population of policies, sampling is at least possible. But there are a variety of ways of defining populations, concerns about duplicates in the population that may distort the sampling process must be addressed, and the link between sample and population when the sample is drawn from one time period but the policies are traced historically must be considered as well.

It seems clear that if we are to analyze the relationship between public opinion and policy, we must have opinion data on the policies in the sample. But rarely will such data exist, and the justification for making do with data on vaguely similar topics gets weaker and weaker as we analyze the relationship more closely. What we really need is a fairly immense effort to collect new data on a sample of policies. Because such data cannot be collected retroactively, it will be necessary to begin with new policy proposals and follow them forward, repeating opinion questions on those that remain on the agenda. Though the field of public opinion has seen much creative experimentation with regard to data collection in recent years (e.g., Ansolabehere, Rodden, and Snyder 2008; Jessee 2009; Lax and Phillips 2009; Sniderman and Grob 1996), it is not obvious how this would work or where the resources would come from. We need more careful theoretical work to help us decide what the minimal requirements for data would be, and careful consideration of the tradeoffs between time and expense on the one side, and likely social scientific payoff on the other.

Then there is the question of what questions to ask. It has been argued here that it is essential to ask questions about the bills actually being considered, rather than about vaguely related topics. Yet there is an intermediate level of opinion, on policy in fairly broad policy domains rather than on specific bills, and, at least for some issues, a global level of opinion on the general direction in which the country should be heading. Legitimate claims may be made about the potential importance of opinion at each level (Erikson et al. 2002; Soroka and Wlezien 2010), and it would be important to gauge the importance of each.

When we think about adding data on advocacy to data on public opinion, there are at least three ways in which future research will have to go beyond what has been done in the past. The first concerns data collection. The data on advocacy used in this book represent an intermediate level of technological development. The data themselves were reported for a period before the development of the World Wide Web, so it was still reasonable to limit data collection to print media; yet it was possible to make use of electronic data bases to search for widely for relevant reports than would have been the case previously. In the future, it will be necessary to collect data from a much wider array of sources, particularly electronic ones. Doing so will raise an interesting issue. There has long been some concern about what it is about events that has an impact – the events themselves, or the fact of their being reported. Back when most people got news from one source (newspapers) or perhaps two, the distinction may not have mattered much. But it is sometimes said now that events become influential when they are reported over and over again on blogs and many other media sources developed on the Web. Data will have to be collected about both the events and the reporting of the events.

It will be necessary also to continue refining our sense of what data should be collected about advocacy in light of what is known about the needs of the targets – elected officials and possibly others in government. Decisions about what data to collect have long been made with little regard for theories about what would be most likely to matter; the findings here about the impact of information provided at committee hearings should encourage further consideration of this issue.

In addition, a concern in the collection of data about public opinion should also be taken into account in the collection of data about advocacy. While it is essential to collect data about advocacy directed at particular policy proposals, it would be a good idea to take into account advocacy still targeting the same general issue, but in not quite so focused a way.

We must also expand the set of determinants of policy change beyond those considered in this book and consider the entire set as a system, not as just different variables operating in isolation. This may seem obvious, but we still see a great deal of work focusing on one type of variable at a time – on public opinion, or lobbying, or protest. We need to consider the impact of political parties and elections on policy, the intensity of attention each policy receives, the overall configuration of populations of interest organizations, the internal structure of Congress, and political leadership, and interactions among them.

It will also be very important to consider the relationship between advocacy and public opinion, and the reciprocal relationship between both of them and policy. It was not practical here to consider how public opinion and policy interact because there was no data on public opinion for so many of the issues. Nevertheless, past research has shown that the interaction between public opinion and advocacy matters – each can influence the impact of the other (Agnone 2007; Burstein 1998b). In addition, if we want to see whether it is possible for organized interests to get what they want against the voice of public opinion, it will be necessary to include both in the same studies – something that occurs surprisingly seldom (Burstein 2003; Gray et al. 2004). We also know that not only do public opinion and advocacy sometimes affect policy, but policy affects public opinion and advocacy as well (Baumgartner et al. 2011; Gray et al. 2005; Soroka and Wlezien 2010); we will have to take these reciprocal effects into account more systematically in future work.

We also need to rethink some conventional views about the nature of politics and the connections between society and government. The impression of politics presented by those who study Congress is that the political process is characterized by intense activity. For members of Congress and their staffs, the flow of information, demands, appeals, complaints, etc., pouring in on them is overwhelming, and much of what they do involves sorting through what they receive and trying to decide what's important enough to warrant their attention (Jones 1994; Krehbiel 1991; Lohmann 1998). It's easy to see why this would be the case. The U.S. Constitution created a House of Representatives with 68 members; with just under four million people counted in the 1790 Census, each member represented approximately 59,000 people (leaving aside issues of who could vote and who was counted as a person). Virginia, the most populous state, had approximately 750,000 people to be represented by its two senators. Today each voting member of the House of Representatives represents around 875,000 people; California, the most populous state, has a population of roughly 37 million; the number and complexity of issues addressed by Congress has increased immeasurably, and so have the means of communicating the public's policy preferences.

What politics looks like out in the countryside, however, is less clear. Though the number of registered lobbyists has increased, many of the organizations they represent are small, and some are entirely inactive; though there have been claims that the United States was becoming a "movement society," with protest becoming increasingly common, recent research (Caren et al. 2011) suggests that's not so. Though there are no widely accepted standards for deciding whether the level of advocacy in the United States as a whole is high or low, it is at least possible that the general state of affairs is well conveyed in the work by Baumgartner et al. (2009) and me here. There's simply not that much going on, especially when one looks for activity on specific policies or issues. This is not inconsistent with Congress being overwhelmed by the pressures it confronts – with such a large population, even a very low rate of participation per capita could translate into more than an organization of modest size can handle. Most bills may fail to move forward in the legislative process not simply because they lose out in the perpetual struggle for attention, but because there is very little pressure for them in the first place.

From a theoretical standpoint, one of the more promising theoretical developments in the study of policy is the "punctuated equilibrium theory" of policy change (Baumgartner et al. 2009:ch. 12; Jones and Baumgartner 2012; Jones, Sulkin, and Larsen 2003). Beginning with the observation of status quo bias, Baumgartner, Jones, and others hypothesize that the forces working against policy change are so powerful that "policymaking institutions are 'sticky' – they do not respond simply or directly to demands or needs" (Jones et al. 2003:152). It takes great effort to overcome such "stickiness," so much that when policy finally does change, the changes are disproportionately likely to be large rather than small. We may thus need to revise our ideas about how public opinion and advocacy are related to policy; they may matter a great deal, but the policy changes they produce may be discontinuous. Thus far the theoretical and empirical work on the theory has focused on its implications for policymaking institutions, such as Congress, as less on the links between those institutions and the larger society. But the work appears to be an especially promising basis for moving forward.

"Democracy works," write Soroka and Wlezien (2010:182) at the conclusion of *Degrees of Democracy*. The public senses what the government is doing, and it responds – calling for less spending when spending is already high, more spending when spending is low. And the government responds to the public, altering its policies in line with public opinion.

But there are some caveats. Democracy works better under some circumstances than others; it works better on issues on which the public has opinions, and on issues that are salient. Its effectiveness depends on institutional arrangements. There are concerns about the capacities of citizens. And Soroka and Wlezien (2010) can speak only to policy domains for which public opinion data exist (pp. 172, 182).

There is "nearly a one-to-one translation of preferences into policy, where policy and preferences are measured in familiar percentage liberal terms," write Erikson et al. (2002:316). "American democracy is real" (p. 447).

But there are some caveats. They examine the relationship between opinion and policy for only a subjectively defined set of "important" laws, and, from among those, only the laws that are clearly liberal or conservative, and do not deal with foreign, defense, or agricultural policy, and have an impact subjectively defined as more local than national – just 57 percent of the original list.

Other observers begin with a different perspective. Focusing on the 2001 and 2003 Bush tax cuts, Hacker and Pierson (2005:49) find that on an issue of monumental importance, Congress more or less ignored the public, to the point that "for those committed to core principles of democratic governance, the picture that emerges is unsettling." Bartels (2005) disagreed, arguing that when Congress voted for the tax cuts it was in line with public opinion – but not exactly in a way that would give anyone confidence in how well democracy was working. According to Bartels (2005:21), the public was so "remarkably ignorant" about the issues that it supported policies completely contrary to its self-interest – and support for democracy rests in part on the assumption that the public is able to recognize its self-interest and act on it.

But when it comes to thinking about the implications of the Bush tax cuts for evaluating American democracy, there's a caveat – though in this case one that's implicit. The Bush tax cuts were selected for analysis precisely because they seemed so egregiously contrary to the principles of democracy. How representative they were of the policy process in general, we do not know.

However well or badly democracy works, *how* does it work? Quantitative work on multiple policies considered over significant periods of time can say something about the impact of parties and elections, but not about advocacy by individuals and organizations, because individuals and organizations don't orient their activities around very broad measures of policy; qualitative work on single issues may describe advocacy, but has no hope of generalizing.

I agree with Soroka and Wlezien. Democracy, in the sense of there being a reciprocal relationship between opinion and policy, does work, sometimes. But what if, across the entire range of issues on the legislative agenda, "sometimes" is not very often – not because the government is ignoring the public, but because the public has no opinion on many issues? And what if it is difficult to establish links between opinion and policy because on most issues, there is very little advocacy – that is, very little activity connecting what the public wants (if anything) to what the government does? Congress may not be responding to the public – but because the public has no opinions and nothing to express, not because Congress favors some organized interests in opposition to the public. Is what we have not democracy? Or is it democracy reconsidered in light of what research can teach us?

Appendix

APPENDIX TABLE 1. *Sample of Policy Proposals from 101st Congress*

Bill Number	Subject
Policy Proposals Eventually Enacted:	
H.R. 1278	Savings and loan bailout
H.R. 1441	Labeling requirements for food with cholesterol
H.R. 1454	Student Right-to-Know and Campus Security Act (followed Title II – CSA)
H.R. 1606	Expanding Rocky Mountain National Park
H.R. 2136	Sets legal standards for incarceration for civil contempt
H.R. 2273	Americans with Disabilities Act
H.R. 2344	Transfer naval vessels to the Philippines
H.R. 2419	Chatahoochee National Forest land exchange
H.R. 2423	Safer tanker traffic in Puget Sound
H.R. 2791	Encouraging remining + reclamation of mining lands
H.R. 2799	Planting of alternate crops
H.R. 3104	Adding Pemigewasset River national status
H.R. 3664	Agriculture research
H.R. 4025	Requires child safety restraint systems on aircraft
H.R. 4520	FDI measurement
H.R. 5322	Expands rights of senior executive service

(continued)

APPENDIX TABLE I *(continued)*

Bill Number	Subject
H.R. 5598	Space patents
H.R. 5740	Expands veterans' health care programs
H.R. 5771	Olympic coins
H.R. 5891	Resolution Trust Corporation funding – second round

Policy Proposals Reported Out of Committee but Not Enacted:

H.R. 3855	Establishing Regional Petroleum Products Reserve
H.R. 3927	Additional immigrant visas for people denied freedom of emigration
H.R. 4328	Textile Trade Act – increasing duties on imports
H.R. 0824	Wetlands conservation
H.R. 2408	Creates Rural Development Administration
H.R. 2655	International Cooperation Act
H.R. 2983	Designates a clinic as Gene Taylor's Veterans' Clinic
H.R. 3016	Inclusion of certain employees in census
H.R. 3264	Prohibits disposal of solid waste in other states
H.R. 3847	Creates Department of Environmental Protection
H.R. 0895	Garnishment of federal pay treated like nonfederal pay
H.R. 3785	Compensation for victims of sexual assault against pornographers
H.R. 0336	Standardization of bolts
H.R. 1449	IRS construction rules
H.R. 1605	Admission of additional refugees from communist countries
H.R. 3120	Permit requirements for overflows
H.R. 4266	Higher pay for federal employees in District of Columbia

Policy Proposals That Never Made It Out of Committee:

H.R. 0072	Requires consultants to register for Department of Defense contracts
H.R. 0178	Reduces federal funding for foster care and adoption
H.R. 0181	Social Security benefit computation formula
H.R. 0337	Extends compensation for veterans' spouses that remarry
H.R. 0376	Requires presidential reports on reforms in Nicaragua
H.R. 0499	Indexing and reduction of capital gains tax
H.R. 0601	Provides income tax refunds to be allotted to incurable disease research
H.R. 1433	Expands benefits for military infertility medical procedures
H.R. 1928	Suspends duty on chemical
H.R. 2302	Reduce requirements for training for nursing aids
H.R. 3077	Promoting education of human rights and freedom

Bill Number	Subject
H.R. 3324	Public interest considered in railroad bankruptcy
H.R. 3643	Requires federal environmental impact statements
H.R. 4547	Suspends duty on red pigment
H.R. 4552	Duke Ellington dollar
H.R. 4603	Amends Medicaid to cover personal care services
H.R. 4634	Vehicle weight limitations on highways
H.R. 4835	Improvement of programs providing health insurance information
H.R. 5120	Prohibits gifts among federal employees
H.R. 5389	Additional requirements for defense procurement system
H.R. 5472	Family violence prevention and services
H.R. 5753	Repeals rules concerning passive foreign investment
H.R. 5966	Regulates greenhouse gas emissions

APPENDIX TABLE 2. *House Bill Numbers, Subject, and Terms Used for Database Searches*

Bill Number	Subject	Search Terms[a]
72	Requires consultants to register for Dept. of Defense contracts	Defense consultant registration
178	Reduces federal funding for foster care and adoption	Foster care AND assistance[b]
181	Social Security benefit computation formula	(social security AND notch) OR "social security notch act"[b]
336	Standardization of bolts	Standardization AND bolts
337	Extends compensation for veterans' spouses that remarry	Veteran AND spouse AND (remarriage OR remarry)[b]
376	Requires presidential reports on reforms in Nicaragua	President AND Nicaragua AND report AND reforms AND (month or monthly)[b]
499	Indexing and reduction of capital gains tax	Indexing AND capital gains[b]

(*continued*)

APPENDIX TABLE 2 *(continued)*

Bill Number	Subject	Search Terms[a]
601	Provides income tax refunds to be allocated for incurable disease research	Tax refunds AND incurable diseases
824	Wetlands conservation	Coastal wetlands AND threatened
895	Garnishment of federal pay treated like nonfederal pay	Federal pay AND garnishment
1278	Savings and loan bailout	Savings and loan AND bailout[b]
1433	Expands benefits for military infertility medical procedures	Infertility AND (military OR armed forces)
1441	Labeling requirements for food with cholesterol	Labeling AND cholesterol AND (Congress OR senate OR government OR "House of Representatives")
1449	IRS construction rules	Construction rules AND income tax; contribution AND "aid of construction"
1454	Student Right-to-Know and Campus Security Act	Crime Awareness AND Campus Security; Higher Education Act of 1965 AND Amendment; campus crime
1605	Admission of additional refugees from communist countries	(refugee OR refugees) AND admissions AND (Soviet Union OR Eastern Europe OR Vietnam OR Near East OR East Asia)[b]
1606	Rocky Mountain National Park	"Rocky Mountain National Park"
1928	Suspends duty on chemical	Tariffs AND chemicals
2136	Sets legal standards for incarceration for civil contempt	Child custody AND contempt AND ("District of Columbia" OR D.C.)[b]

Bill Number	Subject	Search Terms[a]
2273	Americans with Disabilities Act	"Americans with Disabilities Act"; employment AND discrimination AND (disabled OR disability OR disabilities)[b]
2302	Reduce requirements for training for nursing aids	(nursing facility OR nurse aid) AND training[b]
2344	Transfer naval vessels to the Philippines	Naval vessels AND Philippines
2408	Creates Rural Development Administration	"Department of Agriculture" AND rural development[b]
2419	Chatahoochee National Forest land exchange	"Chatahoochee National Forest"
2423	Safer tanker traffic in Puget Sound	Oil spil* AND oil tanker*[b]
2655	International cooperation act	Foreign aid AND "International cooperation act"; foreign aid AND "foreign assistance act"[b,c]
2791	Encouraging remining + reclamation of mining lands	Reclamation AND mined lands[b]
2799	Planting of alternate crops	Alternate crops OR alternative crops
2983	Designates clinic as Gene Taylor Veterans' Clinic	Gene Taylor Veterans' Clinic; Department of Veterans Affairs outpatient clinic; Gene Taylor AND veterans; veterans AND clinic AND Missouri
3016	Inclusion of certain employees in census	Census AND (armed forces OR civilian employees)
3077	Promoting education of human rights and freedom	"Human rights education"
3104	Adding Pemigewasset River national status	Pemigewasset River
3120	Permit requirements for overflows	(sewer AND overlo*) AND (estuaries OR ocean OR marine waters)[b]

(*continued*)

APPENDIX TABLE 2 (*continued*)

Bill Number	Subject	Search Terms[a]
3264	Prohibits disposal of solid waste in other states	(transport OR move OR ship) AND solid waste AND state[b,c]
3324	Public interest considered in railroad bankruptcy	Railroad AND bankruptcy AND public interest
3643	Requires federal environmental impact statements	"Environmental impact statements" AND "Council on Environmental Quality"[b]
3664	Agriculture research	(pecan OR pecans) AND (promotion OR marketing OR research)[b]
3785	Compensation for victims of sexual assault against pornographers	Pornography Victims' Compensation Act, pornography victims AND sexual assault[b]
3847	Creates Dept. of Environmental Protection	"Department of Environmental Protection"[b,c]
3855	Establishing Regional Petroleum Products Reserve	Petroleum reserve AND (region 1 OR New England), "petroleum products reserve" AND (region 1 OR New England), residential heating AND reserve (region 1 OR New England)[b]
3927	Additional immigrant visas for those denied freedom of emigration	"Freedom of emigration" AND visas,[b] "Independent Immigrant Act"
4025	Requires child safety restraint	Child safety AND aircraft[b]
4266	Higher pay for federal employees in the District of Columbia	Federal pay AND (D.C. or "District of Columbia")[b]
4328	Textile trade act	Textile imports[b]

Bill Number	Subject	Search Terms[a]
4520	Foreign direct investment measurement	"Foreign Direct Investment" AND report[b]
4547	Suspends duty on red pigment	Harmonized tariff schedule AND amendment, red pigment duty, naphthalenecarboxamide, red pigment AND tariff
4552	Duke Ellington dollar	Duke Ellington Dollar Coin Act, Duke Ellington Dollar Coin, Duke Ellington Coin
4603	Amends Medicaid to cover personal care services	"Personal care services" AND Medicaid[b]
4634	Vehicle weight limitations	(Load weight OR weight limitations OR weight limits) AND highways[b]
4835	Improve health insurance information	Health insurance AND information AND Medicare[b]
5120	Extends Hatch Act prohibitions of gift giving and campaigning	Hatch Act AND (gift OR "thing of value"); Hatch Act AND political campaigns; federal employees AND gifts[b]
5322	Expands rights of senior executive service	"Senior executive service"[b]
5389	Additional requirements for defense procurement	Defense programs AND accountability; defense procurement AND accountability
5472	Family violence prevention and services	Family violence[b]
5598	Space patents	Space AND patents[b]
5740	Expands veterans' health care programs	Veterans' benefits AND (health OR disability)[b]
5753	Repeals rules concerning passive foreign investment	"Passive foreign investment"; "Export Trade Corporation"

(*continued*)

APPENDIX TABLE 2 *(continued)*

Bill Number	Subject	Search Terms[a]
5771	Olympic coins	1996 Olympic Commemorative Coin Act; Olympic commemorative coin; Atlanta Olympics AND commemorative coin
5891	Resolution Trust Corporation funding – second round	(S&L OR "Savings and Loan") AND bailout AND funding[b]
5966	Regulates greenhouse gas emissions	Carbon dioxide AND credits; carbon dioxide AND offsets; carbon dioxide AND "clean air act"; carbon dioxide AND "control of greenhouse gases"; carbon dioxide AND greenhouse AND (U.S. OR United States OR American)[b]

[a] All included search under bill number.
[b] (Congress OR Senate OR government OR "House of Representatives") also included as search term in all searches for this proposal.
[c] (U.S. OR United States OR American) also included as search term in all searches for this proposal.

APPENDIX TABLE 3. *Publications Reporting Advocacy*

ABA Journal	*Grand Rapids* (Michigan) *Press*
Air Safety Week	*Greensboro* (North Carolina)
American Banker	*News Record*
Anchorage (Alaska) *Daily News*	*Hartford* (Connecticut) *Courant*
Arizona Daily Star	*Houston Chronicle*
Asian Week	*India Abroad*
Atlanta Constitution	*Investment Dealers' Digest*
Atlanta Journal	*Italian Voice*
Austin (Texas) *American-*	*Journal of Accountancy*
Statesman	*Journal Record* (Oklahoma City)
Barron's National Business and	*Journal Star* (Peoria, Illinois)
Financial Weekly	*Lancaster* (Pennsylvania) *New Era*
Billboard	*Las Vegas Review-Journal*
Boston Globe	*Los Angeles Times*
Boston Herald	*Marketplace Magazine*
Buffalo News	*Michigan Citizen* (Highland Park)
Challenge Magazine	*Milwaukee Journal*
Chemical Week	*Mississippi Business Journal*
Chicago Citizen	*Morning Call* (Allentown,
Chicago Sun-Times	Pennsylvania)
Chicago Tribune	*Mortgage Banking*
Chief Executive	*National Journal*
Christian Science Monitor	*National Petroleum News*
Chronicle of Higher Education	*National Review*
Cincinnati Post	*National Tax Journal*
Cleveland Plain Dealer	*Nation's Business*
Colorado Springs Gazette-	*New Republic*
Telegraph	*New York Times*
Columbian (Vancouver,	*Newsday*
Washington)	*Northwest Florida Daily News*
Columbus (Ohio) *Dispatch*	*Octane Week*
Consumers' Research Magazine	*Off Our Backs*
Daily News (Los Angeles)	*Omaha* (Nebraska) *World-Herald*
Dayton (Ohio) *Daily News*	*Orange County* (California) *Register*
Denver Post	*Oregonian* (Portland, Oregon)
Equipment Leasing Today	*Orlando* (Florida) *Sentinel*
Forbes	*Palm Beach* (Florida) *Post*
Fortune	*Pantagraph* (Bloomington, Illinois)
Fresno (California) *Bee*	*Parents*

(*continued*)

APPENDIX TABLE 3 *(continued)*

Patriot-News (Harrisburg,
  Pennsylvania)
Philadelphia Inquirer
Pittsburgh Post-Gazette
Policy Review
Press Democrat (Santa Rosa,
  California)
Providence (Rhode Island) *Journal*
Reason (Los Angeles)
Richmond (Virginia) *Times-
  Dispatch*
Roanoke (Virginia) *Times & World
  News*
Rock Products
Salt Lake (City, Utah) *Tribune*
San Antonio (Texas)
  Express-News
San Diego Tribune
San Diego Union
San Francisco Chronicle
Seattle Times
Spokesman-Review (Spokane,
  Washington)
St. Louis Post-Dispatch
St. Petersburg (Florida) *Times*
Star-Tribune (Minneapolis)
State Journal Register (Springfield,
  Illinois)

Sun Sentinel (Fort Lauderdale,
  Florida)
Tampa (Florida) *Tribune*
*Tax Management Financial
  Planning Journal*
Telegraph & Gazette (Worcester,
  Massachusetts)
The Progressive (Madison,
  Wisconsin)
The Record (Bergen County, New
  Jersey)
The Sun (Baltimore, Maryland)
The Tribune (San Diego)
Times-Picayune (New Orleans)
Tribune Business Weekly (South
  Bend, Indiana)
Tri-State Defender
Tulsa (Oklahoma) *World*
Ukrainian Weekly
Upside (Foster City, California)
USA Today
Village Voice
Virginian Pilot (Norfolk, Virginia)
Wall Street Journal
Washington (D.C.) *Post*
Washington (D.C.) *Times*
Washington Informer
Waste Age

APPENDIX TABLE 4. *Data Collection*

Advocacy Codebook

If an event meets the inclusion criteria, code as follows:

DateCode	Date coded
TimeStrt	Time data entry began
CoderID	Coder identification
PropID	Proposal description
PropNum	Proposal number (four-digit bill number)
PubYear	Publication year (four digits)
PubMonth	Publication month (two digits; if no month, code 99; if seasonal (e.g., summer issue), code first month of season)
PubDate	Publication date (if not dated, code 99)
PageNoB	Page on which article begins (maximum of four digits; use leading zeros; if letters and numbers, as in *New York Times* pagination, including leading zeros also, e.g., 0A21 for an article that begins p. 21 of section A)
PubName	Publication name (max six spaces)

For publications with a locality in the title, use the USPS two-letter state code, the first two letters of the locality (city or otherwise), and first two letters of further title. For example, the *Chicago Tribune* would be ILCHTR, and the *Wall Street Journal* would be NYWSJO.

For publications with two-word city names in their title, use the first letter of each word in the city section.

For other publications, use the first six letters of the title, excluding articles ("the," etc.). If the title consists of generic terms, use an acronym that excludes conjunctions and the like.

For example, *The Atlantic* would be ATLANT; the *Journal of the American Medical Association* would be JAMA. Here the key is consistency. Share codes among coders.

Include   Article inclusion reason

If options 1 or 2 are chosen, continue to next question. If options 3 through 7 are chosen, end coding and go on to next article.

1 Include article; explicit preferences rule clearly met

2 Include article; preferences and subject of preferences quite clear, but implicit

3 Exclude article; repeat of earlier coded event or article (must be published no later than one week following the primary report)

(*continued*)

---

	4 Exclude article; article on topic, no preferences stated implicitly or explicitly
	5 Exclude article; no full text, abstract only
	6 Exclude article; article postdates legislation being signed into law
	7 Exclude article; not on topic
EvntStat	State event occurred
	In what state did the event take place (including D.C.)? For national publications (typically substantive articles), code the location as US.
	(If multiple events are reported, each is reported separately. Events in different locations are counted as separate events, even if jointly organized and sharing a goal.)
	If no state is reported for the event, enter code NS (no state).
EvntType	Event type
	For the first (second, etc.) event reported: What type of event is this?
	1 Delegation
	2 Protest event (combining vigils, marches, other protests/ demonstrations)
	3 Strike or boycott
	4 Riot
	5 Message event: speech (Primarily one-way communication in front of an audience, which may include people participating in a protest event. This includes participation in congressional floor debate speeches.)
	6 Message event: two-way communication (a format with two-way communication, such as a press conference, in which a speaker is asked questions)
	7 Message event: editorial (Article by or on behalf of editors/ owners of a publication that takes a position on federal action on one of the relevant issues. No author is given for editorials.)
	8 Message event: letter to the editor (Letter to the editor that demonstrates an explicit preference on federal action on one of the relevant issues. Letters to the editor are signed at the end.)
	9 Message event: congressional testimony (include here witnesses before congressional committees)
	10 Message event: substantive article (Article in a publication, neither an editorial nor a letter to the editor,

taking a position on federal action on one of the relevant issues. This will include syndicated columns, technical articles assessing the likely success of proposed solutions, etc. The author's name appears at the beginning of the article.)

11 Message event: interview

12 Message event: other (Events that are not protest events, speeches, or press conferences, but communicate preferences about policy change. These can include literature tables, fundraiser, press releases, or other events where the type of event is unclear.)

13 Other (describe briefly)

ActorID   Actor name

Who was the actor? Record name if provided.

ActrType   Type of actor

What type of actor?

1 Interest organization (someone representing an interest organization; include authors of editorials)

2 Interest organizations, or representative of a set of interest organizations

3 Representative of a political party (not an elected official)

4 Representative of a state or local government (includes public universities)

5 Representative of a set of state or local government agencies

6 Representative of U.S. government executive branch, except the president

7 The president

8 Representative of U.S. government judiciary

9 Member of Congress, or staff of member of Congress

10 Unaffiliated individual(s)

ActrRelt   Specificity of reference to proposal

How specifically does the actor refer to the policy proposal? (If the actor refers to it in more than one of the ways described below, code the most specific.)

1 Refers to the specific bill number, identifies the proposal in such detail that it is clear the specific bill being considered in Congress is the object of concern, or makes it clear (is explicit) that the object of concern is a congressional bill with content identical with, or very similar to, the original proposal (of the set of 60).

(continued)

APPENDIX TABLE 4 (*continued*)

	2 Refers to federal (not necessarily congressional only) action on the same general issue in a way that seems consistent with the relevant policy proposal, but not included in category 1 because: (a) The action proposed is executive (including presidential) rather than congressional, (b) The proposal is very significantly stronger or weaker than the original proposal, (c) The proposal proposes a similar outcome for other targets, and/or (d) The proposal broadens the proposed outcome for the same targets. 3 Refers to state level action on the same general issue in a way that seems consistent with the relevant policy proposal, either proposing a similar outcome for other targets, broadening the proposed outcome for the same targets, or both
ActrPstn	Position of actor on the proposal What is the position of the actor with regard to the proposal? 1 Favors enactment of particular policy (described proposal in terms of no. 1 above) 2 Favors government action on the issue, without specifying what particular policy is favored (described proposal in terms of no. 2 or no. 3 above) 3 Opposes government action without specifying particular policy (described proposal in terms of no. 2 or no. 3 above) 4 Opposes enactment of particular policy (described proposal in terms of no. 1 above)
EvntPblc	Degree of publicity Was the action: 1 Public (Communication in the form of a speech, rally, march, demonstration, picket, etc. In these events there is no organized give and take between groups, organizers appeal to broad audience.) 2 Semiprivate (Attendance or audience is somewhat limited either officially or by custom, such as that of congressional hearings, a press conference, public debate requiring ticket for admittance and not presented live in the media, partisan conference, campaign speech directed toward a restricted group, etc.)

3 Private (theoretically) communication with a limited audience. This includes reports of letter-writing campaigns to the president, or representatives, personal correspondence between groups or individuals via letters, phone calls, staff meetings, there is no appeal to a wider audience here and record of correspondence is limited (report in the media makes this public, but that was not nature of original action).

4 Can't tell

EvntLngt Length of event

How long did the event last?

1 Half a day or less

2 More than half a day, no more than one full day (include editorials, letters to the editor, substantive articles in daily publications)

3 Two days

4 Three days

5 More than three days

6 Length not indicated

NoActCat No. of supporters of actor categorical

How many supporters of the actors' position were described? (If more than one number is reported, and the numbers differ by enough to put the result in different categories, below, use the higher number. If no specific number is mentioned, but it's possible to make an educated guess, do so. Guesses should err on the low side.)

1 One

2 Two to ten

3 More than 10 but fewer than 100, or a number that could be accommodated easily in a small space (e.g., in an office, in front of a particular business)

4 100–1,000, or a number requiring a larger space (e.g., a hall, a public square, an auditorium)

5 More than 1,000, less than 10,000, or, a number requiring a commensurate space (e.g., a small stadium, public park)

6 10,000 or more, or, a number requiring a very large space (football stadium, the Mall in Washington, D.C.)

7 Organization (the "actor" is an organization of unspecified size)

8 Author (this is to be used for substantive and editorial articles and letters to the editor in which the article is the event)

9 Unable to determine

(continued)

APPENDIX TABLE 4 (*continued*)

NoActCon	Number of supporters of actor continuous
	If an exact number of supporters of the actors' position was reported, what was it?
	(If more than one number is reported, use the higher number. The voting record of members of Congress cannot be used here.)
ViolSup	Violence by actors
	Did the event feature the use of violence by those taking a stand for or against policy change?
	1 No
	2 Yes, injuries reported
	3 Yes, property damage reported
	4 Yes, injuries and property damage reported
ViolLaw	Violence by law enforcement
	Did the event feature the use of violence by the police or other law-enforcement officials?
	1 No
	2 Yes, injuries reported
	3 Yes, property damage reported
	4 Yes, injuries and property damage reported
ViolByst	Violence by bystanders
	Did the event feature the use of violence by bystanders against those taking a stand for or against policy change?
	1 No
	2 Yes, injuries reported
	3 Yes, property damage reported
	4 Yes, injuries and property damage reported
ActPrdct	Explicit predictions of policy enactment
	Does the actor make explicit predictions about whether the policy proposal will have the intended consequences if enacted?
	1 No (this is the correct response if the actor has referred above to the policy domain, but without making it clear that any particular policy proposal is being described or is preferred)
	2 Yes, that enactment will lead to reasonably deduced consequences that go beyond simple restatement of the bill (consequences to be determined beforehand)
	3 Yes, that enactment will have consequences opposite those intended
PrdtConq	Predicted other consequences

Does the actor predict that the policy proposal, if enacted, will have consequences along some dimension other than that emphasized by the proposal's supporters?

(Examples: a bill intended to increase farmers' income having health consequences for people other than the farmers, or leading to increases in the taxes of people other than the farmers; a bill to increase trade having the effect of increasing unemployment among American workers; a bill to increase the size of national parks having the effect of putting timber companies out of business. This does not mean having an effect opposite that intended along the same dimension.)

1 No (this is the correct response if the actor has referred above to the policy domain, but without making it clear that any particular policy proposal is being described or is preferred)

2 Yes

ActThry   Predictions based on theory

Does the actor argue that the predictions are based on scientific or social scientific theory?

1 No

2 Yes

3 Skip, actor makes no predictions

PrdctRsh   Predictions supported with research?

Does the actor support the predictions with systematic research?

"Systematic research" includes quantitative and qualitative research that might be presented in an academic or scientific context, even if purely descriptive. It does not include testimony in which numbers are provided essentially as anecdotes, without any indication of their source or quality.

1 No

2 Yes

3 Skip, actor makes no predictions

PrdctCom   Predictions supported with comparisons

Does the actor support the predictions with comparisons to similar instances?

"Similar instances" refers to parallel policies that were implemented in comparable political units (e.g., U.S. states, other democratic countries, or the federal government itself)

(continued)

APPENDIX TABLE 4 *(continued)*

---

	1 No
	2 Yes
	3 Skip, actor makes no predictions
PrdctAnc	Predictions supported with anecdotes

Does the actor support the predictions with anecdotes? "Anecdotes" are personal stories or summaries of public opinion that are not based on formal research.

1 No
2 Yes
3 Skip, actor makes no predictions

NumAfft Number of people affected by policy

Does the actor mention the number of people likely to be affected by the policy proposal, not describing them as members of organizations, but rather as demographic categories or types of people? (Examples: mention of how many farmers there are, without regard to whether they belong to farmer organizations; mention of how many Latinos there are who would be affected, or of how many defense workers, professors, single mothers, etc.)

1 No (This is the correct response if the actor has referred above to the policy domain, but without making it clear that any particular policy proposal is being described or is preferred.)
2 Yes

Dispursd How widely dispersed affected people are

Does the actor explicitly mention how geographically dispersed the people potentially affected by the policy proposal are? (Examples: in every state, all over the West, in scores of congressional districts, in cities all over the country, etc.)

1 No (correct response if the actor has referred above to the policy domain, but without making it clear that any particular policy proposal is being described or is preferred)
2 Yes

NoRprsnt If number of people represented stated

Is the number of members in the organization the actor(s) represent mentioned?

1 No, or the actor does not represent an organization
2 Yes (this includes cases in which the actor is an organization, and the number of members is mentioned)

RprsntPol	If political activity of organization stated
	Does the actor mention anything about political activities by the organization he or she represents, its members as individuals, or other similar individuals (this includes cases in which the actor is an organization, and such mentions are attributed to it)? (Examples: mentions how important they are as voters, how votes on the bill may affect their actions at election time, etc.)
	1 No
	2 Yes
ReactCon	What was Congress's reaction to the event as reported in the article?
	1 No reaction was reported
	2 Positive (The reaction expresses some agreement with the goal of the action, or indicates that the goals of the event actors will be considered and/or are important.)
	3 Negative (The reaction expresses some disagreement with the goal of the action, or indicates that the goals of the event actors will not be considered and/or are not important.)
	4 Neutral (There is a reaction but it is either unclear or does not express an opinion either positively or negatively about the action or the goals of the action.)
Note	Note anything especially worthy
	Note anything about the report that seems especially worthy of note, including quotations that are especially striking. Quotations should include the name of actor, title and affiliation, and page number.
TimeEnd	Time data entry finished

SUPPLEMENTAL CODING INSTRUCTIONS

Exclusion/Inclusion

The exclusion or inclusion of articles is one of the most difficult steps of the coding process, and we have created a uniform rule (a "bright-line" rule) to aid in this process. This is an attempt to walk the thin line between over- and underexclusion. If we allow all articles that merely complain (as with the "Notch" issue) about a particular topic, we will have far too many articles to code that fall outside our definition of collective action events (collective action is defined as "action taken in pursuit of a collective good, which in turn is characterized by nonexcludability and jointness of supply," and "events occur when someone states an explicit preference for or against action on one of the 60 specific congressional issues"). If we limit our inclusion to only articles that make specific reference to the particular bill at hand, our results will be driven entirely by our methods, and we will inevitably find little or no collective action.

There are two ways in which an article can be included:

1. Actors must state an absolutely explicit preference for or against the "government" (federal or state) acting on one of the specific policy proposals, a different proposed policy with the same or similar content to one of the specific bills, or a general issue consistent with the specific proposal.
2. Actors' preferences for or against the "government" (federal or state) acting on one of the specific policy proposals, a different proposed policy with the same or similar content to one of the specific bills, or a general issue consistent with the specific proposal are *clearly, but implicitly, evident based on the content of the article alone*. The coder should take the subject of the article into account. For example if an actor makes a statement of preference but fails to state the subject of their preference, we can use the subject of the article (the specific bill) to determine that the actor is making a statement of preference for the bill itself.

Repeat articles are to be excluded. An article is a repeat of a previous article if it is by the same author, reporting on the same event or type of event by the same actors, within one week of the original article.

Repeat events are to be excluded. An event is a repeat of a previous event if the actor and the event are the same and published within one week of one another. The author of the article and the publication need not be the same. An event will be determined to be a repeat by identifying details in the article.

Articles that do not contain full text are to be excluded.

Vagueness of Actors

Some articles make reference to "supporters" or "opponents" of particular policy proposals, without identifying who the supporters or opponents actually are. The rule for this occasion is as follows:

When an article in which a preference is expressed by someone other than the author, but is not attributed to specific individuals or organizations, the statement of preference is not coded. If in the same article the author expresses a preferences, the author's statement is to be coded.

Historical Events

We are concerned primarily with contemporaneous events. If an article refers to a statement of preferences made in the past and the reference is nonspecific (does not refer to specific date), the statement is not to be coded.

If a statement of preferences made in the past is described, and the reference is specific (described as occurring on a specific date), within the time period the policy proposal is on the agenda, and not repeated elsewhere, the statement is to be coded.

Letters to the editor are considered public events.

Interviews

For substantive articles that contain interviews:

If the author does not express preferences, the article is coded once, with the interview counted as the event.

If the interviewee and the author both express preferences, each expression is counted as an event.

If an article contains multiple interviews expressing preferences about a policy proposal, each expression of preferences/interview is considered an event.

Interviews are coded as public events.

Event Length

Interviews: Code the actual length of the interview (typically half a day).

Rallies are to be coded 2, full day

If there is not enough information about an event to make an inference about its length, use the "not stated" option.

Event Type

When actors are quoted but the source of the quote (e.g., speech, interview, press release, etc.) is not given, and there are no other details that indicate the sources, the event is coded as event type 12, message event: other, the length of event should be coded as category 1, half a day or less, unless otherwise specified.

When actors are described as "issuing a statement" or other similar but differently worded behavior, this is considered category 12, message event: other.

The introduction of a bill is *not* considered an event. Sponsorship of a bill plus a statement about the bill *does* constitute an event.

When someone is reported as being present at an event (including a demonstration) but not saying anything, that does *not* constitute an instance of collective action – do not code. (Presence does not necessarily signify agreement.)

Actor Type

Option #1 [represents an organization] for the actor type [actrtype] is to be used only if the actor is described in the article as a "spokesperson" or other title conferring official capacity. If an actor is otherwise associated with an organization but is not representing the organization (e.g., professors identified by university affiliation but expressing preferences based on professional expertise rather than as representatives of the university), the actor type is to be coded as category 10 (unaffiliated)

Businesses are coded as interest organizations.

No prior knowledge from other articles should be used to make determinations about actor type.

Specificity of Reference

When determining the specificity of the actor's reference to the proposal (specific bill, federal action, state action), the context of the article should be considered. For example, if the focus of the article is explicitly on a specific federal bill and actors are quoted as saying "the legislation is great and will have far reaching impacts," it should be understood that they mean the specific bill in question, despite not explicitly saying so.

Numbers of Actors and Events

When someone speaks at a demonstration and relevant statements of preferences can be attributed to the speaker and demonstrators separately, the speech and the demonstration are counted as separate events. This avoids attributing the number at the demonstration to each of multiple speakers.

Event Location

When the article itself is the event, the state in which the publication is published is the state. When the article reports *on* an event, the state in which the event occurs held is the state. When the article reports on an event but no state is mentioned, code as NS rather than the state of publication.

Event Publicity

For articles that quote actors but do not give the source of the quote (speech, interview, press release, etc.) and give no other details from which the source is indicated, which are coded as event type 12, message event: other, they must be coded as category 4: can't tell.

Events held for members of an organization or organizations, open to significant numbers of people but seemingly limited to organization members, are to be coded as semi-private. Examples would include "union breakfast" or "breakfast for members" of a particular union.

Congressional Reaction

If a congressional reaction is coded, it must be in response to the event coded from the article (or the article itself, theoretically), and not the legislation or some other nonevent incident.

Actor Predictions

Simple restatement of the purpose of the legislation does not count as prediction.

The "reasonably deduced consequences" will be determined beforehand by both coders in concert.

Number of Supporters

The number of supporters does not include the primary actor. For example, the number of supporters for 1 actor with 3 indicated supporters would be 3, not 4.

Reliability

Ideally, calculating reliability requires that coders "work independently from each other" using "explicit and communicable instructions" (Hayes and Krippendorff 2007:428; also see Krippendorff 2004). Measures of reliability should correct for the likelihood that coders will agree by chance – the fewer categories and the less even the distribution of responses, the more likely coders will agree (Krippendorff 2004:413; Scott 1955:332). Krippendorff's α does especially well at addressing these and other problems, whereas "percent agreement" among coders – a commonly used measure – does not (Gamson 1990:26), nor do measures developed for other purposes (such as Cronbach's α).

In some research using content analysis to study policy change, coders work independently and reliability is calculated with Krippendorff's α (McCammon et al. 2001). Often, however, reliability is assessed by percent agreement (Larson and Soule 2009:310; Walker, Martin, and McCarthy 2008:46–47); other problematic measures are used (Koopmans et al. 2005:265); disagreements among coders are resolved by supervisors, meaning that coding is not done independently (Larson and Soule 2009:310; Walker et al. 2008:46–47; Koopmans et al. 2005:264; cf. McCammon et al. 2007:738); only one coder is used, making calculation of intercoder reliability impossible (Koopmans et al. 2005:264, for data on the United Kingdom); or reliability is calculated from an extremely tiny sample of the material (Koopmans et al. 2005:260, 265, on Germany).

Fifteen percent of the events here were coded independently by two coders. Reliability was measured using Scott's π, a relatively conservative measure which gauges how much the observed agreement between coders exceeds what would be expected by chance. (For the two-observer, nominal data situation here, Krippendorff's α is asymptotically equal to Scott's π.)

APPENDIX TABLE 5. *Congressional Hearings on Policy Proposals*

Proposal, 101st Congress, and Subject	All Hearings on Proposal
H.R. 2273, Americans with Disabilities Act[a]	S541-21, 1979; H341-4, 1987; S541-17, 1988; H341-81, 1989; H341-2, 1990; H341-4, 1989; H341-3, 1989; H361-20, 1990; H361-19, 1989; H521-37, 1989; H641-25, 1989; S541-37, 1989; H721-24, 1990
H.R. 4520, Foreign Investment in the United States[a]	H361-22, 1987; S261-48, 1988; S261-2, 1990; H361-46, 1990; S261-4, 1989
H.R. 2655, International Cooperation Act	H381-80, 1989
H.R. 5891, Resolution Trust Corp.[a]	S241-24, 1991
H.R. 1606, Rocky Mountain National Park[a]	S311-52, 1989
H.R. 1454, Campus Security[a]	H341-62, 1989; H341-31, 1990; S541-12, 1989
H.R. 4328, Textile Imports	H381-37.1, 1985; S361-32, 1986; H781-8, 1988; S361-45, 1988
H.R. 5598, Patents in Outer Space[a]	H701-20, 1986; H521-26, 1989; H701-13, 1989
H.R. 1278, Savings and Loan Bailout[a]	H241-35, 1989; H241-36, 1989; H241-47, 1989; H241-48, 1989; H781-41, 1989
H.R. 3847, Department of Environmental Protection	S401-56, 1990; S321-17, 1993; S401-50, 1993
H.R. 5771, Olympic Coins[a]	H241-79, 1992
H.R. 181, Social Security Benefits	H781-19, 1989; S141-9, 1988; H781-5, 1993
H.R. 336, Standardization of Bolts	H701-56, 1989
H.R. 1449, IRS Construction Rules	H781-47, 1990
H.R. 2136, Civil Contempt Legal Standards[a]	S401-54, 1989; H301-2, 1990
H.R. 2344, Naval Vessels to the Philippines[a]	H381-103, 1989
H.R. 2408, Rural Development Administration	H161-18, 1987

Proposal, 101st Congress, and Subject	All Hearings on Proposal
H.R. 2423, Tankers in Puget Sound	H561-49, 1989
H.R. 2791, Surface Mining Reclamation[a]	H441-53, 1989
H.R. 3104, Pemigewassett River Study[a]	S331-7, 1989
H.R. 3120, Permit Requirements for Overflows	H561-64, 1990
H.R. 3927, Visas for Immigrants	H521-4, 1989; H521-36, 1990; H521-55, 1989
H.R. 3264, Solid Waste Disposal	S321-5, 1999
H.R. 3785, Victims of Sexual Assault	S521-25, 1992; S521-25.1, 1992; S521-25.2, 1991
H.R. 3855, Petroleum Products Reserve	H361-76, 1990; S311-27, 1990; S311-34, 1996
H.R. 4025, Child Safety on Aircraft[a]	H641-3, 1991
H.R. 4266, Federal Employee Pay	H621-8, 1987; H621-7, 1988

[a] Proposal eventually enacted.

References

Adelman, Robert M., Hui-shien Tsao, Stewart E. Tolnay, and Kyle D. Crowder. 2001. "Neighborhood Disadvantage among Racial and Ethnic Groups: Residential Location in 1970 and 1980." *Sociological Quarterly* 42: 603–32.

Agnone, Jon. 2007. "Amplifying Public Opinion: The Policy Impact of the U.S. Environmental Movement." *Social Forces* 85: 1593–1620.

Alba, Richard D., and John. R. Logan. 1992. "Analyzing Locational Attainments: Constructing Individual-Level Regression Models Using Aggregate Data." *Sociological Methods and Research* 20: 367–97.

Althaus, Scott L. 2003. *Collective Preferences in Democratic Politics: Opinion Surveys and the Will of the People.* New York: Cambridge University Press.

Amenta, Edwin, and Neal Caren. 2004. "The Legislative, Organizational, and Beneficiary Consequences of State-Oriented Challengers." Pp. 461–88 in *The Blackwell Companion to Social Movements*, edited by David A. Snow, Sarah A. Soule, and Hanspeter Kriesi. Malden, MA: Blackwell Publishing.

Amenta, Edwin, Neal Caren, Elizabeth Chiarello, and Yang Su. 2010. "The Political Consequences of Social Movements." *Annual Review of Sociology* 36: 287–307.

Amenta, Edwin, Neal Caren, and Sheera Joy Olasky. 2005. "Age for Leisure? Political Mediation and the Impact of the Pension Movement on U.S. Old-Age Policy." *American Sociological Review* 70: 516–38.

Amenta, Edwin, Neal Caren, Sheera Joy Olasky, and James E. Stobaugh. 2009. "All the Movements Fit to Print: Who, What, When, Where, and Why SMO Families Appeared in the *New York Times* in the Twentieth Century." *American Sociological Review* 74: 636–56.

Amenta, Edwin, Bruce Carruthers, and Yvonne Zylan. 1992. "A Hero for the Aged? The Townsend Movement, the Political Mediation Model, and U.S. Old-Age Policy, 1934–1950." *American Journal of Sociology* 98: 303–39.

Andrews, Kenneth T. 2001. "Social Movements and Policy Implementation." *American Sociological Review* 66: 71–95.

Andrews, Kenneth T., and Bob Edwards. 2004. "Advocacy Organizations in the U.S. Political Process." *Annual Review of Sociology* 30: 479–506.

Ansolabehere, Stephen, John de Figueiredo, and James M. Snyder, Jr. 2003. "Why Is There So Little Money in U.S. Politics?" *Journal of Economic Perspectives* 17: 105–30.

Ansolabehere, Stephen, and Philip Edward Jones. 2010. "Constituents' Responses to Congressional Roll-Call Voting." *American Journal of Political Science* 54: 583–97.

Ansolabehere, Stephen, Jonathan Rodden, and James M. Snyder, Jr. 2008. "The Strength of Issues: Using Multiple Measures to Gauge Preference Stability, Ideological Constraint, and Issue Voting." *American Political Science Review* 102: 215–32.

Arnold, R. Douglas. 1990. *The Logic of Congressional Action*. New Haven: Yale University Press.

Austen-Smith, David. 1993. "Information and Influence: Lobbying for Agendas and Votes." *American Journal of Political Science* 37: 799–833.

Barkey, Karen, and Sunita Parikh. 1991. "Comparative Perspectives on the State." *Annual Review of Sociology* 17: 523–49.

Bartels, Larry M. 2005. "Homer Gets a Tax Cut: Inequality and Public Policy in the American Mind." *Perspectives on Politics* 3: 15–32

Baumgartner, Frank R., Jeffrey M. Berry, Marie Hojnacki, David C. Kimball, and Beth L. Leech. 2009. *Lobbying and Public Policy*. Chicago: University of Chicago Press.

Baumgartner, Frank R., and Bryan D. Jones. 1993. *Agendas and Instability in American Politics*. Chicago: University of Chicago Press.

Baumgartner, Frank R., Heather A. Larsen-Price, Beth L. Leech, and Paul Rutledge. 2011. "Congressional and Presidential Effects on the Demand for Lobbying." *Political Research Quarterly* 64: 3–16.

Baumgartner, Frank R., and Beth L. Leech. 1998. *Basic Interests*. Princeton: Princeton University Press.

2001. "Interest Niches and Policy Bandwagons: Patterns of Interest Group Involvement in National Politics." *Journal of Politics* 63: 1191–1213.

Becker, Howard. 1998. *Tricks of the Trade: How to Think about Your Research While You're Doing It.* Chicago: University of Chicago Press.

Bernhagen, Patrick, and Brett Trani. 2012. "Interest Group Mobilization and Lobbying Patterns in Britain: A Newspaper Analysis." *Interest Groups and Advocacy* 1:48–66.

Best, Rachel Kahn. 2012. "Disease Politics and Medical Research Funding: Three Ways Advocacy Shapes Policy." *American Sociological Review* 77: 780–803.

Boli-Bennett, John, and John Meyer. 1978. "Ideology of Childhood and the State." *American Sociological Review* 43: 797–812.

Bradley, Robert B. 1980. "Motivations in Legislative Information Use." *Legislative Studies Quarterly* 5: 393–406.

Brooks, Clem, and Jeff Manza. 2007. *Why Welfare States Persist: The Importance of Public Opinion in Democracies.* Chicago: University of Chicago Press.

Browne, William P., and Delbert J. Ringquist. 1985. "Sponsorship and Enactment: State Lawmakers and Aging Legislation, 1956–1978." *American Politics Quarterly* 13: 447–66.

Burstein, Paul. 1998a. "Interest Organizations, Political Parties, and the Study of Democratic Politics." Pp. 39–56 in *Social Movements and American Political Institutions*, edited by Anne N. Costain and Andrew S. McFarland. Lanham, MD: Rowman & Littlefield.

1998b. *Discrimination, Jobs, and Politics.* Chicago: University of Chicago Press.

1998c. "Bringing the Public Back In: Should Sociologists Consider the Impact of Public Opinion on Public Policy?" *Social Forces* 77: 27–62.

1999. "Social Movements and Public Policy." Pp. 3–21 in *How Social Movements Matter*, edited by Marco Giugni, Doug McAdam, and Charles Tilley. Minneapolis: University of Minnesota Press.

2002. "Public Opinion and Congressional Action on Labor Market Opportunities, 1942–2000." Pp. 86–105 in *Navigating Public Opinion: Polls, Policy, and the Future of American Democracy*, edited by Jeff Manza, Fay Lomax Cook, and Benjamin Page. New York: Oxford University Press.

2003. "The Impact of Public Opinion on Public Policy: A Review and an Agenda." *Political Research Quarterly* 56: 29–40.

2011. "How Our Understanding of Policy Change Is Affected by the Measurement of Public Policy, Hypothetical Determinants of Change, and the Relationship between Them." Paper presented at the annual meeting of the American Political Science Association, Seattle.

Burstein, Paul, Shawn Bauldry, and Paul Froese. 2005. "Bill Sponsorship and Congressional Support for Policy Proposals, from Introduction to Enactment or Disappearance." *Political Research Quarterly* 58: 295–302.

Burstein, Paul, and R. Marie Bricher. 1997. "Problem Definition and Public Policy." *Social Forces* 76: 135–68.

Burstein, Paul, R.Marie Bricher, and Rachel L. Einwohner. 1995. "Policy Alternatives and Political Change: Work, Family, and Gender on the Congressional Agenda, 1945–1990." *American Sociological Review* 60: 67–83.

Burstein, Paul, Rachel Einwohner, and Jocelyn Hollander. 1995 "Political Movements and Their Consequences: Lessons from the U.S. Experience." Pp. 275–95 in *The Politics of Social Protest*, edited by J. Craig Jenkins and Bert Klandermans. Minneapolis: University of Minnesota Press.

Burstein, Paul, and William Freudenburg. 1978. "Changing Public Policy: The Impact of Public Opinion, War Costs, and Anti-War Demonstrations on Senate Voting on Vietnam War Motions, 1964–73." *American Journal of Sociology* 84: 99–122.

Burstein, Paul, and C. Elizabeth Hirsh. 2007. "Interest Organizations, Information, and Policy Innovation in the U.S. Congress." *Sociological Forum* 22: 174–99.

Burstein, Paul, and April Linton. 2002. "The Impact of Political Parties, Interest Groups, and Social Movement Organizations on Public Policy." *Social Forces* 81: 380–408.

Burstein, Paul, and Sarah Sausner. 2005. "The Incidence and Impact of Policy-Oriented Collective Action." *Sociological Forum* 20: 403–19.

Campbell, James E. 1982. "Cosponsoring Legislation in the U.S. Congress." *Legislative Studies Quarterly* 7: 415–22.

Caren, Neal, Raj Andrew Ghoshal, and Vanesa Ribas. 2011. "A Social Movement Generation: Cohort and Period Trends in Protest Attendance and Petition Signing." *American Sociological Review* 76: 125–51.

Chalmers, Adam. 2013. "Trading Information for Access: Informational Lobbying Strategies and Interest Group Access to the European Union." *Journal of European Public Policy* 20: 39–58.

Clemens, Elisabeth S. 1997. *The People's Lobby: Organizational Innovation and the Rise of Interest Group Politics in the United States*. Chicago: University of Chicago Press.

Cmiel, Kenneth. 1999. "The Emergence of Human Rights Politics in the United States." *Journal of American History* 86: 1231–50.

Converse, Philip E. 1964. "The Nature of Belief Systems in Mass Publics." Pp. 206–61 in *Ideology and Discontent*, edited by David E. Apter. New York: Free Press.

Dahl, Robert A. 1956 *A Preface to Democratic Theory*. Chicago: University of Chicago Press.

1989. *Democracy and Its Critics*. New Haven: Yale University Press.

DeGregorio, Christine. 1998. "Assets and Access: Linking Lobbyists and Lawmakers in Congress." Pp. 137–53 in *The Interest Group Connection*, edited by Paul S. Herrnson, Ronald G. Shaiko, and Clyde Wilcox. Chatham, NJ: Chatham House.

della Porta, Donatella. 2008. "Protest on Unemployment: Forms and Opportunities." *Mobilization* 13: 279–95.

Diermeier, Daniel, and Timothy J. Feddersen. 2000 "Information and Congressional Hearings." *American Journal of Political Science* 44: 51–65.

Domhoff, G. William. 1998. *Who Rules America? Power and Politics in the Year 2000*. Mountain View, CA: Mayfield Publishing.

2002a. *Who Rules America?* 4th edition. New York: McGraw-Hill.

2002b. "The Power Elite, Public Policy, and Public Opinion." Pp. 124–37 in *Navigating Public Opinion*, edited by Jeff Manza, Fay Lomax Cook, and Benjamin I. Page. New York: Oxford University Press.

Downs, Anthony. 1957. *An Economic Theory of Democracy*. New York: Harper.

"Dynamics of Collective Action Project." Stanford University (http://www.stanford.edu/group/collectiveaction/cgi-bin/drupal/).

"Dynamics of Collective Protest in the U.S., 1960–1995: Manual for Microfilm Copying and Event Coding." 2009. (http://www.stanford.edu/group/collectiveaction/cgi-bin/drupal/).

Earl, Jennifer, Andrew Martin, John D. McCarthy, and Sarah A. Soule. 2004. "The Use of Newspaper Data in the Study of Collective Action." *Annual Review of Sociology* 30: 65–80.

Earl, Jennifer, Sarah A. Soule, and John D. McCarthy. 2003. "Protest under Fire? Explaining the Policing of Protest." *American Sociological Review* 68: 581–606.

Edwards, George C., III, and B. Dan Wood. 1999. "Who Influences Whom? The President, Congress, and the Media." *American Political Science Review* 93: 327–44.

Ellis, Christopher, and James A. Stimson. 2012. *Ideology in America*. New York: Cambridge University Press.

Erikson, Robert S. 1976. "The Relationship between Public Opinion and State Policy: A New Look Based on Some Forgotten Data." *American Journal of Political Science* 20: 25–36.

Erikson, Robert S., Michael B. MacKuen, and James A. Stimson. 2002. *The Macro Polity.* New York: Cambridge University Press.

Erikson, Robert S., Gerald C. Wright, and John P. McIver. 1993. *Statehouse Democracy.* New York: Cambridge University Press.

Fording, Richard C. 2001. "The Political Response to Black Insurgency: A Critical Test of Competing Theories of the State." *American Political Science Review* 95: 115–30.

Francia, Peter L. 2010. "Organized Interests: Evolution and Influence." Pp. 611–28 in *The Oxford Handbook of American Elections and Political Behavior,* edited by Jan E. Leighley. New York: Oxford University Press.

Frank, David John, Bayliss J. Camp, and Steven A. Boutcher. 2010. "Worldwide Trends in the Criminal Regulation of Sex, 1945 to 2005." *American Sociological Review* 75: 867–93.

Frank, David John, and Elizabeth H. McEneaney. 1999. "The Individualization of Society and the Liberalization of State Policies on Same-Sex Sexual Relations, 1984–1995." *Social Forces* 77: 911–44.

Gamson, William A. 1990 [originally published 1975]. *The Strategy of Social Protest.* Homewood, IL: Dorsey.

Gamson, William A., and Andre Modigliani. 1987. "The Changing Culture of Affirmative Action." *Research in Political Sociology* 3: 137–77.

1989. "Media Discourse and Public Opinion on Nuclear Power." *American Journal of Sociology* 95: 1–37.

Ginsberg, Benjamin. 1976. "Elections and Public Policy." *American Political Science Review* 70: 41–49.

Gormley, William T., Jr. 1998. "Witnesses for the Revolution." *American Politics Quarterly* 26: 174–95.

Granados, Francisco J., and David Knoke. 2005. "Organized Interest Groups and Policy Networks." Pp. 287–309 in *Handbook of Political Sociology: States, Civil Societies, and Globalization,* edited by Thomas Janoski, Robert R. Alford, Alexander M. Hicks, and Mildred A. Schwartz. New York: Cambridge University Press.

Grattet, Ryken, Valerie Jenness, and Theodore R. Curry. 1998. "The Homogenization and Differentiation of Hate Crime Law in the United States, 1978 to 1995." *American Sociological Review* 63: 286–307.

Gray, Virginia, and David Lowery. 2000. *The Population Ecology of Interest Representation: Lobbying Communities in the American States.* Ann Arbor: University of Michigan Press.

Gray, Virginia, David Lowery, Matthew Fellowes, and Jennifer L. Anderson. 2005. "Legislative Agendas and Interest Advocacy:

Understanding the Demand Side of Lobbying." *American Politics Research* 33: 404–34.

Gray, Virginia, David Lowery, Matthew Fellowes, and Andrea McAtee. 2004. "Public Opinion, Public Policy, and Organized Interests in the American States." *Political Research Quarterly* 57: 411–20.

Gray, Virginia, David Lowery, and Erik K. Godwin. 2007. "Public Preferences and Organized Interests in Health Policy: State Pharmacy Assistance Programs as Innovations." *Journal of Health Politics, Policy and Law* 32: 89–129.

Hacker, Jacob S. 2004. "Privatizing Risk without Privatizing the Welfare State: The Hidden Politics of Social Policy Retrenchment in the United States." *American Political Science Review* 98: 243–60.

Hacker, Jacob S., and Paul Pierson. 2005. "Abandoning the Middle: The Bush Tax Cuts and the Limits of Democratic Control." *Perspectives on Politics* 3: 33–54.

Hansen, John Mark. 1991. *Gaining Access: Congress and the Farm Lobby, 1919–1981*. Chicago: University of Chicago Press.

Hansen, Wendy L., and Neil J. Mitchell. 2000. "Disaggregating and Explaining Corporate Political Activity: Domestic and Foreign Corporations in National Politics." *American Political Science Review* 94: 891–903.

Harris, Frederick, and Daniel Gillion. 2010. "Expanding the Possibilities: Reconceptualizing Political Participation as a Toolbox." Pp. 144–61 in *The Oxford Handbook of American Elections and Political Behavior*, edited by Jan E. Leighley. New York: Oxford University Press.

Hayes, Andrew F., and Klaus Krippendorff. 2007. "Answering the Call for a Standard Reliability Measure for Coding Data." *Communication Methods and Measures* 1: 77–89.

Heitshusen, Valerie. 2000. "Interest Group Lobbying and U. S. House Decentralization: Linking Informational Focus to Committee Hearing Appearances." *Political Research Quarterly* 53: 151–76.

Hero, Rodney E., and Robert R. Preuhs. 2007. "Immigration and the Evolving Welfare State: Examining Policies in the U.S. States." *American Journal of Political Science* 51: 498–517.

Hicks, Alexander, and Joya Misra. 1993. "Political Resources and the Growth of Welfare in Affluent Capitalist Democracies, 1960–1982." *American Journal of Sociology* 99: 668–710.

Hilgartner, Steven, and Charles Bosk. 1988. "The Rise and Fall of Social Problems." *American Journal of Sociology* 94: 53–78.

Hirsch, Alexander V., and Kenneth W. Shotts. 2012. "Policy-Specific Information and Informal Agenda Power." *American Journal of Political Science* 56: 67–83.

Horne, Cale. 2012. "The Consistency of Policy with Opinion in the Russian Federation, 1992–2006." *Journal of Elections, Public Opinion, & Parties* 22: 215–44.

Huber, Evelyne, and John D. Stephens. 2000. "Partisan Governance, Women's Employment, and the Social Democratic Service State." *American Sociological Review* 65: 323–42.

Inglehart, Ronald, and Gabriela Catterberg. 2002. "Trends in Political Action." *International Journal of Comparative Sociology* 18: 300–16.

Jacobs, David, and Jason T. Carmichael. 2002. "The Political Sociology of the Death Penalty: A Pooled Time-Series Analysis." *American Sociological Review* 67: 109–31.

Jacobs, David, and Daniel Tope. 2007. "The Politics of Resentment in the Post-Civil Rights Era: Minority Threat, Homicide, and Ideological Voting in Congress." *American Journal of Sociology* 112: 1458–94.

Jacobs, Lawrence R., and Suzanne Mettler. 2011. "Why Public Opinion Changes: The Implications for Health and Health Policy." *Journal of Health Politics, Policy, and Law* 36: 917–33.

Jacobs, Lawrence R., and Benjamin I. Page. 2005. "Who Influences U.S. Foreign Policy?" *American Political Science Review* 99: 107–23.

Jenkins, J. Craig. 1983. "Resource Mobilization Theory and the Study of Social Movements." *Annual Review of Sociology* 9: 527–53.

Jenkins, J. Craig, David Jacobs, and Jon Agnone. 2003. "Political Opportunities and African-American Protest, 1948–1997." *American Journal of Sociology* 109: 277–303.

Jenkins, J. Craig, Kevin T. Leicht, and Heather Wendt. 2006. "Class Forces, Political Institutions, and State Intervention: Subnational Economic Development Policy in the United States, 1971–1990." *American Journal of Sociology* 111: 1122–80.

Jenkins-Smith, Hank C., Gilbert K. St. Clair, and Brian Woods. 1991. "Explaining Change in Policy Subsystems." *American Journal of Political Science* 35: 851–80.

Jenness, Valerie. 1999. "Managing Differences and Making Legislation." *Social Problems* 46: 548–71.

Jennings, Will, and Christopher Wlezien. 2011. "Distinguishing between Most Important Problems and Issues?" *Public Opinion Quarterly* 75: 545–55.

Jessee, Stephen A. 2009. "Spatial Voting in the 2004 Presidential Election." *American Political Science Review* 103: 59–81.

Johnson, Charles W. 2003. *How Our Laws Are Made*. Washington, D.C.: U.S. Government Printing Office (also at http://thomas.loc.gov/home/lawsmade.toc.html).

Johnson, Diane Elizabeth. 1995 "Transactions in Symbolic Resources: A Resource Dependence Model of Congressional Deliberation." *Sociological Perspectives* 38: 151–73.

Johnson, Erik W., Jon Agnone, and John D. McCarthy. 2010. "Movement Organizations, Synergistic Tactics, and Environmental Public Policy." *Social Forces* 88: 2267–92.

Jones, Bryan D. 1994. *Reconceiving Decision-Making in Democratic Politics*. Chicago: University of Chicago Press.

Jones, Bryan D., and Frank R. Baumgartner. 2005. *The Politics of Attention: How Government Prioritizes Problems*. Chicago: University of Chicago Press.

    2012. "From There to Here: Punctuated Equilibrium to the General Punctuation Thesis to a Theory of Government Information Processing." *Policy Studies Journal* 40: 1–19.

Jones, Bryan D., Heather Larsen-Price, and John Wilkerson. 2009. "Representation and American Governing Institutions." *Journal of Politics* 71: 277–90.

Jones, Bryan D., Tracy Sulkin, and Heather A. Larsen. 2003. "Policy Punctuations in American Political Institutions." *American Political Science Review* 97: 151–69.

Jones, Michael D., and Hank C. Jenkins-Smith. 2009. "Trans-Subsystem Dynamics: Policy Topography, Mass Opinion, and Policy Change." *Policy Studies Journal* 37: 37–58.

Jones, Philip Edward. 2011. "Which Buck Stops Here? Accountability for Policy Positions and Policy Outcomes in Congress." *Journal of Politics* 73: 764–82.

Kaplan, Karen. 2012. "Americans Too Confused by Healthcare Act to Like It, Survey Finds." *Los Angeles Times*, October 26. http://www.latimes.com.offcampus.lib.washington.edu/health/boostershots/la-heb-health care-act-misperceptions-survey-20121026,0,4862086.story.

Kessler, Daniel, and Keith Krehbiel. 1996. "Dynamics of Cosponsorship." *American Political Science Review* 90: 555–66.

King, Brayden G., Keith G. Bentele, and Sarah Anne Soule. 2007. "Protest and Policymaking: Explaining Fluctuation in Congressional Attention to Rights Issues, 1960–1986." *Social Forces* 86: 137–63.

King, Brayden G., Marie Cornwall, and Eric C. Dahlin. 2005. "Winning Woman Suffrage One Step at a Time: Social Movements and the Logic of the Legislative Process." *Social Forces* 83: 1211–34.

King, Gary, Robert O. Keohane, and Sidney Verba. 1994. *Designing Social Inquiry: Scientific Inference in Qualitative Research*. Princeton: Princeton University Press.

Kingdon, John W. 1981. *Congressmen's Voting Decisions*. 2nd edition. New York: Harper and Row.

    1995. *Agendas, Alternatives, and Public Policy*. 2nd edition. New York: HarperCollins Publishers.

Klein, Rudolf, and Theodore R. Marmor. 2008. "Reflections on Policy Analysis." Pp. 892–912 in *The Oxford Handbook of Public Policy*, edited by Michael Moran, Martin Rein, and Robert E. Goodin. New York: Oxford University Press.

Knoke, David. 1988. "Incentives in Collective Action Organizations." *American Sociological Review* 53: 311–29.

Knoke, David, Franz Urban Pappi, Jeffrey Broadbent, and Yutaka Tsujinaka. 1996. *Comparing Policy Networks*. New York: Cambridge University Press.

Kollman, Ken. 1998. *Outside Lobbying: Public Opinion and Interest Group Strategies*. Princeton: Princeton University Press.

Koopmans, Ruud. 2002. "Codebook for the Analysis of Political Mobilisation and Communication in European Public Spheres." (http://europub.wz-berlin.de).

2007a. "Who Inhabits the European Public Sphere?" *European Journal of Political Research* 46: 183–210.

2007b. "Social Movements." Pp. 693–707 in *Oxford Handbook of Political Behavior*, edited by Russell Dalton and Hans-Dieter Klingemann. New York: Oxford University Press.

Koopmans, Ruud, and Dieter Rucht. 2002. "Protest Event Analysis." Pp. 231–59 in *Methods of Social Movement Research*, edited by Bert Klandermans and Suzanne Staggenborg. Minneapolis: University of Minnesota Press.

Koopmans, Ruud, and Paul Statham. 1999. "Political Claims Analysis: Integrating Protest Event and Political Discourse Approaches." *Mobilization* 4: 203–22.

Koopmans, Ruud, and Paul Statham, editors. 2010a. *The Making of a European Public Sphere: Media Discourse and Political Contention*. New York: Cambridge University Press.

2010b. "Theoretical Frameworks, Research Design, and Methods." Pp. 34–59 in *The Making of a European Public Sphere*, edited by Ruud Koopmans and Paul Statham. New York: Cambridge University Press.

Koopmans, Ruud, Paul Statham, Marco Giugni, and Florence Passy. 2005. *Contested Citizenship: Immigration and Cultural Diversity in Europe*. Minneapolis: University of Minnesota Press.

Krehbiel, Keith. 1991. *Information and Legislative Organization*. Ann Arbor: University of Michigan Press.

1995. "Cosponsors and Wafflers from A to Z." *American Journal of Political Science* 39: 906–23.

Kriesi, Hanspeter, Ruud Koopmans, Jan Willem Dyvendak, and Marco G. Giugni. 1995. *New Social Movements in Western Europe*. Minneapolis: University of Minnesota Press.

Krippendorff, Klaus. 2004. "Reliability in Content Analysis: Some Common Misperceptions and Recommendations." *Human Communication Research* 30: 411–33.

Labaton, Stephen. 1991. "House Backs Bailout Bill, Sending It to Bush." *New York Times*, late East Coast edition, March 22, p. D1.

Larson, Jeff A., and Sarah A. Soule. 2009. "Sector-Level Dynamics and Collective Action in the United States, 1965–1975." *Mobilization* 14: 293–314.

Laumann, Edward O., and David Knoke. 1987. *The Organizational State*. Madison: University of Wisconsin Press.

Lax, Jeffrey R., and Justin H. Phillips. 2009. "Gay Rights in the States: Public Opinion and Policy Responsiveness." *American Political Science Review* 103: 367–86.

2012. "The Democratic Deficit in the States." *American Journal of Political Science* 56: 148–66.

Leech, Beth. 2010. "Lobbying and Influence." Pp. 534–51 in *The Oxford Handbook of American Political Parties and Interest Groups*, edited by L. Sandy Maisel and Jeffrey M. Berry. New York: Oxford University Press.

Leifeld, Philip, and Volker Schneider. 2012. "Information Exchange in Policy Networks." *American Journal of Political Science* 56: 731–44.

Lexis-Nexis Congressional Universe. n.d. Dayton, OH: Lexis-Nexis.

Leyden, Kevin M. 1995. "Interest Group Resources and Testimony at Congressional Hearings." *Legislative Studies Quarterly* 20: 431–39.

Lichbach, Mark Irving. 1995. *The Rebel's Dilemma*. Ann Arbor: University of Michigan Press.

Lohmann, Susanne. 1993 "A Signaling Model of Informative and Manipulative Political Action." *American Political Science Review* 87: 319–33.

1994 "The Dynamics of Information Cascades: The Monday Demonstrations in Leipzig, East Germany, 1989–91." *World Politics* 47: 42–101.

1998. "An Information Rationale for the Power of Special Interests." *American Political Science Review* 92: 809–28.

2003. "Representative Government and Special Interest Politics." *Journal of Theoretical Politics* 15: 299–319.

Long, J. Scott, and Jeremy Freese. 2001. *Regression Models for Categorical Dependent Variables Using Stata*. College Station, TX: Stata Press.

Lopipero, Peggy, Dorie E. Apollonio, and Lisa A. Bero. 2007–8. "Interest Groups, Lobbying, and Deception: The Tobacco Industry and Airline Smoking." *Political Science Quarterly* 122: 635–56.

Lowery, David, and Virginia Gray. 2004. "A Neopluralist Perspective on Research on Organized Interests." *Political Research Quarterly* 57: 163–75.

Lowery, David, Virginia Gray, and Frank R. Baumgartner. 2010. "Policy Attention in State and Nation: Is Anyone Listening to the Laboratories of Democracy?" *Publius* 41: 286–310.

Luskin, Robert C., and John G. Bullock. 2011. "'Don't Know' Means 'Don't Know': DK Responses and the Public's Level of Political Knowledge." *Journal of Politics* 73: 547–57.

Maier, Pauline. 2011. *Ratification: The People Debate the Constitution, 1787–1788*. New York: Simon and Schuster.

Manza, Jeff, and Clem Brooks. 2012. "How Sociology Lost Public Opinion: A Genealogy of a Missing Concept in the Study of the Political." *Sociological Theory* 30: 89–113.

Manza, Jeff, and Fay Lomax Cook. 2002a. "A Democratic Polity? Three Views of Policy Responsiveness to Public Opinion in the United States." *American Politics Research* 30: 630–67.

2002b. "The Impact of Public Opinion on Public Policy." Pp. 17–32 in *Navigating Public Opinion*, edited by Jeff Manza, Fay Lomax Cook, and Benjamin I. Page. New York: Oxford University Press.

Markoff, John. 1999. "Where and When Was Democracy Invented?" *Contemporary Studies in Society and History* 41 (1999): 660–90.

Mattei, Laura R. Winsky. 1998. "Gender and Power in American Legislative Discourse." *Journal of Politics* 60: 440–61.

Mayhew, David. 1974. *Congress: The Electoral Connection*. New Haven: Yale University Press.

1991. *Divided We Govern*. New Haven: Yale University Press.

McAdam, Doug, and Hilary Schaffer Boudet. 2012. *Putting Social Movements in Their Place: Explaining Opposition to Energy Projects in the United States, 2000–2005*. New York: Cambridge University Press.

McAdam, Doug, and Yang Su. 2002. "The War at Home: Antiwar Protests and Congressional Voting, 1965 to 1973." *American Sociological Review* 67: 696–721.

McAdam, Doug, Sidney Tarrow, and Charles Tilly. 1996. "To Map Contentious Politics." *Mobilization* 1: 17–34.

McCammon, Holly J. 2012. *The U.S. Women's Jury Movements and Strategic Adaptation: A More Just Verdict*. New York: Cambridge University Press.

McCammon, Holly J., Karen E. Campbell, Ellen M. Granberg, and Christine Mowery. 2001. "How Movements Win: Gendered Opportunity Structures and U.S. Women's Suffrage Movements, 1866–1919." *American Sociological Review* 66: 49–70.

McCammon, Holly J., Soma Chaudhuri, Lyndi Hewitt, Courtney Sanders Muse, and Harmony D. Newman. 2008. "Becoming Full Citizens: The U.S. Women's Jury Rights Campaigns, the Pace of Reform, and Strategic Adaptation." *American Journal of Sociology* 113: 1104–47.

McCammon, Holly J., Harmony D. Newman, Courtney Sanders Muse, and Teresa M. Terrell. 2007. "Movement Framing and Discursive Opportunity Structures: The Political Successes of U.S. Women's Jury Movements." *American Sociological Review* 72: 725–49.

McCarthy, John, Clark McPhail, and Jackie Smith. 1996. "Images of Protest: Dimensions of Selection Bias in Media Coverage of Washington Demonstrations, 1982 and 1991." *American Sociological Review* 61: 478–99.

McCarthy, John, and Mayer Zald. 1977. "Resource Mobilization and Social Movements." *American Journal of Sociology* 82: 1212–41.

Meyer, David S., and Debra C. Minkoff. 2004. "Conceptualizing Political Opportunity." *Social Forces* 82: 1457–92.

Monogan, James, Virgina Gray, and David Lowery. 2009. "Public Opinion, Organized Interests, and Policy Congruence in Initiative and Noniniative U.S. States." *State Politics and Policy Quarterly* 9: 304–24.

Monroe, Alan D. 1998. "Public Opinion and Public Policy, 1980–1993." *Public Opinion Quarterly* 62: 6–28.

Moran, Michael, Martin Rein, and Robert E. Goodin, editors. 2008. *The Oxford Handbook of Public Policy*. New York: Oxford University Press.

Nam, Taehyun. 2006. "What You Use Matters: Coding Protest Data." *PS: Political Science and Politics* 39: 281–87.

Nash, Nathaniel C. 1989a. "Can the U.S. Bail Out Thrifts without Sinking Real Estate?" *New York Times*, 14 May, p. A4.

1989b. "The Savings and Loan Crisis: 'Arizona is Lost, Next is San Francisco'." *New York Times*, 7 May, p. A2.

Nicholson-Crotty, Sean. 2009. "The Politics of Diffusion: Public Policy in the American States." *Journal of Politics* 71: 191–205.

Oliver, Pamela E. 1993. "Formal Models of Collective Action." *Annual Review of Sociology* 19: 271–300.

Oliver, Pamela E., and Daniel J. Myers. 1999. "How Events Enter the Public Sphere: Conflict, Location, and Sponsorship in Local Newspaper Coverage of Public Events." *American Journal of Sociology* 105: 38–87.

Olson, Mancur. 1971 [originally published 1965]. *The Logic of Collective Action*. Cambridge, MA: Harvard University Press.

Olzak, Susan. 1989. "Analysis of Events in the Study of Collective Action." *Annual Review of Sociology* 15: 119–41.

Olzak, Susan, and Emily Ryo. 2007. "Organizational Diversity, Vitality, and Outcomes in the Civil Rights Movement." *Social Forces* 85: 1561–91.

Olzak, Susan, and Sarah A. Soule. 2009. "Cross-Cutting Influences of Environmental Protest and Legislation." *Social Forces* 88: 201–25.

Opp, Karl-Dieter. 2009. *Theories of Political Protest and Social Movements.* New York: Routledge.

Page, Benjamin I. 2002. "The Semi-Sovereign Public." Pp. 325–44 in *Navigating Public Opinion,* edited by Jeff Manza, Fay Lomax Cook, and Benjamin I. Page. New York: Oxford University Press.

Page, Benjamin I., and Robert Y. Shapiro. 1982. "Changes in Americans' Policy Preferences, 1935–1979." *Public Opinion Quarterly* 46: 24–42.

   1983. "Effects of Opinion on Policy." *American Political Science Review* 77: 175–90.

   1992. *The Rational Public: Fifty Years of Trends in Americans' Policy Preferences.* Chicago: University of Chicago Press.

Pampel, Fred C., and John B. Williamson. 1988. "Welfare Spending in Advanced Industrial Democracies, 1950–1980." *American Journal of Sociology* 93:1424–56.

Parsons, Talcott. 1960. *Structure and Process in Modern Societies.* New York: Free Press.

Pierson, Paul. 2004. *Politics in Time: History, Institutions, and Social Analysis.* Princeton: Princeton University Press.

Polsby, Nelson. 1984. *Political Innovation in America.* New Haven: Yale University Press.

Potters, Jan, and Randolph Sloof. 1996. "Interest Groups: A Survey of Empirical Models That Try to Assess Their Influence." *European Journal of Political Economy* 12: 403–42.

Prakash, Aseem, and Mary Kay Gugerty. 2010. "Advocacy Organizations and Collective Action: An Introduction." Pp. 1–28 in *Advocacy Organizations and Collective Action,* edited by Aseem Prakash and Mary Kay Gugerty. New York: Cambridge University Press.

Proquest LLC. 1990–2012. Ann Arbor, MI: Proquest. (http://proquest .umi.com).

Quinn, Jane Bryant. 1999. "Notch Lobby Donations Benefit Only Fund-Raisers." *Sunday Patriot-News* (Harrisburg, Pennsylvania), March 21, p. D02.

Rabb, Will. 1990. "Finally in Office, Idea Man Gil Carmichael May Have the Idea to Save Area's Rail Line." *Mississippi Business Journal,* February 26, section 1, p. 10.

Randolph, Eleanor. 1989. "Students Say Colleges Hide Bad News." *San Francisco Chronicle*, December 2, p. A8.

Regens, James L. 1989. "Congressional Cosponsorship of Acid Rain Controls." *Social Science Quarterly* 70: 505–12.

Riker, William H. 1986. *The Art of Political Manipulation*. New Haven: Yale University Press.

Riker, William, and Peter Ordeshook. 1968. "A Theory of the Calculus of Voting." *American Political Science Review* 72: 25–42.

Rosenfeld, Rachel, and Kathryn Ward. 1996. "Evolution of the Contemporary U.S. Women's Movement." Pp. 51–73 in *Research in Social Movements, Conflict, and Change*, edited by Louis Kreisberg. Greenwich, CT: JAI Press.

Rucht, Dieter. 1999. "The Impact of Environmental Movements in Western Societies." Pp. 204–24 in *How Social Movements Matter*, edited by Marco Giugni, Doug McAdam, and Charles Tilly. Minneapolis: University of Minnesota Press.

Santoro, Wayne A. 2002. "The Civil Rights Movement's Struggle for Fair Employment: A 'Dramatic Events-Conventional Politics' Model." *Social Forces* 81: 177–206.

2008. "The Civil Rights Movement and the Right to Vote: Black Protest, Segregationist Violence and the Audience." *Social Forces* 86: 1391–1414.

Schattschneider, E. E. 1960. *The Semi-Sovereign People*. New York: Holt, Rinehart, and Winston.

Schickler, Eric, Kathryn Pearson, and Brian D. Feinstein. 2010. "Congressional Parties and Civil Rights Politics from 1933 to 1972." *Journal of Politics* 72: 672–89.

Schiller, Wendy J. 1995. "Senators as Political Entrepreneurs: Using Bill Sponsorship to Shape Legislative Agendas." *American Journal of Political Science* 39: 186–203.

Schlozman, Kay Lehman, Sidney Verba, and Henry E. Brady. 2012. *The Unheavenly Chorus: Unequal Voice and the Broken Promise of American Democracy*. Princeton: Princeton University Press.

Schneider, Anne and Helen Ingram. 1988. "Systematically Pinching Ideas." *Journal of Public Policy* 8: 61–80.

Schroedel, Jean Reith. 1986. "Campaign Contributions and Legislative Outcomes." *Western Political Quarterly* 39: 371–89.

Schumaker, Paul. 1975. "Policy Responsiveness to Protest Group Demands." *Journal of Politics* 37: 488–521.

Schuman, Howard, and Stanley Presser. 1996. *Questions and Answers in Attitude Surveys*. Thousand Oaks, CA: Sage.

Scott, William A. 1955. "Reliability of Content Analysis: The Case of Nominal Scale Coding." *Public Opinion Quarterly* 19: 321–25.

Segal, Jeffrey A., Charles M. Cameron, and Albert D. Cover. 1992. "A Spatial Model of Roll Call Voting." *American Journal of Political Science* 36: 96–121.

Segal, Mady Wechsler, and Amanda Faith Hansen. 1992. "Value Rationales in Policy Debates on Women in the Military." *Social Science Quarterly* 73: 296–309.

Shapiro, Robert Y. 1998. "Public Opinion, Elites, and Democracy." *Critical Review* 12: 501–28.

2011. "Public Opinion and American Democracy." *Public Opinion Quarterly* 75: 982–1017.

Shipan, Charles R., and Craig Volden. 2006. "Bottom-Up Federalism: The Diffusion of Antismoking Policies from U.S. Cities to States." *American Journal of Political Science* 50: 825–43.

Sinnott, Richard. 2000. "Knowledge and the Position of Attitudes toward a European Foreign Policy on the Real-to-Random Continuum." *International Journal of Public Opinion Research* 12: 113–37.

Smith, Mark A. 2000. *American Business and Political Power*. Chicago: University of Chicago Press.

Smith, Richard A. 1984. "Advocacy, Interpretation, and Influence in the U.S. Congress." *American Political Science Review* 78: 44–63.

1995. "Interest Group Influence in the U.S. Congress." *Legislative Studies Quarterly* 20: 89–139.

Sniderman, Paul M., and Douglas B. Grob. 1996. "Innovations in Experimental Design in Attitude Surveys." *Annual Review of Sociology* 22: 377–99.

Snijders, Tom A. B., and Roel J. Bosker. 1999. *Multilevel Analysis*. Thousand Oaks, CA: Sage.

Snow, David A., Sarah A. Soule, and Hanspeter Kriesi. 2004. "Mapping the Terrain." Pp. 3–16 in *The Blackwell Companion to Social Movements*, edited by David A. Snow, Sarah A. Soule, and Hanspeter Kriesi. Malden, MA: Blackwell Publishing.

Soroka, Stuart N., and Christopher Wlezien. 2005. "Opinion-Policy Dynamics: Public Preferences and Public Expenditure in the United Kingdom." *British Journal of Political Science* 35: 665–89.

2010. *Degrees of Democracy: Politics, Public Opinion, and Policy*. New York: Cambridge University Press.

Soule, Sarah A. 1997. "The Student Divestment Movement in the United States and Tactical Diffusion: The Shantytown Protest." *Social Forces* 75: 855–82.

Soule, Sarah A., and Jennifer Earl. 2005. "A Movement Society Evaluated: Collective Protest in the United States, 1960–1986." *Mobilization* 10: 345–64.

Soule, Sarah A., Doug McAdam, John McCarthy, and Yang Su. 1999. "Protest Events: Cause or Consequence of State Action?" *Mobilization* 4: 239–55.

Soule, Sarah A., and Susan Olzak. 2004. "When Do Movements Matter? The Politics of Contingency and the Equal Rights Amendment." *American Sociological Review* 69: 473–97.

Statham, Paul, and Andrew Geddes. 2006. "Elites and the 'Organized Public': Who Drives British Immigration Politics and in What Direction?" *West European Politics* 29: 248–69.

Steinberg, Ronnie J. 1982. *Wages and Hours: Labor and Reform in Twentieth-Century America.* New Brunswick, NJ: Rutgers University Press.

Stimson, James A. 1999. *Public Opinion in America: Moods, Cycles, and Swings.* 2nd edition. Westview Press.

2004. *Tides of Consent: How Public Opinion Shapes American Politics.* New York: Cambridge University Press.

Stimson, James, Michael B. MacKuen, and Robert S. Erikson. 1995. "Dynamic Representation." *American Political Science Review* 89: 543–65.

Stone, Deborah. 1989. "Causal Stories and the Formation of Policy Agendas." *Political Science Quarterly* 104: 281–300.

Talbert, Jeffrey C., and Matthew Potoski. 2002. "Setting the Legislative Agenda: The Dimensional Structure of Bill Cosponsoring and Floor Voting." *Journal of Politics* 64: 864–91.

Tarrow, Sidney. 1994. *Power in Movement: Social Movements, Collective Action, and Politics.* New York: Cambridge University Press.

Therien, Jean-Philippe, and Alain Noel. 2000. "Political Parties and Foreign Aid." *American Political Science Review* 94: 151–62.

Tilly, Charles. 1976. "Major Forms of Collective Action in Western Europe, 1500–1975." *Theory and Society* 3: 365–75.

1997. "Parliamentarization of Popular Contention in Great Britain, 1758–1834." *Theory and Society* 26: 245–73.

2005. "Introduction to Part II: Invention, Transformation, and Diffusion of the Social Movement Repertoire." *European Review of History* 12: 307–20.

2008. "Describing, Measuring, and Explaining Struggle." *Qualitative Sociology* 31: 1–13.

Tilly, Charles, and Sidney Tarrow. 2007. *Contentious Politics.* Boulder, CO: Paradigm.

Tolnay, Stewart E., Kyle D. Crowder, and Robert M. Adelman. 2000. "Narrow and Filthy Alleys of the City? The Residential Settlement Patterns of Black Southern Migrants to the North." *Social Forces* 78: 989–1015.

United States House of Representatives, Committee on Banking, Finance, and Urban Affairs, Subcommittee on Financial Institutions Supervision, Regulation, and Insurance. 1989. Hearing on Financial Institutions Reform, Recovery, and Enforcement Act of 1989 (H.R. 1278), Part 1. CIS number 1989-H241–35.

United States House of Representatives, Committee on Education and Labor, Subcommittee on Postsecondary Education. 1990. Hearing on HR3344, The Crime Awareness and Campus Security Act of 1989. Y 4.Ed 8/1:101–75.

United States Library of Congress, Congressional Research Service. 1998. *Vital Statistics on Congress*. Washington, D.C.: U.S. Library of Congress.

United States Library of Congress. 2001. *Thomas Legislative Information on the Internet*. (http://thomas.loc.gov).

Vasi, Ion Bogdan, and Michael Macy. 2003. "The Mobilizer's Dilemma: Crisis, Empowerment, and Collective Action." *Social Forces* 81: 983–98.

Verba, Sidney, Norman H. Nie, and Jae-on Kim. 1978. *Participation and Political Equality: A Seven-Nation Comparison*. Chicago: University of Chicago Press.

Verba, Sidney, Kay Lehman Schlozman, and Henry E. Brady. 1995. *Voice and Equality*. Cambridge, MA: Harvard University Press.

Walker, Edward T., Andrew W. Martin, and John D. McCarthy. 2008. "Confronting the State, the Corporation, and the Academy: The Influence of Institutional Targets on Social Movement Repertoires." *American Journal of Sociology* 114: 35–76.

Warshaw, Christopher, and Jonathan Rodden. 2012. "How Should We Measure District-Level Public Opinion on Individual Issues?" *Journal of Politics* 74: 203–19.

Wawro, Gregory. 2000. *Legislative Entrepreneurship in the U.S. House of Representatives*. Ann Arbor: University of Michigan Press.

Weeks, Elaine L., Jacqueline M. Boles, Albeno P. Garbin, and John Blount. 1986. "The Transformation of Sexual Harassment from a Private Trouble into a Public Issue." *Sociological Inquiry* 56: 432–55.

Wilensky, Harold L. 2002. *Rich Democracies: Political Economy, Public Policy, and Performance*. Berkeley: University of California Press.

Wilson, Rick K., and Cheryl D. Young. 1997. "Cosponsorship in the U.S. Congress." *Legislative Studies Quarterly* 22: 25–43.

Winters, Jeffrey A., and Benjamin I. Page. 2009. "Oligarchy in the United States?" *Perspectives on Politics* 7: 731–51.

Wittman, Donald A. 1995. *The Myth of Democratic Failure*. Chicago: University of Chicago Press.

Wlezien, Christopher. 2004. "Patterns of Representation." *Journal of Politics* 66: 1–24.

2005. "On the Salience of Political Issues: The Problem with 'Most Important Problem'." *Electoral Studies* 24: 555–79.

Wlezien, Christopher, and Stuart N. Soroka. 2012. "Political Institutions and the Opinion-Policy Link." *West European Politics* 35: 1407–32.

Woolley, John T. 2000. "Using Media-Based Data in Studies of Politics." *American Journal of Political Science* 44: 156–73.

Wootton, David. 1992. "The Levellers." Pp. 71–89 in *Democracy: The Unfinished Journey, 508 BC to AD 1993*, edited by John Dunn. New York: Oxford University Press.

Workman, Samuel, Bryan D. Jones, and Ashley E. Jochim. 2009. "Information Processing and Policy Dynamics." *Policy Studies Journal* 37: 75–92.

Wright, John R. 1996. *Interest Groups and Congress*. Boston: Allyn & Bacon.

Zaller, John R. 1992. *The Nature and Origins of Mass Opinion*. New York: Cambridge University Press.

Index